CW01425050

POCKET
LISBON

written and researched by
MATTHEW HANCOCK
with additional accounts by Amanda Tomlin

Samsonite

PROXIS
MADE WITH ROXKIN™ TECHNOLOGY

samsonite.co.uk

CONTENTS

LISBON

Set across a series of hills overlooking the broad estuary of the Rio Tejo (River Tagus), Lisbon's stunning location and effortless beauty immediately strike most first-time visitors. It's an instantly likeable place, a big city with a population of around two million, but one that remains human enough in pace and scale to be easily taken in over a long weekend. That said, many visitors visit again and again, smitten by a combination of old-world charm and cosmopolitan vibrancy that makes it one of Europe's most exciting cities.

View of Lisbon from Cristo Rei

What's new

One of Lisbon's premier museums, the Gulbenkian (see page 95), is reopening following a revamp, which includes a fabulous structure for the Centro de Arte Moderna (CAM) within its grounds. Also new to the Guide is the Berardo – Museu Arte Deco (B-MAD; see page 78), showcasing the art movement that had a defining impact on Lisbon. And getting around is easier than ever with the opening of another street lift, the Funicular da Graça (see page 41), which whisks passengers up to a wonderful viewpoint over the city.

Although one of the EU's least expensive capitals, Lisbon was once one of the continent's wealthiest, controlling a maritime empire that stretched from Brazil to Macau. The iconic Torre de Belém, Mosteiro dos Jerónimos and dramatic Moorish castle survive from these times, though many other buildings were destroyed in the Great Earthquake of 1755. Today, much of the historic centre – the Baixa, Chiado and Bairro Alto – dates from the late eighteenth and nineteenth centuries. The biggest attraction in these quarters is the street life: nothing beats watching the city's comings and goings from a pavement café over a powerful *bica* coffee or Portuguese beer.

If you're fit enough to negotiate its hills, Lisbon is a great place to explore on foot: venture off the beaten track and you'll discover atmospheric neighbourhoods sheltering aromatic *pastelarias* (patisseries), traditional shops, and shuttered houses faced with beautiful *azulejo* tiles. Getting around by public transport can be fun in itself, whether you're cranking uphill on one of the city's ancient trams, riding a ferry across the Rio Tejo, or speeding across town on the metro, whose stations are decorated with adventurous contemporary art.

Lisbon also boasts excellent museums – from the Gulbenkian, with its amazing collection of arts through the ages, to the Berardo, whose modern paintings are the envy of Europe, via the Museu Nacional de Arte Antiga, the national gallery, filled with a plethora of top Portuguese and European masterpieces.

Lisbon's eclectic nightlife scene ranges from the traditional fado clubs of the Alfama district to glitzy venues in the Bairro Alto and along the riverfront, many of them playing African and Brazilian beats influenced by immigrants from Portugal's former colonies.

Elsewhere, the city offers a pleasing mishmash of the

Best places for alfresco dining

The best way to soak up Lisbon's atmosphere is to grab an outdoor table and sit back with a coffee or something more substantial. Sample tapas at *Pharmacia Felicidade*, with a fine little garden overlooking the Tagus (see page 66), or enjoy a pizza-with-a-view at riverside *Casanova* (see page 46). It's hard to find a lovelier lunch spot than the sleek, riverside *Á Margem* (see page 89). Alternatively, head to one of Lisbon's squares or *miradouros* (viewpoints), many of which have cafés, bars or restaurants, such as *Portas do Sol* (see page 49).

Portas do Sol restaurant

traditional and modern: chequered-tiled bars full of old-timers supping brandies adjacent to boutiquey clubs pumping out the latest sounds; tiny *tascas* with bargain menus scrawled in white chalk on boards rubbing shoulders with gourmet restaurants eyeing the latest Michelin awards, and artisanal stores that wrap purchases in paper and string sitting alongside malls packed with high-street and designer stores.

Should city life begin to pall, take the train out to the beautiful hilltop town of Sintra, whose lush, wooded heights and royal palaces comprise a UNESCO World Heritage Site. Alternatively, the lively resorts of Estoril and Cascais are just half an hour away, with the best beaches lying south of the city, along the Costa da Caparica, where Atlantic breakers crash on kilometre after kilometre of superb dune-backed sands.

When to visit

Lisbon is comfortably warm from April to October (average daily temperature 20–28ºC), with cooling Atlantic breezes making it less hot than Mediterranean cities on the same latitude. Most Lisbon residents take their holidays in July and August (27–28ºC), which means that some shops, bars and restaurants close for the period and the local beaches are heaving. Lower temperatures of 22–26ºC mean September and October are good times to visit, as is June, when the city enjoys its main festivals. Even in midwinter it is rarely cold and, as one of Europe's sunniest capitals, the sun usually appears at some stage to light up the city.

Where to...

Shop

Suburban Lisbon has some of Europe's largest shopping malls, but the city centre is a pleasing mixture of quirky local stores and smaller independent outlets. The top end of **Avenida da Liberdade** features the likes of Armani and Louis Vuitton, and Chiado is the place to head for glass and jewellery. Antique shops cluster round **São Bento**, **Príncipe Real** and **Campo de Santa Clara**, while off-the-wall clothing and accessories are to be found in the independent boutiques of the **Bairro Alto**. **Santos** has become the district of design, with several stores dedicated to contemporary jewellery and high-end home products.
OUR FAVOURITES: Embaixada, see page 64. Ler Devagar, see page 81. Manuel Tavares, see page 32.

Eat

You're never far from a restaurant in Lisbon. For diversity, head to the **Bairro Alto** district where an eclectic array of inexpensive diners sits alongside ultrahip venues. The **Baixa** caters to Lisbon's workers and has a whole street, Rua das Portas de Santo Antão, largely given over to seafood restaurants. International flavours can be sampled by the Tejo at the **Parque das Nações** and the dockside developments at **Santa Apolónia** and **Doca de Santo Amaro**, while fashionistas head to the cool haunts of **Cais do Sodré**. Some of the best dining experiences, however, are in local neighbourhood restaurants highlighted in the Guide.
OUR FAVOURITES: Black Pavilion, see page 32. Mini Bar, see page 65. O Barbas, see page 122.

Drink

The most historic cafés are scattered throughout the **Baixa** and **Chiado** districts, where you'll find locals getting their caffeine fixes throughout the day. You can also pick up beer, wine or food at these places, though many bars only open after dark. Portuguese beers – largely Sagres and Super Bock – are inexpensive and recommended, while local wines are invariably excellent. Worth sampling too are local brandies; the white variety of port, which makes an excellent aperitif; and a powerful cherry brandy called *ginginha* – several bars in the Baixa specialize in the stuff. Finally, don't miss trying a *caipirinha*, a punchy Brazilian cocktail.
OUR FAVOURITES: Catch Me, see page 75. Chapitô, see page 48. Park, see page 68.

Go out

Lisbon has a pulsating nightlife, with the highest concentration of clubs and bars in the **Bairro Alto**. Many locals prefer the less frenetic vibe of the **Cais do Sodré** district, which has a handful of cool clubs and happening bars; while the city's biggest clubs are to be found near the river, especially *LuxFrágil* near **Santa Apolónia** and the upmarket venues of **Alcântara**. There are various excellent live music venues, with the **Bairro Alto** and **Alfama** famed for their fado houses.
OUR FAVOURITES: Casa Independente, see page 48. Páginas Tantas, see page 69. Pink Street, see page 53.

Lisbon at a glance

◁ Sintra see page 108.
With its fairy-tale palaces, the hilltop town of Sintra is a must-see day-trip from the capital.

Avenida, Parque Eduardo VII and the Gulbenkian see page 90.
The grand Avenida da Liberdade leads to the leafy Parque Eduardo VII; beyond, the Gulbenkian displays an extraordinarily rich collection of ancient and modern art.

◁ The Lisbon coast see page 118.
In less than an hour you can reach superb beaches at Estoril, Cascais or south to Caparica, famed for its surf and miles of sands.

Estrela, Lapa and Santos see page 70.
Well-to-do Estrela and Lapa boast gardens and excellent museums, while earthy Santos is the riverside district of design.

Belém and Ajuda see page 82.
Many of Portugal's maritime explorers set sail from Belém, home to some of the city's finest monuments and museums.

Alcântara and the docks see page 76.
Lisbon's docks shelter appealing riverside bars, clubs, restaurants and a couple of top museums.

| 0 | metres | 500 |
| 0 | yards | 500 |

▷ **Parque das Nações** see page 102.
This futuristic park occupies the former
Expo '98 site, with a range of modern
attractions including a huge oceanarium.

Bairro Alto and São Bento see page 58.
The Bairro Alto, or Upper Town, shelters the city's
best restaurants, bars and clubs, a short walk from
the parliament building at São Bento.

The Sé, Castelo and Alfama see page 36.
Next to the Sé cathedral, Alfama is an ancient
warren of steep streets leading up to the
city's stunning Moorish castle.

Chiado and Cais do Sodré see page 50.
Lisbon's upscale shopping area, Chiado,
rubs shoulders with down-to-earth Cais
do Sodré, site of the main market.

The Baixa and Rossio see page 24.
The heart of the modern city, an elegant
grid of eighteenth-century streets
running down to the River Tejo.

N

15

Things not to miss

It is not possible to see everything that Lisbon has to offer on one trip – and we don't suggest you try. What follows, in no particular order, is a selection of the city's unmissable highlights, including fascinating museums, historical buildings, and custard tarts to die for.

> Alfama

See page 44

A maze of streets and tortuous alleys where life continues much as it has for centuries.

< Castelo de São Jorge

See page 40

A former Moorish castle then later a palace and prison, the Castelo is now one of Lisbon's best viewpoints.

∨ Mosteiro dos Jerónimos

See page 83

Packed with flamboyant Manueline architectural features, this sixteenth-century monastery commemorates Vasco da Gama's discovery of a sea route to India.

< **Praça do Comércio**
See page 24
The city's grandest square, beautifully arcaded and facing the Tagus.

∨ **Oceanário**
See page 103
This spectacular oceanarium has a massive central tank and is home to all kinds of marine creatures, from sea otters to sharks.

∧ **Mercado da Ribeira (Time Out Market)**

See page 51
Part colourful fruit, veg and fish market and part vibrant food hall packed with stalls selling all kinds of dishes and drinks.

< **Museu Nacional de Arte Antiga**

See page 71
Portugal's national gallery is packed with fine works by the likes of Nuno Gonçalves and Hieronymus Bosch.

∧ A ride on a tram
See page 137
The vintage trams are the best way to negotiate Lisbon's steepest slopes and cobbled streets.

∨ Pink Street
See page 53
This is the place to be seen in the evening, filled with clubs, hip bars and fado joints.

∧ Torre de Belém
See page 86
An iconic Lisbon building, this fabulously ornate tower was built to defend the mouth of the Rio Tejo.

< Pastéis de Belém
See page 89
Head to this famous *pastelaria* for the best custard tarts in town.

< **A day out in Sintra**

See page 108

A UNESCO World Heritage Site, this attractive wooded hilltop town was the summer retreat for Portuguese royalty whose fabulous palaces can still be visited today.

∨ **A day at the beach**

See page 118

It's just a short hop from Lisbon to a string of excellent Atlantic beaches: those at Cascais and Estoril are easiest to reach.

THINGS NOT TO MISS

Day one in Lisbon

Confeitaria Nacional. See page 34. Start the day with a punchy *bica* coffee in one of Lisbon's most historic cafés, where the decor is as alluring as the pastries.

The Baixa. See page 28. Head down main Rua da Augusta and explore the lively streets and cafés of the Baixa grid.

Chiado. See page 50. Stroll up Rua do Carmo and Rua Garrett where many of Lisbon's best shops can be found.

Lunch. See page 56. Try *Leitaria Académica*, with a simple menu and tables outside a lovely square.

Tram #28. See page 45. This is Lisbon's most famous tram route, grinding back through the Baixa and up towards the Castelo through the Alfama.

Castelo de São Jorge. See page 40. Walk up to the ruined Moorish castle, the heart of historic Lisbon.

Alfama. See page 44. Take the steps into the Alfama, Lisbon's village within a city where traditional life still holds sway.

Museu do Fado. See page 44. Gain an insight into the history and sounds of Portugal's distinctive music at this informative museum.

Dinner. See page 49. Try one of the Alfama's fado houses, where you can dine while listening to live music; *A Baiuca* is a good place to start.

Drinks. See page 48. End the night by the riverside at *Lux*, one of Europe's coolest clubs.

Armazéns do Chiado shopping centre

Tram #28

Museu do Fado

Day two in Lisbon

Museu Calouste Gulbenkian: Centro de Arte Moderna (CAM).
See page 95. Take the metro to this superb arts complex showcasing modern art in beautifully manicured grounds.

Parque Eduardo VII. See page 95. It's a short walk from the museums to Lisbon's main central park famed for its *estufas* – hothouses filled with exotic plants.

Praça do Comércio. See page 24. Hop on the metro or bus to the city's graceful riverside square and walk along the riverside path for ten minutes to Cais do Sodré.

Lunch. See page 51. Pick up lunch from one of the many food stalls in the Time Out Mercado da Ribeira, Lisbon's main market.

Mosteiro dos Jerónimos. See page 83. Take the tram to Belém's fantastic monastery, built to give thanks to the success of Portugal's great navigators.

Museu de Arte Contemporânea MAC/CCB. See page 84. Don't miss this superb collection of modern art, featuring the likes of Andy Warhol and Francis Bacon.

Torre de Belém. See page 86. Climb the elaborate sixteenth-century riverside tower that has become the symbol of the city.

Dinner. See page 66. Eat at *Taberna*, a buzzy restaurant serving modern takes on Portuguese classics.

Drinks. See page 67. Stick around the Bairro Alto and wait for the nightlife to crank up at its hundreds of little bars and clubs.

Centro de Arte Moderna Gulbenkian

Greenhouse garden in Parque Eduardo

Praça do Comércio

Lisbon viewpoints

Built on seven hills, Lisbon has some fantastic *miradouros*, or viewpoints, each with its own distinctive outlook over the city's skyline – here we list the best.

Miradouro de Santa Luzia. See page 40. The best place to see over the terracotta rooftops of the Alfama and the eastern riverfront.

São Vicente de Fora. See page 42. Climb to the top of this historic church for dizzying views over the eastern city from its extensive roof.

Castelo de São Jorge. See page 40. Not quite Lisbon's highest hill, but clamber around the old ramparts to glimpse all sides of the city.

Parque Eduardo VII. See page 95. The top of the park offers an exhilarating panorama encompassing Lisbon and beyond.

Lunch. See page 101. Chill out by a tranquil lake at *A Linha d'Água*, which serves good-value buffet lunches at the top of the park.

Miradouro da Graça. See page 42. Superb views over the Castelo and the city can be had from this breezy terrace by the church of Graça.

Miradouro de São Pedro de Alcântara. See page 61. A broad, tree-lined viewpoint from where you can gaze down on the Baixa and the castle opposite.

Miradouro de Santa Catarina. See page 62. Tucked-away *miradouro* with sweeping views over the Tejo, a popular hangout for Lisbon's alternative crowd.

Dinner. See page 67. *Noobai* is hidden beneath the lip of Miradouro de Santa Catarina and serves inexpensive food and drinks; grab a table on the terrace on summer evenings.

Cityscape from Miradouro de Santa Luzia

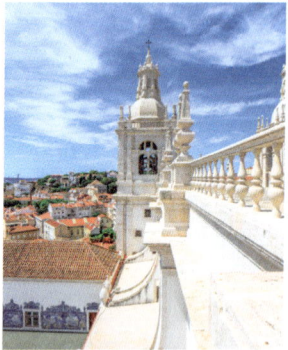

View from São Vicente de Fora

Linha d'Água

Lisbon for families

Lisbon is very family-friendly, and children are welcomed everywhere. Below are some of the best attractions for those with kids.

Boat trips. See page 138. Take to the water to see Lisbon from a new perspective; an experience that kids always love.

Oceanário. See page 103. One of the largest oceanariums in Europe, with sharks, rays, otters, penguins and fish galore.

Pavilhão do Conhecimento. See page 102. This science museum has fantastic hands-on experiments and challenges for people of all ages, together with informative exhibits.

Lunch. See page 107. The traffic-free restaurants of Parque das Nações are great for kids – try the popular *ZeroZero* pizzeria for an inexpensive lunch.

Segway tour. See page 138. Zip around the city on two wheels for a fun way to see the sights.

Museu da Marioneta. See page 72. From medieval marionettes to contemporary satirical puppets, this museum trumpets an art form that satisfied children long before computer games.

Museu da Carris. See page 78. Lisbon's trams are great fun to ride on, but here kids can clamber about trams, buses and metro trains with fewer crowds.

Caparica. See page 121. Lisbon's best beaches are just south of the city, great at any time of the year for a walk or day by the sea.

Sintra. See page 108. Horse and carriage rides, castles and fantasy palaces make this a great day out.

Dinner. See page 32. Spacious, early-opening *Bom Jardim* has tables inside and out and affordable food that kids love.

Segway tour

Museu da Marioneta

Parque das Nações

PLACES

Castelo de São Jorge

The Baixa and Rossio

The tall, imposing buildings that make up the Baixa (Lower Town, pronounced bye-sha) house some of Lisbon's most interesting shops. With plenty of hotels and guesthouses, this is also the tourist epicentre, whose needs are served by a range of cafés, restaurants and street entertainers. Facing the river, this area felt the full force of the 1755 earthquake that destroyed much of what was then one of Europe's wealthiest capitals. The king's minister, the Marquês de Pombal, swiftly redesigned the sector with the grid pattern evident today, framed by a triangle of broad squares. Praça do Comércio sits to the south, with Praça da Figueira and Rossio to the north, the latter having been the city's main square since medieval times.

Praça do Comércio

MAP PAGE 26, POCKET MAP E13

The beautiful, arcaded **Praça do Comércio** represents the climax of Pombal's design. Its classical buildings were once a royal palace and the square is centred on an exuberant bronze equestrian statue of Dom José, monarch during the earthquake and the period of the capital's rebuilding. Two of Portugal's last royals came to a sticky end in this square: in 1908 King Carlos I and his eldest son were shot dead here, clearing the way for the declaration of the Republic two years later.

The square has been partly pedestrianized in recent years in a successful attempt to make it more

Aerial view of Praça do Comércio

Rua Augusta

tourist-friendly, with a panoply of cafés and shops on either side. The secluded Patio da Galé, tucked into the western arcades, hosts frequent events, while the **Torreão Poente**, at the southwest corner of the square, is part of the Museu de Lisboa and holds temporary exhibits – see Ⓦ bit.ly/Torreao. The north side of the square is where you can start tram tours of the city. However, it is the square's riverfront that is perhaps most appealing, especially in the hour or two before sunset, when people linger in the golden light to watch the orange ferries ply between the Estação Fluvial ferry station and Barreiro on the other side of the Tejo. An attractive walk is to head west along the pedestrianized riverfront to Cais do Sodré (see page 50).

Lisbon Story Centre

MAP PAGE 26, POCKET MAP E13
Praço do Comércio 79 Ⓜ Terreiro de Paço
Ⓦ lisboastorycentre.pt, charge.
This is the highlight of a group of touristy cafés and shops that fill the square's historic eastern arcades. The **Lisbon Story Centre** gives a potted, visual account of the city's

history – good for a rainy day, though somewhat pricey. There are six zones, each dedicated to a phase in Lisbon's past. The multimedia displays include models, paintings, photos, narrations and filmed re-enactments – the highlight is a somewhat gory 4D film depicting the 1755 earthquake, and a "virtual" scale model of the modern city.

Arco da Rua Augusta

MAP PAGE 26, POCKET MAP E13
Rua Augusta 2 Ⓜ Terreiro de Paço
Ⓦ visitlisboa.com, charge.
Praça do Comércio's most prominent landmark is a huge arch, the **Arco da Rua Augusta**, adorned with statues of historical figures, including the Marquês de Pombal and Vasco da Gama. Acting as a gateway to the city, the arch was built to celebrate Lisbon's reconstruction after the earthquake, though it wasn't completed until 1873. You can take a lift up to just below the Clock Room, a small exhibition space centred round the workings of a nineteenth-century clock. From here, you can squeeze up a spiral staircase to the flat roof

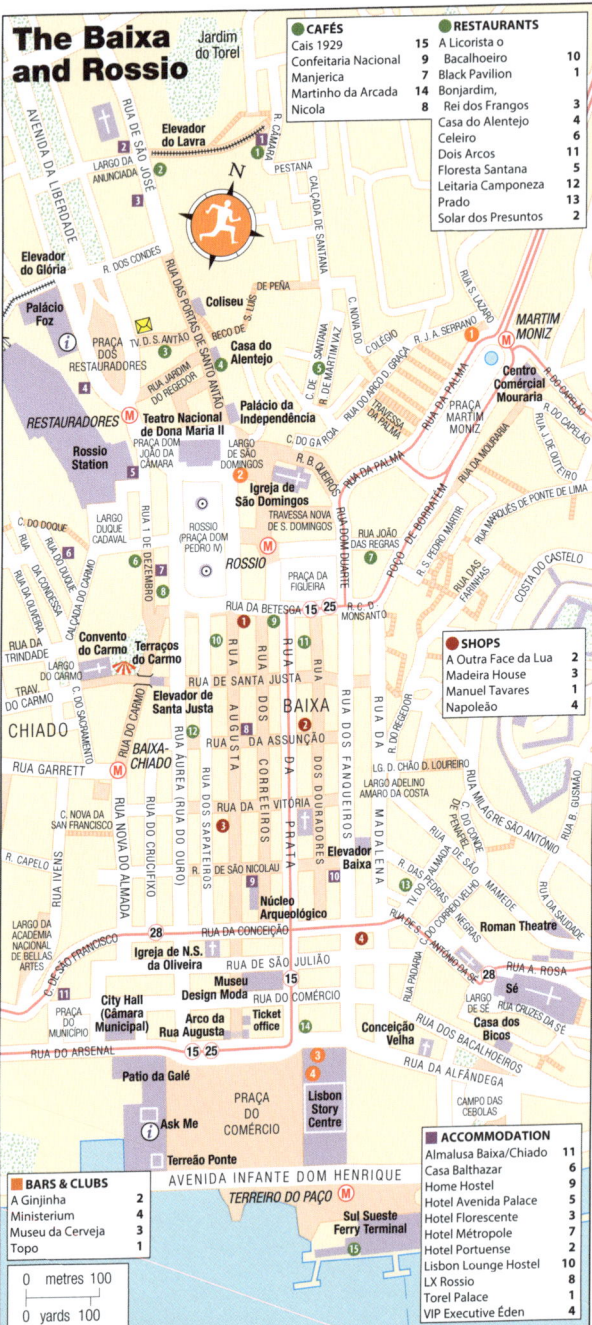

The Baixa and Rossio

Jardim do Torel

CAFÉS
Cais 1929	15
Confeitaria Nacional	9
Manjerica	7
Martinho da Arcada	14
Nicola	8

RESTAURANTS
A Licorista o Bacalhoeiro	10
Black Pavilion	1
Bonjardim, Rei dos Frangos	3
Casa do Alentejo	4
Celeiro	6
Dois Arcos	11
Floresta Santana	5
Leitaria Camponeza	12
Prado	13
Solar dos Presuntos	2

SHOPS
A Outra Face da Lua	3
Madeira House	2
Manuel Tavares	1
Napoleão	4

BARS & CLUBS
A Ginjinha	2
Ministerium	4
Museu da Cerveja	3
Topo	1

ACCOMMODATION
Almalusa Baixa/Chiado	11
Casa Balthazar	6
Home Hostel	9
Hotel Avenida Palace	3
Hotel Florescente	5
Hotel Métropole	7
Hotel Portuense	2
Lisbon Lounge Hostel	10
LX Rossio	8
Torel Palace	1
VIP Executive Éden	4

of the monument where you'll be greeted by unmissable views across the Praça do Comércio and the Baixa. Don't be tempted to stand under the bell here – when it strikes, you'll regret it.

Rua Augusta

MAP PAGE 26, POCKET MAP D11

Completely paved in mosaics, the broad **Rua Augusta** runs from Praça do Comércio up to Rossio and is the Baixa's main pedestrianized thoroughfare. Filled with shops, cafés, bars, market stalls and touristy restaurants, it can get pretty packed, but its buskers and street performers are always entertaining.

Museu Design Moda

MAP PAGE 26, POCKET MAP E13
Rua Augusta 24 ⓦ mude.pt.

Housed in a superbly remodelled former bank, the **Museu Design Moda** is an impressive collection of around 2500 design and fashion classics from the early 1900s to today, amassed by former stockbroker and media mogul Francisco Capelo. The museum's ever-changing exhibitions include design classics, such as furniture by Charles and Ray Eames, Phillipe Starck, Oscar Niemeyer and Frank Gehry, and also features Capelo's fashion collection – including haute couture from the 1950s, 1960s street fashion and the brand

Historic café *Martinho da Arcada*

labelling of the 1990s. Designers who are represented include Pierre Cardin, Zandra Rhodes, Stella McCartney, Christian Dior, Alexander McQueen, Jean Paul Gaultier and Portuguese talent Ana Salazar.

The huge building itself is something of a design icon, much of it pared back to its original brickwork; some of the exhibits are even arranged in the basement vaults behind bars and huge iron doors. There's also a first-floor shop, second-floor café and top-floor restaurant and roof terrace.

The Lisbon earthquake

Eighteenth-century Lisbon had been one of the most active and important ports in Europe, making the Great Earthquake of 1755 all the more tragic. The quake, which was felt as far away as Jamaica, struck Lisbon at 9.30am on November 1 (All Saints' Day), when most of the city's population was at Mass. Within the space of ten minutes there had been three major tremors, and the candles of a hundred church altars had started fires that raged throughout the capital. A vast tidal wave later swept the waterfront and, in all, 40,000 of the 270,000-population died. The destruction of the city shocked the continent and prompted religious debate between philosophers Voltaire and Rousseau. For Portugal, it was a disaster that ended its capital's golden age.

Praça do Município

MAP PAGE 26, POCKET MAP D13

The attractive, mosaic-paved **Praça do Município** houses the Neoclassical nineteenth-century Câmara Municipal (City Hall), where the Portuguese Republic was declared in 1910, flatteringly described by one of Portugal's greatest poets as "one of the finest buildings in the city". The square adjoins Rua do Arsenal, an atmospheric street lined with pungent shops selling dried cod and grocers stocked with cheap wines, port and brandy.

The Baixa Grid

MAP PAGE 26, POCKET MAP D11–12

Pombal designed the **Baixa** to have three main streets dissected by nine smaller streets. Many of these took their names from the crafts and businesses carried out there, like Rua da Prata (Silversmiths' Street) and Rua dos Sapateiros (Cobblers' Street). Modern banks and shops have disturbed these divisions somewhat, though plenty of traditional stores remain; the central section of Rua da Conceição, for example, is still lined with shops selling beads and sequins. Some of the most interesting streets to explore are the smaller ones running south to north – Rua dos Correeiros, Rua dos Dourados and Rua dos Sapateiros. Pombal also wanted the grid's churches to blend in with his harmonious design, so much so that they are almost invisible – wander along Rua de São Julião and the facade of the Church of Nossa Senhora da Oliveira is barely distinguishable from the new offices huddled alongside it, though its tiled interior is delightful.

Núcleo Arqueológico (NARC)

MAP PAGE 26, POCKET MAP E12

Rua dos Correeiros 21 ⓦ bit.ly/NARCLisbon, hourly tours (not Sun), advance bookings required ☏ 211 131 070, free.

Recently renovated, one of Lisbon's smallest but most fascinating museums lies beneath the streets of Baixa. The remnants of Roman fish-preserving tanks, a fifth-century Christian burial place and Moorish ceramics can all be seen in the tiny **Núcleo Arqueológico**, containing the remains of excavations revealed during building work on the BCP bank. Most exhibits are viewed through glass floors or from cramped walkways under the modern bank during a 50-minute tour (hourly, alternate between English and Portuguese). Pombal

Fernando Pessoa

Martinho da Arcada, the café at the north end of Praça do Comércio, was the favoured haunt of Fernando Pessoa (1888–1935), Portugal's greatest contemporary poet and a leading figure of twentieth-century Modernism. Born in Lisbon, Pessoa grew up in South Africa before returning to Portugal in 1905 to work as a translator. He spent much of his time composing poems in Lisbon's cafés. Many of his works are about identity – he wrote under various alter-egos or "heteronyms", each with their own personality and style. The most famous are Alberto Caeiro, Ricardo Reis and Alvaro de Campos, though his most iconic work is the *Book of Disquiet* penned under the heteronym Bernardo Soares. The partly autobiographical work is full of extraordinary philosophical ruminations that have cemented his reputation as a leading existentialist artist.

Exhibits in Núcleo Arqueológico

actually rebuilt most of the Baixa on a riverbed, and you can even see the wooden piles driven into the waterlogged soil to support the buildings, the same device that is used in Venice.

If you're interested in discovering more about Lisbon's underground ruins, ask the museum about early summer visits to the amazing Roman tunnels that lie beneath the Baixa. Access is restricted to the 2000-year-old tunnels, whose purpose remains unclear, because they are usually flooded. As a result, they are open for just three days a year and attract enormous queues. It's a bizarre sight watching people enter the tunnels, which can only be accessed through a manhole cover between tram tracks on Rua da Conceição.

Elevador de Santa Justa

MAP PAGE 26, POCKET MAP D11
Rua de Santa Justa, charge.
Raul Mésnier's extraordinary and eccentric **Elevador de Santa Justa** was built in 1902 by a disciple of Eiffel. Its giant lift whisks you 32m up the inside of a latticework metal tower, depositing you on a platform high above the Baixa. Before taking the upper exit on to the Largo do Carmo, head up the dizzying spiral staircase to the pricey rooftop café for great views over the city.

Rossio

MAP PAGE 26, POCKET MAP C11
Praça Dom Pedro IV (popularly known as **Rossio**) has been the city's main square since medieval times and it remains the hub of commercial Lisbon. Its central space sparkles with Baroque fountains and polished, mosaic-cobbled pavements. During the nineteenth century, Rossio's plethora of cafés attracted Lisbon's painters and writers, though many of the artists' haunts were converted to banks in the 1970s. Nevertheless, the outdoor seats of the square's remaining cafés are perennially popular meeting points. On the northwestern side of the square, there's a horseshoe-shaped entrance to Rossio station, a mock-Manueline complex with the train platforms an escalator ride above the street-level entrances.

Teatro Nacional de Dona Maria II

MAP PAGE 26, POCKET MAP D10
Rossio Ⓦ tndm.pt.

Rossio's biggest concession to grandeur is the **Teatro Nacional de Dona Maria II**, built along its north side in the 1840s, and heavily restored after a fire in 1964. Inside, there is a good café. Prior to the earthquake, the Inquisitional Palace stood on this site, in front of which public hangings and *autos-da-fé* (ritual burnings of heretics) took place.

Igreja de São Domingos

MAP PAGE 26, POCKET MAP D11
Largo de São Domingos ☎ 213 428 275.

The **Igreja de São Domingos** stands on the site of the thirteenth-century Convento de São Domingos, where sentences were read out during the Inquisition. The convent was destroyed in the earthquake of 1755, though its portal was reconstructed soon after as part of the current Dominican church. For over a century it was

Praça dos Restauradores

the venue for royal marriages and christenings, though it lost this role after the declaration of the Republic and was then gutted by a fire in the 1950s.

Some say the flames purged the unsavoury acts that took place on the spot, such as the massacre of forcibly converted Jews (known as "New Christians") which began here in 1506. It was reopened in 1997 after partial restoration to replace the seats and some statues; however, the rest of the cavernous interior and the scarred pillars remain powerfully atmospheric.

Praça da Figueira

MAP PAGE 26, POCKET MAP D11

Praça da Figueira is a historic square (once the site of Lisbon's main market), though the unfortunate addition of an underground car park has detracted from its former grandeur. Nevertheless, it is slightly quieter than Rossio and still offers appealing views of the green slopes of the Castelo de São Jorge.

Praça dos Restauradores

MAP PAGE 26, POCKET MAP C10

The elongated **Praça dos Restauradores** (Square of the Restorers) takes its name from the renewal of independence from Spain in 1640. To the south sits the superb Art Deco frontage of the old Eden cinema, now an apartment-hotel (see page 127). The square is dominated by the pink Palácio de Foz on the western side, built for a count in 1777 and housed the Ministry of Propaganda under the Salazar regime (1932–74). It is now home to the Portuguese Tourist Office (see page 141). Its ornate mirror room hosts occasional concerts.

Rua das Portas de Santo Antão

MAP PAGE 26, POCKET MAP D10

The pedestrianized **Rua das Portas de Santo Antão** is well

Casa do Alentejo

known for its seafood restaurants. Despite the tourist trappings on this street and the adjacent Rua Jardim Regedor (you're likely to get waiters trying to smooth-talk you into their premises), it is worth eating here at least once to sample its seafood. The thoroughfare is also home to several theatres, and the domed **Coliseu dos Recreios** at no. 96 (ⓦcoliseulisboa.com), which opened in 1890 as a circus but has since been reimagined as one of Lisbon's main concert venues.

Casa do Alentejo

MAP PAGE 26, POCKET MAP D10
Rua de Santo Antão 58 ⓜ Terreiro de Paço
ⓦ casadoalentejo.pt, free.
A cultural centre with its own café-bar and restaurant (see page 32), the **Casa do Alentejo** is a sumptuously decorated pseudo-Moorish palace, little changed for decades. Originally a seventeenth-century mansion and later a casino, it has been a centre

dedicated to culture from the Alentejo district since the 1930s. You can just wander in and peek at the beautifully tiled interior but most visitors head upstairs to the dining room or café-bar, with its neighbouring ballroom, an amazing, slightly rundown room hung with chandeliers.

Elevador do Lavra

MAP PAGE 26, POCKET MAP K5
Largo da Anunciada, charge.
Rua das Portas de Santo Antão ends next to the lower platform of one of the city's classic *elevadores*, **Elevador do Lavra**. The funicular opened in 1884 and is Lisbon's oldest and least tourist-frequented *elevador*, though its future is currently uncertain following the tragic accident at the Elevador da Glória in 2025. At the top, a short walk down Travessa do Torel takes you to **Jardim do Torel**, a tiny park above a series of ornate terraces offering exhilarating views over the city.

Shops

A Outra Face da Lua
MAP PAGE 26, POCKET MAP E12
Rua da Assunção 22.
This small, buzzy family-run space specializes in retro fashion – fab vintage clothes, tin toys and so on.

Madeira House
MAP PAGE 26, POCKET MAP D12
Rua Augusta 133.
Linens and embroidery from Madeira feature, along with attractive ceramics, tiles and souvenirs from the mainland.

Manuel Tavares
MAP PAGE 26, POCKET MAP D11
Rua da Betesga 1a.
Small 1860-opened treasure trove, with a fine array of nuts, chocolate and cheeses, and a basement stuffed with vintage wines and ports, some from the early 1900s.

Napoleão
MAP PAGE 26, POCKET MAP E12
Rua dos Fanqueiros 68–70.
This spruce shop offers a fine range of quality port and wine from Portugal's main regions, and its enthusiastic, English-speaking staff can advise on what to buy.

Restaurants

A Licorista o Bacalhoeiro
MAP PAGE 26, POCKET MAP D11
Rua dos Sapateiros 222–224 ☎ 213 431 415.
Dating back to the 1920s and once a favoured haunt of Pessoa, this pleasant tile-and-brick restaurant is a popular lunchtime stop, when locals flock in for inexpensive set meals or mains such as *bacalhau à brás*. €€

Black Pavilion
MAP PAGE 26, POCKET MAP J5
Rua Câmara Pestana 45
ⓦ blackpavilion.com.pt.
Inside the luxurious *Torel Palace* hotel, set within a historic glass pavilion, *Black Pavilion* offers surprisingly affordable top-quality food with fantastic views over the city, either inside or on a beautiful terrace. Dishes include scallop ravioli, duck with sweet potato, pork with orange sauce and an amazing baked goat's cheese starter. Service is second to none and there are also vegetarian options. €€€

Bonjardim, Rei dos Frangos
MAP PAGE 26, POCKET MAP C10
Trav de Santo Antão 11–18 ☎ 213 424 389.
A Lisbon institution thanks to its spit-roast chicken, in an attractive building tucked down a pedestrianized alley. There are plenty of tables outdoors too. A half-chicken is the dish to go for, though it also serves other meat and fish at less-generous prices. €

Casa do Alentejo
MAP PAGE 26, POCKET MAP D10
Rua das Portas de Santo Antão 58
ⓦ casadoalentejo.pt.
A centre dedicated to Alentejan culture (see page 31), with its own restaurant in a beautifully tiled upstairs dining room. Alentejo specialities include rice with lamb and mushrooms and *carne de porco à alentejana* (grilled pork with clams); or just pop in for a drink in the superb bar or courtyard taverna. €€

Celeiro
MAP PAGE 26, POCKET MAP D11
Rua 1° de Dezembro 65 ⓦ celeiro.pt.
Just off Rossio, this inexpensive self-service restaurant sits in the basement of a health-food supermarket and offers tasty vegetarian spring rolls, quiches, pizza and the like. There's also a streetside café offering snacks and drinks. €

Dois Arcos
MAP PAGE 26, POCKET MAP D11
Rua dos Douradores 163 ☎ 218 879 689.
The "Two Arches" is one of the more historic restaurants on

Casa do Alentejo cultural centre

this bustling Baixa street – with historic prices too. Expect simple, well-prepared grilled meat and fish dishes, such as salmon steaks and generous portions of *febras* (pork steak). €€

Floresta Santana

MAP PAGE 26, POCKET MAP D10
Calçada Santana 18 ☎ 963 945 338.
A short (uphill) walk from the hustle of the Baixa, but a world away in terms of atmosphere, this friendly, family-run restaurant plates up excellent-value meals. The fish and meat dishes are fresh and generous, and desserts are home-made and huge. Gets particularly busy at lunchtimes with local residents. €€

Leitaria Camponeza

MAP PAGE 26, POCKET MAP D12
Rua dos Sapateiros 155–157 ☎ 923 132 488.
Formerly a *leitaria* (dairy shop) and still displaying the Art Nouveau decor from its past existence, this is now a simple restaurant with a short, moderately priced menu – the grilled meat *espetadas* (skewers) are particularly good. A great spot for a chilled dinner along a local crowd. €€

Prado

MAP PAGE 26, POCKET MAP E12
Travessa das Pedras Negras 2
Ⓦ pradorestaurante.com.
Chef António Galapito whips up Modern Portuguese cuisine using local, seasonal produce, served to patrons in an airy high-ceilinged space with low-hanging lights. As you'd expect, menus change regularly but might feature cockles with chard or oyster mushrooms with fermented pepper and buckwheat; and there's even a mushroom ice cream for dessert. Prices are reasonable considering the quality, and there are decent organic wines. €€

Solar dos Presuntos

MAP PAGE 26, POCKET MAP J5
Rua das Portas de Santo Antão 150
Ⓦ solardospresuntos.com.
The "Manor House of Hams" is, not surprisingly, best known for its smoked ham from the Minho region in northern Portugal, served cold as a starter. There are also excellent, if expensive, meat and seafood dishes, many using traditional recipes. Popular with celebrities, it's best to book a table. €€€

Confeitaria Nacional

Cafés

Cais 1929

MAP PAGE 26, POCKET MAP F13
Estação Sul Sueste, Terreiro do Paço ⓣ 911 929 276.

Part of the beautiful Arc Deco Sul Sueste ferry terminal – which now acts as a base for boat tours – *Cais 1929* sits in a 1930s *building* renovated by architect Ana Costa. It serves pricy seafood, but most people forgive the steep prices for its outdoor seating, right up by the waterfront – also a great spot for a coffee or cocktail. €€

Confeitaria Nacional

MAP PAGE 26, POCKET MAP D11
Praça da Figueira 18B.

Opened in 1829 as the royal confectioner and little changed since, with a stand-up counter selling pastries and sweets below mirrors and stucco ceilings. There's a little side room and outdoor seating for sit-down coffees and snacks. €

Manjerica

MAP PAGE 26, POCKET MAP E11
Rua das Regras 5A.

This simple café with a few outdoor tables serves a good range of vegetarian and vegan dishes at very good prices and is a good destination for breakfast, brunch or lunch. Expect the likes of pancakes, banana bread, toasties, eggs benedict and scrambled tofu. €

Martinho da Arcada

MAP PAGE 26, POCKET MAP E13
Praça do Comércio 3.

One of Lisbon's oldest café-restaurants, first opened in 1782 and declared a national monument in 1910. It has been a gambling den, a meeting place for political dissidents and, later, a more reputable hangout for politicians, writers and artists. It is now divided into a simple stand-up café and a slightly pricey restaurant. The outdoor tables under the arches are a perfect spot for a coffee and a *pastel de nata*. €€

Nicola

MAP PAGE 26, POCKET MAP D11
Rossio 24–25.

The only surviving Rossio coffee house from the early twentieth century, once the haunt of some of Lisbon's great literary figures. The outdoor tables overlooking the bustle of Rossio are the main calling card; sadly, it has sacrificed

A starter for ten euros?

At restaurants, don't feel you're being ripped off when you're served an array of starters before you even order your main course, then get a bill for what you've eaten at the end. This is normal practice in Portugal, and no waiter will take offence if you politely decline whatever you're offered. Starters can vary from simple bread, butter and olives to prawns, cheeses and cured meats. If you're tempted, it's a good idea to ask the waiter how much each item costs. Check your bill, too, to ensure you've not been charged for anything you declined.

much of its period interior in the name of modernization. €

Bars

A Ginjinha
MAP PAGE 26, POCKET MAP D11
Largo de São Domingos 8.
Everyone should try *ginjinha* – Portuguese cherry brandy – once. There's just about room in this microscopic joint to walk in, down a glassful and stagger outside to see the city in a new light.

Ministerium
MAP PAGE 26, POCKET MAP E13
Ala Nascente 72, Praça do Comércio
Ⓦ ministerium.pt.
The grand and historic buildings of the former Ministry of Finance partly make up the stylish backdrop to this hip club, mostly playing house and techno and attracting top-name DJs. There's a spacious dancefloor plus quieter zones and a great rooftop café-bar – check the website for events and parties.

Museu da Cerveja
MAP PAGE 26, POCKET MAP E13
Terreiro do Paço Ala Nascente 62–65.
Undoubtedly touristy but indisputably fun, this bar-restaurant serves not bad food, but most people visit to sample some of its 100 beers, sourced from around the country and Portugal's former colonies. Try one of the highly rated craft beers such as Sovina

from Porto or Letra from Braga, inside or out on a table by the square. If you want to learn more about the history of Portuguese brewing, *visit the upstairs museum (*charge).

Topo
MAP PAGE 26, POCKET MAP E10
Sixth floor, Centro Comercial Martim Moniz, Praça Martim Moniz Ⓣ 215 881 322.
Set on the top floor of a shopping centre, this contemporary bar-restaurant has great views towards the castle from both the light and airy interior and its outdoor terrace. The drinks and cocktail list is as long as the bar, and it also dishes up light snacks or pricier mains. At weekends there are often DJs.

Historic *Nicola* coffee house

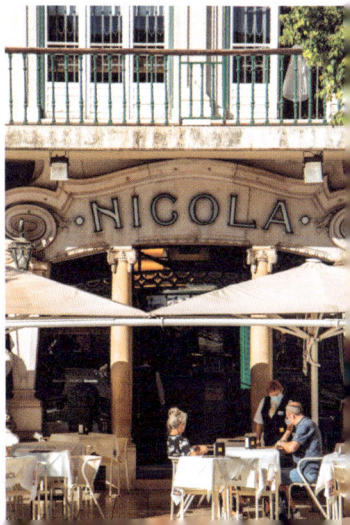

The Sé, Castelo and Alfama

East of the Baixa, the streets climb past the capital's ancient cathedral, or Sé, to the dramatic remains of the Castelo de São Jorge, an oasis of tranquillity high above the city. East of the castle lie two of Lisbon's most prominent churches, São Vicente de Fora and Santa Engrácia. The districts around the castle – Mouraria, Santa Cruz and particularly the Alfama – represent the oldest and most atmospheric corners of Lisbon, served by famous tram #28, which wends its way round the castle and down to the fashionable district of Intendente. Down below, Santa Apolónia, the international train station, is situated by the riverfront that boasts the glitzy *Lux* club, while a little further east is a historic steam pumping station and a surprisingly fascinating tile museum.

The Sé

MAP PAGE 38, POCKET MAP F12
Largo da Sé, Tram #28 ⓦ sedelisboa.pt, charge.

Lisbon's main cathedral, **the Sé**, was founded in 1150 to commemorate the city's Reconquest from the Moors on the site of their main mosque. It's a Romanesque structure with a suitably fortress-like appearance. The great rose window and twin towers form a simple and effective facade, although there's nothing particularly exciting inside: the building was once splendidly embellished on the orders of Dom João V, but his Rococo whims were swept away by the 1755 earthquake and subsequent restorers. All that remains is a group of Gothic tombs behind the high altar and the decaying thirteenth-century **cloister**, whose archeological excavations have revealed the remains of a sixth-century Roman house and Moorish public buildings.

The Baroque **Treasury** (charge) holds a small museum of treasures including the relics of St Vincent, brought to Lisbon in 1173 in a boat that was piloted by ravens,

according to legend. Ravens were kept in the cloisters for centuries afterwards, but the tradition halted when the last one died in 1978. To this day, the birds remain one of the city's symbols.

Igreja de Santo António and Museu Antoniano

MAP PAGE 38, POCKET MAP E12
Largo S. António da Sé 22, Tram #28 ⓣ 218 860 447.

The small eighteenth-century church of **Santo António** (open daily) is said to have been built on the spot where the city's most popular saint was born as Fernando Bulhões; after his death in Italy in 1231 he became known as St Anthony of Padua. The tiny neighbouring **museum** (charge) chronicles the saint's life, including his enviable skill at fixing marriages, though only devotees will find interest in the statues and endless images.

Casa dos Bicos

MAP PAGE 38, POCKET MAP F13
Rua dos Bacalhoeiros 10
ⓦ museulisboa.pt, charge.

The **Casa dos Bicos** means the "House of Points", and its curious walls – set with diamond-shaped stones – give an idea of the richness of pre-1755 Lisbon. It was built in 1523 for the son of the Viceroy of India, though only the lower facade of the original building survived the earthquake. It is now owned by the Saramago organization, which uses the venue for recitals and a permanent exhibition dedicated to the Nobel Prize-winning Portuguese author José Saramago, who died in 2010.

The ground floor has been maintained as an archeological area where you can view sections of a third-century Roman wall and fish-processing plant, excavated from beneath the building.

Museu do Aljube – Resistência e Liberdade

MAP PAGE 38, POCKET MAP F12
Rua de Augusta Rosa 42
Ⓦ museudoaljube.pt, charge.

This small but engaging and moving **museum** is dedicated to **resistance and freedom**, commemorating those who have been censored or repressed, in particular people who risked their lives during the dictatorship of Salazar (1926–68). Housed in a former political prison, it details the drastic and often brutal lengths Salazar's regime went to hold onto its former colonies and preside over an increasingly weary population up until the 1974 revolution. Exhibits over three floors include old photos and newsreels, radio broadcasts and personal statements from people who were imprisoned here, including Mário Soares (later the Portuguese president) and author Miguel Torga – you can also duck inside their former windowless cells, just one by two metres in size.

Museu do Teatro Romano

MAP PAGE 38, POCKET MAP F12
Entrance on Patio de Aljube 5, Tram #28
Ⓦ bit.ly/TeatroLisbon, charge.

The **Museu do Teatro Romano** displays a wealth of Roman coins, spoons and fragments of pots, statues and columns excavated from the ruins of a Roman theatre, dating from 57 AD, which are fenced off just north of Rua Augusto Rosa. Roman Lisbon – Olisipo – became the administrative capital of Lusitania, the western part of Iberia, under Julius Caesar in 60 BC, and the

Quirky Casa dos Bicos

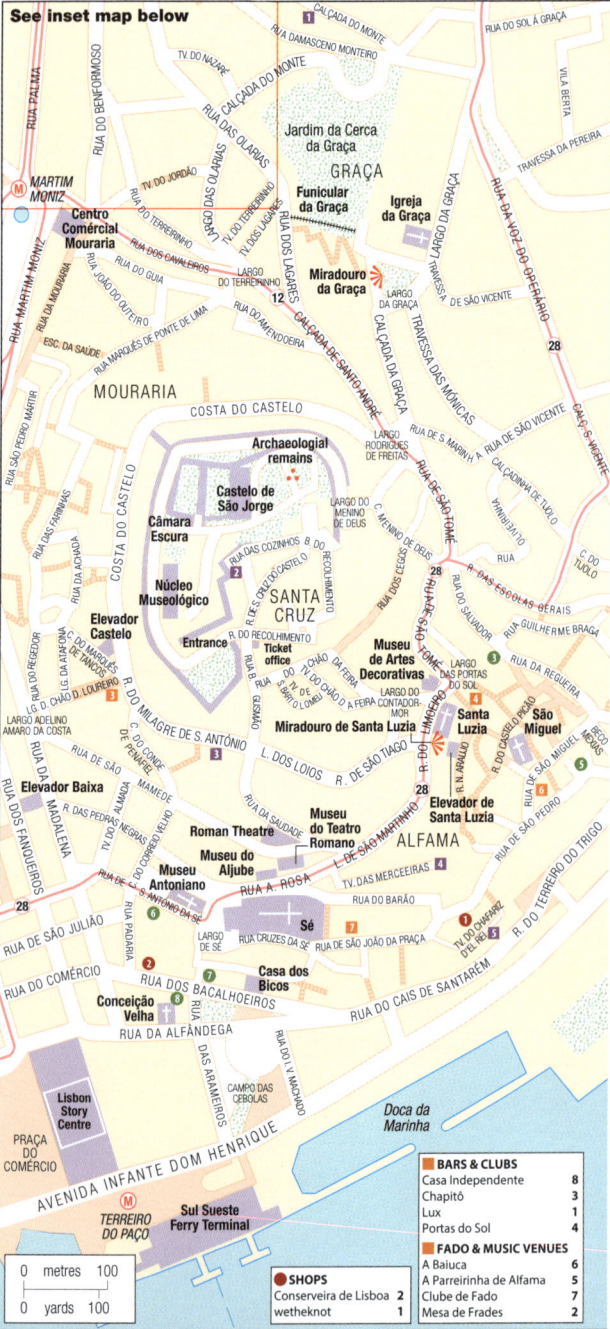

THE SÉ, CASTELO AND ALFAMA

See inset map below

CALÇADA DO MONTE
RUA DAMASCENO MONTEIRO
RUA DO SOL À GRAÇA
TV. DO NAZARÉ
RUA DE BENFORMOSO
RUA DAS OLARIAS
VILA BERTA
CALÇADA DO MONTE
Jardim da Cerca da Graça
GRAÇA
TRAVESSA DA PEREIRA
MARTIM MONIZ
Centro Comércial Mouraria
Funicular da Graça
Igreja da Graça
RUA DA GRAÇA
RUA DO TERREIRINHO
TV. DO JORDÃO
RUA DOS CAVALEIROS
LARGO DO TERREIRINHO
TV. DO TERREIRINHO
TV. DOS LAGARES
RUA DOS LAGARES
Miradouro da Graça
Largo da Graça
TRAVESSA DAS MÓNICAS
RUA DA VOZ DO OPERÁRIO
RUA DO GUIA
RUA DO AMENDOAL
DE SÃO VICENTE
RUA JOÃO DO OUTEIRO
ESC. DA SAÚDE
RUA MARQUÊS DE PONTE DE LIMA
CALÇADA DE SANTO ANDRÉ
CALÇADA DA GRAÇA
28
CALÇADA DE SÃO VICENTE
MOURARIA
COSTA DO CASTELO
Largo RODRIGUES DE FREITAS
RUA DE S. MARINH A
RUA DE SÃO VICENTE
CALÇADINHA DE TIJOLO
Archaeologial remains
Castelo de São Jorge
Largo DO MENINO DE DEUS
C. MENINO DE DEUS
RUA DE SÃO TOMÉ
28
VOZINHO
C. DO TIJOLO
Câmara Escura
RUA DAS COZINHAS
B. DO RECOLHIMENTO
RUA DOS EGIDOS
R. DAS ESCOLAS GERAIS
COSTA DO CASTELO
RUA DAS FARINHAS
Núcleo Museológico
RUA DA ADIAÇA
B. DO CASTELO
SANTA CRUZ
R. DO SALVADOR
RUA GUILHERME BRAGA
Elevador Castelo
R. R.S. DO RECOLHIMENTO
R. DO RECOLHIMENTO
Entrance
Ticket office
Museu de Artes Decorativas
RUA DA REGUEIRA
C. DO REGEDOR
C. DO MARQUÊS DE TANCOS
R. DO MILAGRE DE S. ANTÓNIO
DO CHÃO DA FEIRA
TV. DO CHÃO DA FEIRA
B. DO CHÃO DA FEIRA
Largo DAS PORTAS DO SOL
LARGO DO CONTADOR-MOR
Santa Luzia
São Miguel
C. DO CONDE DE PENAFIEL
R. DO LIMOEIRO
Miradouro de Santa Luzia
R. N. ARRÚDO
R. DO SÃO MIGUEL
LARGO ADELINO AMARO DA COSTA
LG. D. CHÃO D. LOUREIRO
RUA DE SÃO
MAMEDE
L. DOS LOIOS
R. DE SÃO TIAGO
Elevador de Santa Luzia
Elevador Baixa
R. DAS PEDRAS NEGRAS
RUA DA SAÚDE
Museu do Teatro Romano
R. DE SÃO MARTINHO
RUA DE SÃO PEDRO
RUA DOS FANQUEIROS
RUA DA MADALENA
Roman Theatre
ALFAMA
R. DO TERREIRO DO TRIGO
TV. DO CORREIO VELHO
Museu Antoniano
Museu do Aljube
RUA A. ROSA
TV. DAS MERCEEIRAS
R. DO CHAFARIZ D'EL REI
RUA PADARIA
LARGO DE SÉ
Sé
RUA DO BARÃO
RUA DE SÃO JULIÃO
S. ANTÓNIO DA SÉ
RUA CRUZES DA SÉ
RUA DE SÃO JOÃO DA PRAÇA
Casa dos Bicos
Conceição Velha
RUA DO COMÉRCIO
RUA DOS BACALHOEIROS
RUA DA ALFÂNDEGA
RUA DAS ARAMEIROS
R. DO M. MACHADO
RUA DO CAIS DE SANTARÉM
CAMPO DAS CEBOLAS
Doca da Marinha
Lisbon Story Centre
PRAÇA DO COMÉRCIO
AVENIDA INFANTE DOM HENRIQUE
TERREIRO DO PAÇO
Sul Sueste Ferry Terminal

| metres | 100 |
| yards | 100 |

◼ BARS & CLUBS
Casa Independente 8
Chapitô 3
Lux 1
Portas do Sol 4

◼ FADO & MUSIC VENUES
A Baiuca 6
A Parreirinha de Alfama 5
Clube de Fado 7
Mesa de Frades 2

◆ SHOPS
Conserveria de Lisboa 2
wetheknot 1

The Sé, Castelo and Alfama

Barbadinhos Steam
Pumping Station (200m),
Museu Nacional do
Azulejo (1.3km)

RUA DA SENHORA DA GLÓRIA
RUA LEITE DE VASCONCELOS
RUA DO VALE DE S. ANTÓNIO
R. DA CRUZ DE S. APOLÓNIA
RUA DIOGO DE COUTO
RUA DE ENTREMUROS DO MIRANTE
BECO DO MIRANTE
RUA DA VERÓNICA
TRAVESSA DAS PEDRAS
TRAVESSA DAS FREIRAS
RUA DO MIRANTE
CAMPO DE SANTA CLARA

Feira da Ladra Market (Tues & Sat)
Jardim Botto
Mercado de Santa Clara
CAMPO DE SANTA CLARA
LARGO DR. BERNARDINO ANTÓNIO GOMES
ARCO GRANDE DE CIMA
C. D. CARDEAL
RUA DOS CAMINHOS DE FERRO

São Vicente de Fora
Santa Engrácia (Panteão Nacional)
CAMPO DE SÃO VICENTE
TV. DO ZAGALO
TV. DO PAIÓ
CASCÃO
RUA DO PARAÍSO
R. DOS CORVOS

Santa Apolónia Station
Ⓜ *SANTA APOLÓNIA*
C. DE SÃO VICENTE
C. DO FORTE
RUA DA M. DE ARTILHARIA
Museu Militar

Santo Estevão
RUA DO VIGÁRIO
RUA DE SANTO ESTEVÃO
BECO DA LAPA
RUA DOS REMÉDIOS
RUA DA LAPA
R. DA REGUEIRA
RUA DO JARDIM DO TABACO
Museu do Fado
AVENIDA INFANTE DOM HENRIQUE
LARGO DO CHAFARIZ DE DENTRO

Cruise Terminal
Doca do Jardim do Tabaco

Ⓜ *INTENDENTE*
RUA ANDRADE
RUA MARIA
RUA MARIA DA FONTE
RUA ANTERO DE QUENTAL
RUA DOS ANJOS
AVENIDA ALMIRANTE REIS
LARGO DO INTENDENTE PINA MANIQUE
RUA MARIA DA FONTE

Miradouro da Senhora do Monte
RUA PALMA
RUA DO BENFORMOSO
RUA DA BOMBARDA
RUA DAM ASCENSO MONTEIRO
C. DO MONTE

■ ACCOMMODATION
1908 Lisboa Hotelo	6
Albergaria Senhora do Monte	1
Memmo Alfama	4
Palacete Chafariz d'el Rei	5
Solar do Castelo	2
Solar dos Mouros	3

● RESTAURANTS
Barracão de Alfama	5
Casanova	2
Casa da Tia Helena	3
Cervejaria Ramiro	10
Delfina Café	7
Estrela da Sé	6
Infame	9
Pateo 13	4
Sála de João Sá	8
Santa Clara dos Cogemelos	1

metres 100
yards 100

Museu de Artes Decorativas

theatre shows the wealth that quickly grew thanks to its fish-preserving industries.

Miradouro de Santa Luzia

MAP PAGE 38, POCKET MAP F12
Largo de Santa Luzia.
The church of Santa Luzia marks the entry to the **Miradouro de Santa Luzia**, a spectacular viewpoint where elderly Lisboetas play cards and tourists gather to take in the sweeping views across the Alfama and the river beyond.

Museu de Artes Decorativas

MAP PAGE 38, POCKET MAP F11
Largo das Portas do Sol 2, Tram #28 or #12
Ⓦ fress.pt, charge.
Set in the seventeenth-century Azurara Palace, this fascinating **museum** contains some of the best examples of sixteenth- to eighteenth-century applied art in the country. Founded by a wealthy banker and donated to the nation in 1953, the galleries boast unique pieces of furniture, major collections of gold, silver and porcelain, magnificent paintings and textiles. The rambling building covers five floors, set around a stairway decorated with spectacular *azulejos*. Highlights include a stunning sixteenth-century tapestry depicting a parade of giraffes, beautiful carpets from Arraiolos in the Alentejo district, and Eastern-influenced quilts that were all the rage during the seventeenth and eighteenth centuries. There's also a small café with a patio garden.

Castelo de São Jorge

MAP PAGE 38, POCKET MAP F11
Bus #37 from Praça da Figueira
Ⓦ castelodesaojorge.pt, charge (includes visit to Câmara Escura and Núcleo Museológico).
Reached by a confusing but well-signposted series of twisting roads, the **Castelo de São Jorge** is perhaps the most spectacular building in Lisbon, as much because of its position as anything else. Now Lisbon's most-visited tourist site, the castle was once the heart of a walled city that spread downhill as far as the river. The original Moorish stronghold was besieged in 1147 by a particularly ruthless gang of Crusaders who, together with King Alfonso I of Portugal, conquered Lisbon after some four hundred years of Moorish rule. Badly damaged during the siege, its fortifications were rebuilt. From the fourteenth century, Portuguese kings took up residence in the old Moorish palace, or Alcáçova, within the ramparts, but by the early sixteenth century they had moved to the new royal palace on Praça do Comércio. Subsequently, the castle was used as a prison and then as an army barracks until the 1920s. The walls were partly renovated by Salazar in the 1930s and further restored for Expo '98. A series of gardens, walkways and **viewpoints** hidden within the old Moorish ramparts makes this an enjoyable place in which to wander for a couple of hours, with spectacular views over the city from its towers.

Câmara Escura

MAP PAGE 38, POCKET MAP F11
Castelo de São Jorge, charge (included in visit to Castelo de São Jorge).

One of the castle towers, the **Tower of Ulysses**, now holds a kind of periscope which projects sights from around the city onto a white disc, accompanied by commentary in English. Unless you like being holed up in dark chambers with up to fifteen other people, though, you may prefer to see the view in the open air.

Núcleo Museológico and Archeological Remains

MAP PAGE 38, POCKET MAP F11
Castelo de São Jorge, charge (includes visit to Castelo de São Jorge and Câmara Escura).

Only a much-restored shell remains of the old Moorish Alcáçova. This now houses the **Núcleo Museológico**, a small museum containing items unearthed during excavations in the castle, including Moorish lamps, Roman storage jars and coins, and pottery and tiles from the seventeenth century. Included in the ticket price is a 15-minute guided tour of the **Archeological Remains**, an excavation site that includes the scant remnants of an Iron

Age house, an eleventh-century Moorish quarter and the ruins of the fifteenth-century Palácio dos Condes de Santiago, built for the Bishops of Lisbon.

Santa Cruz and Mouraria

MAP PAGE 38, POCKET MAP F11
Crammed within the castle's outer walls, but free to enter, is the tiny medieval quarter of **Santa Cruz**. This remains a village in its own right, with its own school, bathhouse and church. Leaving Santa Cruz, a tiny arch at the end of Rua do Chão da Feira leads through to Rua dos Cegos and down to Largo Rodrigues de Freitas, which marks the eastern edge of **Mouraria**, the district to which the Moors were relegated after the siege of Lisbon – hence the name. Today Mouraria is an atmospheric residential area.

Funicular da Graça

MAP PAGE 38, POCKET MAP F10
The **Funicular da Graça**, Lisbon's newest, was finally completed in 2024. Its distinctive sleek yellow design is a modern take on the traditional carriage, though its opening was not without controversy: the project took fifteen

The Mouraria district

years and ran over budget by a staggering seven million euros. The fourteen-person, tinted-windowed cuboid glides down to Rua dos Lagares in the historic Mouraria district – a picturesque trundle that saves a steep walk, though the run takes under two minutes.

Miradouro da Graça

MAP PAGE 38, POCKET MAP F10
Calçada da Graça.

The **Miradouro da Graça** provides superb views over Lisbon and the castle. To reach it you can take tram #28 (see page 45) to the broad Largo da Graça and then walk past Nossa Senhora da Graça. The viewpoint also has a small kiosk café-bar. Beneath the *miradouro*, steps lead down to the Jardim da Cerca da Graça. There's a children's play area, lawns and appealing walkways.

Igreja da Graça

MAP PAGE 38, POCKET MAP F10
Largo da Graça.

Behind the *miradouro* sits the imposing **Igreja da Graça**, originally built as a convent in 1271 by Afonso III. Peek inside the church (free) to see its huge painted vaulted ceilings, marble pillars and arches. You can also climb up to the huge terrace

(charge) for views over the city; the ticket includes access to the church cloisters and high altar, where there's a small exhibition of religious art.

Intendente

MAP PAGE 38, POCKET MAP K5
Served by tram #28, **Intendente** was recently down-at-heel and best avoided, certainly after dark, but is now a district to be seen. Its turnaround was driven by the opening of the superb Art Nouveau *1908 Lisboa Hotel* (see page 128) on one side of its pedestrianized square, and the hip Casa Independent (see page 48) cultural centre on the other. Now, the *praça* and its surrounding streets are abuzz with cafés, bars and restaurants, many in beautiful, tile-fronted buildings. You can climb the stepped alleys to the east of the square for a steep 15-minute walk up to Miradouro Senhora do Monte, Lisbon's highest point and a great lookout spot.

São Vicente de Fora

MAP PAGE 38, POCKET MAP G11
Largo de São Vicente, Tram #28
Ⓦ mosteirodesaovicentedefora.com,
church free, charge for monastery.

The church of **São Vicente de Fora** stands as a reminder of the extent

Santa Engrácia

Fado

Fado (literally "fate") is often described as a kind of Portuguese blues. Popular themes are love, death, bullfighting and indeed fate itself. It is believed to derive from music that was popular with eighteenth-century immigrants from Portugal's colonies who first settled in Alfama. Famous singers like Maria Severa and Amália Rodrigues grew up in Alfama, which since the 1930s has hosted some of the city's most authentic fado houses – stroll around after 8pm and you'll hear magical sounds emanating from venues, or better still, enjoy a meal at one of the places listed on page 46. The big contemporary names are Ana Moura; Mariza, who grew up in neighbouring Mouraria; and Cuca Roseta. Other notable singers of the genre include Mísia (1955–2024), Carminho, Helder Moutinho, Carlos do Carmo (1939–2021), Maria da Fé, Raquel Tavares, Camané and Cristina Branco.

of the sixteenth-century city; its name means "Saint Vincent of the Outside". It was built during the years of Spanish rule by Philip II's Italian architect, Felipe Terzi (1582–1629), its geometric facade an important Renaissance innovation. Of more interest is the adjoining monastery, home to the world's largest collection of Baroque tiles. Head through the beautiful cloisters, decorated with *azulejos* representing scenes from Portugal's history, to visit the old monastic refectory, which since 1855 has formed the pantheon of the Bragança dynasty. Here, in more or less complete sequence, are the **tombs** of all the Portuguese kings from João IV, who restored the monarchy in 1640, to Manuel II, the last Portuguese monarch who died in exile in England in 1932. Among them is Catherine of Bragança, the widow of England's Charles II, who is credited with introducing the concept of "teatime" to the British. If you have energy, climb to the roof for spectacular views out over the city. There's also a lovely café by the entrance if you do fancy a cup of tea.

Feira da Ladra

MAP PAGE 38, POCKET MAP H10
Campo de Santa Clara, Tram #28.
The leafy square of Campo de Santa Clara is home to the **Feira da Ladra** ("Thieves' Market"), Lisbon's main flea market, held every Saturday and Tuesday morning. It's not the world's greatest market, but it does turn up some interesting things, like oddities from the former African colonies and old Portuguese prints. Out-and-out junk – from broken alarm clocks to old postcards – is spread on the ground above Santa Engrácia, with cheap clothes, CDs and half-genuine antiques at the top end of the *feira*. The covered *mercado* (market) building has a fine array of fresh fruit and vegetables.

Santa Engrácia

MAP PAGE 38, POCKET MAP H10
Campo de Santa Clara, Tram #28, charge.
The white dome of **Santa Engrácia**, crowning the loftiest church in the city, has become synonymous with unfinished work – begun in 1682, it was only finally completed in 1966. It is now the **Panteão Nacional**, housing the tombs of eminent Portuguese figures, including writer Almeida Garrett (1799–1854), fado extraordinaire Amália Rodrigues (1920–99) and football legend Eusébio (1942–2014). You can take the stairs up to the terrace, from where there are great views over eastern Lisbon.

44

THE SÉ, CASTELO AND ALFAMA

The Alfama

MAP PAGE 38, POCKET MAP G12

In Moorish times, the **Alfama** was
the grandest part of the city, but as
Lisbon expanded, the new Christian
nobility moved out, abandoning
it to the local fishing community.
None of today's houses date from
before the Christian Reconquest, but
you'll notice a kasbah-like layout.
Although an increasing number of
fado restaurants are moving in, the
quarter retains a quiet, charming
village-like quality.

Life continues much as it has
done for years, with people buying
groceries and fish from hole-in-
the-wall stores and householders
stoking small outdoor charcoal
grills. Half the fun of exploring
here is getting lost in its tangle of
cobbled streets, but head for Rua
de São Miguel – off which shoot
some of the most interesting *becos*
(alleys) – and for the parallel Rua
de São Pedro.

Igreja de Santo Estêvão

MAP PAGE 38. POCKET MAP G11

Largo de Santo Estêvão, Tram #28 ☎ 213
912 600, free.

The handsome church of **Santo
Estêvão**, built in 1733, was partly
damaged in the 1755 earthquake,

leaving it with one of its two
original towers. Its Baroque interior
is impressive but is usually open
only for Mass (Sunday at 10am).
However, it's worth a visit if only
to see the view over the river from
its terrace.

Museu do Fado

MAP PAGE 38, POCKET MAP G12

Largo do Chafariz de Dentro 1
Ⓦ museudofado.pt, charge.

Set in the renovated Recinto da
Praia, a former water cistern and
bathhouse, the **Museu do Fado**
provides an excellent introduction
to this quintessentially Portuguese
art form (see box, page 43). A
series of rooms in the museum
contains wax models, photographs,
famous paintings of fado scenes
and descriptions of the leading
singers. It also traces the history of
the Portuguese guitar, an essential
element of the performance.

Interactive displays allow you
to listen to the different types of
music (Lisbon has its own kind,
differing from that of the northern
city of Coimbra), varying from
mournful to positively racy. There
is also a good restaurant on site and
a shop stocking a great selection
of CDs.

Tram 28 in the Alfama

Tram #28

The picture-book tram #28 (6am–10.30pm, every 15min) is one of the city's greatest experiences, though its popularity is such that there are usually queues to board and standing-room-only is more than likely. Built in England in the early twentieth century, the trams are all polished wood and chrome, but give a distinctly rough ride up and down Lisbon's steepest streets, at times coming so close to shops that you could almost take a can of sardines off the shelves. From Graça, the tram plunges down through Alfama to the Baixa and up to Prazeres, to the west of the centre. Take care of belongings as pickpockets also enjoy the ride.

Barbadinhos Steam Pumping Station

MAP PAGE 38, POCKET MAP M5
Rua do Alviela 12 Ⓦ **epal.pt, charge.**
Ten minutes' walk from Santa Apolónia metro, off Calçada dos Barbadinhos, the **Barbadinhos Steam Pumping Station** is a small but engaging museum housed in an attractive old pumping station filled with shiny brass, polished wood and Victorian ingenuity. It was built in 1880 to pump water from a nearby river up Lisbon's steep hills, depositing it in a reservoir hollowed out from a former Franciscan convent. It used four steam-powered engines that worked nonstop until 1928 and which you can see demonstrated today. The museum is the main branch of Lisbon's Museu da Água (see page 62), whose exhibits give a fascinating insight into the evolution of the city's water supply.

Museu Nacional do Azulejo

MAP PAGE 38, POCKET MAP M5
Rua da Madre de Deus 4. Bus #794 from Praça do Comércio/Santa Apolónia Ⓦ **museunacionadoazulejo.pt, charge.**
The **Museu Nacional do Azulejo** traces the development of Portuguese *azulejo* tiles from fifteenth-century Moorish styles to the present day, with each room representing a different period. Diverse styles range from seventeenth-century portraits of the English King Charles II with his Portuguese wife, Catherine of Bragança, to the 1720 satirical panel depicting a man being given an injection in his bottom. The museum is housed inside the stunning church of Madre de Deus, whose eighteenth-century tiled scenes of St Anthony are among the best in the city. Many of the rooms are arranged round the church's cloisters – look for the spire in one corner of the main cloister, itself completely tiled. The highlight upstairs is Portugal's longest *azulejo* – a wonderfully detailed 40-metre panorama of Lisbon, completed in around 1738. There is also a good café-restaurant and shop.

Patio of the Museu Nacional do Azulejo

Shops

Conserveira de Lisboa

MAP PAGE 38, POCKET MAP E13

Rua dos Bacalhoeiras 34.

Wall-to-wall tins stuffed into
wooden cabinets make this
colourful 1930s shop a bizarre but
intriguing place to stock up on
preserved sardines, squid, salmon,
mussels and just about any other
sea beast you can think of.

wetheknot

MAP PAGE 38, POCKET MAP G12

Rua São João da Praça 41.

This small company sells sustainable
fashion and accessories, ethically
made in Portugal from the likes of
organic cotton and vegan leather
or silk, or upcycled from reused
and preloved items. Founded by a
fashion and graphic designer, the
company's style is minimalist and
simple but hardwearing.

Restaurants

Barracão de Alfama

MAP PAGE 38, POCKET MAP G12

Rua de S. Pedro 16 ☎ 218 866 359.

Conserveira de Lisboa

An unpretentious local *tasca*
popular with locals, with non-
touristy prices. Portions are
generous, with fine fish and grilled
meats. Grab one of the outdoor
tables in summer. €€

Casanova

MAP PAGE 38, POCKET MAP M6

Avda Infante Dom Henrique, Loja 7
Armazém B, Cais da Pedra à Bica do Sapato
Ⓦ pizzeriacasanova.pt.

Very popular Italian serving pizza,
pasta and *crostini* with sumptuous
river views from its terrace (when
the cruise ships aren't blocking the
view). You can't book, so turn up
early. €€

Casa da Tia Helena

MAP PAGE 38, POCKET MAP G11

Rua do Castelo Picão 55–57
☎ 218 861 180.

This cosy local restaurant has tables
spilling out onto the steps outside.
The short menu features traditional
Portuguese dishes, such as oven-
baked cod with potatoes, octopus
rice and grilled sardines, as well as
smaller *petiscos* plates (tapas-style
dishes). There's also a fish counter
so you can see that day's catch
before it's grilled on the barbecue. €

Eggs at *Santa Clara dos Cogumelos*

Cervejaria Ramiro

MAP PAGE 38, POCKET MAP K5
Avenida Almirante Reis 1
ⓦ **cervejariaramiro.com.**
Fabulous, famous and extremely
popular seafood restaurant, whose
decor has changed little since it
opened in 1956. It's set across
three floors; the basement is full of
bubbling tanks, while the ground
floor is usually rammed with clients
downing its famed garlic prawns,
lobster and crab. There are some
meat dishes, but no fish. Live
soccer is likely to be on TV. Queue
for a table. €€

Delfina Café

MAP PAGE 38, POCKET MAP F13
Rua dos Bacalhoeiros 16 ☎ **218 770 200.**
Small but amazing-quality
café-restaurant attached to
the *AlmaLusa Hotel* serving an
alluring range of tapas and *petiscos*
(don't miss the garlic prawns or
mushroom *bulhão pato*) as well as
substantial meals – think codfish
pregos in a bun, Iberian pork
wellington or marinated partridge.
You may also be tempted by one
of its classy cocktails with fun
names like White Port, Why
not? (white port, lime juice and
cinnamon). €€€

Estrela da Sé

MAP PAGE 38, POCKET MAP E12
Largo S. António da Sé 4 ☎ **218 870 455.**
Beautiful *azulejo*-plastered
restaurant near the Sé that's been
serving inexpensive and tasty dishes
like *alheira* (chicken sausage),
salmon and Spanish-style tapas
to loyal patrons since 1857. Its
wooden booths – perfect for
discreet trysts – date from the
nineteenth century. €€

Infame

MAP PAGE 38, POCKET MAP H8
Largo do Intendente Pina Manique 4
ⓦ **infame.pt.**
Inside the classy *1908 Lisboa Hotel*,
this Art Nouveau gem has a fine
galleried interior. Dishes feature the
likes of *açorda de camarão* (bread
stew with prawn) or duck with
gnocchi, and there are vegetarian
options. Don't miss a drink in the
adjacent bar. €€€

Pateo 13

MAP PAGE 38, POCKET MAP G12
Calcadinha de Santo Estevão 13
☎ **210 503 434.**
Apart from the kitchen, *Pateo 13* is
formed entirely of outdoor seating
– so opening is weather-dependent.
But for most of the year, the

charming terrace is the perfect spot for excellent-value grilled fish, including sea bass and sardines. The house wine is very affordable. €

Sála de João Sá

MAP PAGE 38, POCKET MAP E13
Rua dos Bacalhoeiros 103
Ⓦ https://restaurantesla.pt.

Cosy and inviting, "The Room of Jão Sá" is named after the head chef who wants to welcome patrons as if to his own home – and he's gained a Michelin star for his efforts. There's a five- or eight-course menu – the former seafood, the latter comprising 'full gastronomic' dishes – with a distinctly Eastern influence; think Goan curry, red prawn tom yum or sea urchin with couscous. The desserts are equally memorable: try the blackberry with wasabi and pistachio nuts. €€€

Santa Clara dos Cogumelos

MAP PAGE 38, POCKET MAP H10
Mercado de Santa Clara 7
Ⓦ santaclaradoscogumelos.com.

In a lovely room above the market building, this very good Italian-run restaurant specializes in mushroom-themed dishes. Try the mushroom

Chapitô

risotto, steak with portobello mushrooms, or the porcini ice cream. €€

Bars and clubs

Casa Independente

MAP PAGE 38, POCKET MAP K5
Largo do Intendente Pina Manique 45
Ⓦ casaindependente.com.

Unassuming from the outside, this wonderful rambling building is credited with kick-starting Independente's cool credentials. Part club, part music venue and part cultural centre, it consists of various rooms where you can admire works of art, listen to surf rock or Zouk bass (check the website for what's on) or simply chat over a drink. Great terrace.

Chapitô

MAP PAGE 38, POCKET MAP E12
Costa do Castelo 7 Ⓦ www.chapito.org.

Multipurpose venue incorporating a theatre, circus school, restaurant and tapas bar. The restaurant, *Chapitô à Mesa*, is in an upstairs dining room, reached via a spiral staircase, and serves mains such as black pork with ginger and mushroom risotto. The outdoor esplanade commands terrific views over Alfama and most people come here to drink and take in the view; reservations advised. Check the website for upcoming live music, films and readings.

Lux

MAP PAGE 38, POCKET MAP M6
Armazém A, Cais da Pedra a Santa Apolónia
Ⓦ luxfragil.com.

This converted former meat warehouse is one of Europe's most fashionable spaces, attracting A-list visitors such as Cameron Diaz. Part-owned by actor John Malkovich, it was the first place to venture into the docks opposite Santa Apolónia station. There's a rooftop terrace with amazing views, various bars, projection screens, a

Clube de Fado

frenzied downstairs dancefloor, and music from pop and trance to jazz and dance. The club is also on the circuit for touring bands.

Portas do Sol

MAP PAGE 38, POCKET MAP G12
Largo Portas do Sol Ⓦ **www.portasdosol.pt.**
As you might guess from the name, this hip spot is an obligatory venue for anyone into sunsets. Hiding under the lip of the road, it's a chic indoor space, though most people head for the outside seats on the giant terrace with grandstand views over the Alfama. Pricey drinks, coffees and cocktails, but worth it. DJs on Fridays and Saturdays.

Fado and music venues

A Baiuca

MAP PAGE 38, POCKET MAP G12
Rua de São Miguel 20 Ⓣ **218 867 284.**
Nightly *fado vadio* ("casual" fado) is performed in this great little tiled *tasca*, which serves decent fresh fish and grills; minimum spend is €25. Reservations advised.

A Parreirinha de Alfama

MAP PAGE 38, POCKET MAP G12
Beco do Espírito Santo 1
Ⓦ **parreirinhadealfama.com.**
One of the best fado venues in a former charcoal shop, often attracting leading stars and an enthusiastic local clientele. Reservations are advised when the big names appear.

Clube de Fado

MAP PAGE 38, POCKET MAP F12
Rua de São João da Praça 86–94 Ⓦ **clube-de-fado.com.**
Intimate fado club with stone pillars, an old well as a decorative feature, and a mainly local clientele. It attracts small-time performers, up-and-coming talent and the occasional big name. Expect to pay €60 (including food).

Mesa de Frades

MAP PAGE 38, POCKET MAP L7
Rua dos Remédios 139a Ⓦ **mesadefrades.pt.**
Set in a beautiful former chapel and richly adorned with decorative tiles, this intimate space was in the spotlight in 2018 when Madonna popped in for an impromptu singalong. Less illustrious performers are usually just as engaging.

Chiado and Cais do Sodré

The well-to-do district of Chiado (pronounced she-ar-doo) is famed for its smart shops and cafés, along with the city's main museum for contemporary arts. Down on the waterfront, Cais do Sodré (kaiysh-doo-soodray) is one of the capital's "in" districts. Many of its waterfront warehouses have been converted into upmarket cafés and restaurants and by day, in particular, a stroll along its characterful riverfront is very enjoyable. Nearby Lisbon's main market, Mercado da Ribeira, aka Time Out Market, is also big on atmosphere, as is the hillside Bica district, which is served by one of the city's classic funicular street lifts – Elevador da Bica. Cais do Sodré is also where you can catch ferries across the Tejo to the little port of Cacilhas, which not only has some great seafood restaurants with views over Lisbon, but is also the bus terminus for some of the region's best beaches and for the spectacular Cristo Rei statue of Christ.

Rua Garrett

MAP PAGE 52, POCKET MAP C12

Chiado's most famous street, **Rua Garrett**, is where you'll find some of the oldest shops and cafés in the city, including *A Brasileira* (see page 56). Close by, the **Igreja dos Mártires** (Church of the Martyrs) is named after the English Crusaders who were killed during the siege of Lisbon. Some of the area's best shops can also be found in nearby Rua do Carmo. This was the heart of the area that was greatly damaged by a fire in 1988, although the original

Belle Époque atmosphere has since been superbly recreated under the direction of eminent Portuguese architect Álvaro Siza Vieira.

Museu Nacional de Arte Contemporânea do Chiado

MAP PAGE 52, POCKET MAP C13
Rua Serpa Pinto 4 Ⓦ museuarte contemporanea.gov.pt, charge.

The **Museu Nacional de Arte Contemporânea do Chiado** (National Museum of Contemporary Art) traces the history of art from Romanticism to Modernism. It

Tram #25 to Prazeres

You can catch another of Lisbon's classic tram rides, the #25, from Praça da Figueira (Mon–Fri 6.30am–8.30pm, every 15min). This sees far fewer tourists than tram #28 (see page 45), but takes almost as picturesque a route. From here it trundles along the riverfront and up through Lapa and Estrela to the suburb of Prazeres, best known as the site of one of Lisbon's largest cemeteries. You can stroll round the enormous plot where family tombs are movingly adorned with trinkets and photos of the deceased.

Mercado da Ribeira

is housed in a stylish building with a pleasant courtyard café and rooftop terrace, constructed around a nineteenth-century biscuit factory. Within the gallery's permanent collection are works by some of Portugal's most influential artists since the nineteenth century, along with foreign talent influenced by Portugal including Rodin. Highlights include Almada Negreiros' 1920s panels from the old São Carlos cinema, showing Felix the Cat; a beautiful sculpture, *A Viúva* (The Widow), by António Teixeira Lopes; and some evocative early twentieth-century Lisbon scenes by watercolourist Carlos Botelho. There are also frequent temporary exhibitions.

Elevador da Bica

MAP PAGE 52, POCKET MAP B13
Entrance on Rua de São Paulo, charge.
With its entrance tucked into an arch on Rua de São Paulo, the **Elevador da Bica** is one of the city's most atmospheric funicular railways. Built in 1892 – and originally powered by water counterweights, but now electrically operated – the *elevador* leads up towards the Bairro Alto, via a steep residential street. Following the tragic accident at

the nearby Elevador da Glória in 2025, however, its future remains uncertain. Take time to explore the steep side-streets of the Bica neighbourhood too, a warren of characterful houses, little shops and fine local restaurants.

Mercado da Ribeira/ Time Out Market

MAP PAGE 52, POCKET MAP B13
Main entrance on Avda 24 de Julho
Ⓦ timeoutmarket.com/lisboa. Fruit, fish and vegetable market Mon–Sat 6am–2pm; food stalls daily 10am–midnight.
Built originally on the site of an old fort at the end of the nineteenth century, the **Mercado da Ribeira** is Lisbon's most historic market, though most of the current structure dates only from 1930. Inside, stalls sell an impressive array of fresh fish, fruit and vegetables, with a separate, aromatic flower section. However, much of the building is now given over to the vibrant Time Out Market, filled with an impressive range of food stalls and plenty of communal benches; it's a great place to sample dishes from some of the city's top chefs, such as Vincent Farges and Henrique Sá Pessoa, or you can choose something simple like a *prego* (steak sandwich)

Chiado and Cais do Sodré

Convento do Carmo

Elevador de Santa Justa

Teatro da Trindade

CHIADO

BAIXA-CHIADO

Nossa Senhora do Loreto

LARGO DO CHIADO

Igreja dos Mártires

RUA GARRETT

BAIXA-CHIADO

LARGO DO BARÃO DE QUINTELA

Teatro de São Luís

Teatro de São Carlos

Museu Nacional de Arte Contemporânea do Chiado

LARGO DA ACADEMIA NACIONAL DE BELAS ARTES

City Hall (Câmara Municipal)

PRAÇA DO MUNICÍPIO

BICA

Elevador da Bica

PRAÇA DE SÃO PAULO

Rua Cor-de-Rosa (Pink Street)

TRAVESSA DO FERRAGIAL

PRAÇA DOM LUÍS

Mercado da Ribeira (Time Out Market)

PRAÇA DUQUE DE TERCEIRA

CAIS DO SODRÉ

Cais do Sodré Station

Bus Terminal

CAIS DO SODRÉ

Estação Fluvial

CAIS DO GÁS

AVENIDA DE BRASÍLIA

Rio Tejo

0 metres 100
0 yards 100

Ferry to Cacilhas

0 metres 200
0 yards 200

Ferry to Cais do Sodré

Rio Tejo

Bus Station

Bus stop to Caparica

CACILHAS

Dom Fernando II e Glória Frigate (Boat Museum)

Elevador Panorâmico da Boca da Vento

25 DE ABRIL

ALMADA

GIL VICENTE

Caparica (9.5km)

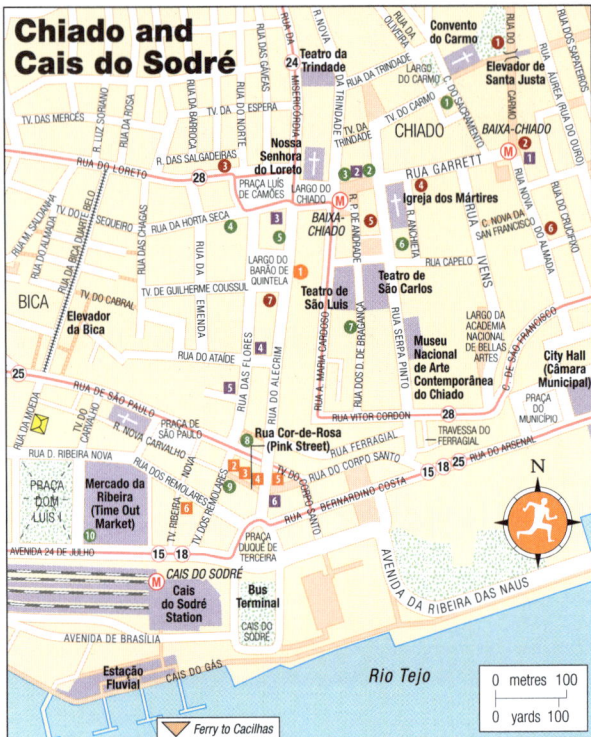

ACCOMMODATION		RESTAURANTS		BARS		SHOPS	
Hotel Bairro Alto	3	26 Vegan Food Project	4	A Tabacaria	6	A Vida Portuguesa	6
Hotel Borges	2	Cantinho do Avillez	7	Music Box	5	Armazéns do Chiado	2
Hotel do Chiado	1	Cervejaria Farol	11	Palácio Chiado	1	Burel Factory	5
Lost Inn	5	Encanto	6	Pensão Amor	2	Fábrica Sant'Anna	7
LX Boutique	6	La Brasserie L'Entrecôte	5	Povo	2	Livraria Bertrand	4
Martinhal Chiado	4	Pap'Açôrda	10	Sol e Pesca	3	Luvaria Ulisses	1
		Rio Grande	9			Manteigaria	3
		Vicente	8				
		CAFÉS					
		Benard	2				
		Café a Brasileira	3				
		Leitaria Académica	1				

Travel to Cacilhas and beyond

Cais do Sodré is the main departure point for ferries over the Tejo to the largely industrial suburbs to the south. Ferries to Cacilhas (transtejo.pt, 5.35am–1.40am, last return 1.20am, every 15–20min, charge) dock by a bus and tram depot from where buses run to Costa da Caparica (see page 121).

or pizza. You pay above the norm for the concept and ambience, but with everything from hams, cheeses and grilled chicken to gourmet burgers, seafood, organic salads and chocolates (not to mention champagne and cocktail bars), you might well find yourself tempted back here again and again.

On Sunday mornings there's a collectors' market, while additional outlets line up around the outside of the market building.

Rua Cor-de-Rosa

MAP PAGE 52, POCKET MAP C13

Rua Nova do Carvalho's once dodgy clubs and bars have now (largely) been revamped into some of the city's coolest hangouts. The rebranding has extended to the colour of the street, which is now pink, hence the nickname **Rua Cor-de-Rosa** (Pink Street). We list some of the best places on page 56.

Cacilhas and Almada

MAP PAGE 52, POCKET MAP J8

The short, blustery ferry ride from Lisbon's Cais do Sodré over the Tejo to Cacilhas is great fun and grants wonderful views of the city. **Cacilhas** is little more than a somewhat rundown bus, tram and ferry terminal with a pretty church, surrounded by lively stalls and cafés, but is well known for its seafood restaurants. You can also visit the wooden-hulled, fifty-gun **Dom Fernando II e Glória frigate** (ccm.marinha.pt, charge) on Largo Alfredo Diniz. Built in India in 1843, it's now a museum showing what life at sea was like in the mid-nineteenth century. A good riverside walk is to head west towards

the bridge along the waterfront. It's around fifteen minutes' walk to the **Elevador Panorâmico da Boca do Vento** (cm-almada.pt, daily 10am–9pm, charge), a sleek lift that whisks you 30m up the cliff face to the attractive old part of **Almada**, giving fantastic views.

Cristo Rei

MAP PAGE 52, POCKET MAP H9

Bus #101 from outside the Cacilhas ferry terminal cristorei.pt, charge for lift.

On the heights above Almada stand the outstretched arms of **Cristo Rei** (Christ the King). Inspired by Rio's famous *Cristo Redentor* statue, it was built in 1959 as a pilgrimage site to grace Portugal's non-participation in World War II. A lift shuttles you 80m up the plinth, where a few stairs lead to a dramatic viewing platform at the foot of the statue, from which, on a clear day, you can catch a glimpse of the glistening roof of the Pena palace at Sintra.

Cristo Rei

Shops

A Vida Portuguesa

MAP PAGE 52, POCKET MAP D12
Rua Nova do Almada 72.

An expensive but evocative collection of retro toys, crafts and ceramics, beautifully displayed and packaged in a historic shop – don't miss the basement room.

Armazéns do Chiado

MAP PAGE 52, POCKET MAP D12
Rua do Carmo 2.

This six-floor swish shopping centre sits above metro Baixa-Chiado in a structure that has risen from the ashes of the Chiado fire, though it retains its traditional facade. The top floor has a series of cafés and restaurants, most with great views.

Burel Factory

MAP PAGE 52, POCKET MAP C12
Rua Serpa Pinto 17a ⓦ burelfactory.com.
Beautiful blankets, throws, rugs, bedspreads, scarves and shawls all made from local wool in its Serra d'Estrela factory. This flagship shop sells a range of different colours, or you can have a design made up in any pattern or colour you like. You

Livraria Bertrand

can also ask for woollen suits, coats and jackets made to order.

Fábrica Sant'Anna

MAP PAGE 52, POCKET MAP C13
Largo Barão de Quintela, 4, off Rua do Alecrim ⓦ santanna.com.
A great place to find out more about Portuguese *azulejos*, and to buy a few souvenirs to take home. Founded in 1741, the factory shop still makes ceramics using traditional techniques and sells a wide range of handmade designs, plus copies of classics.

Livraria Bertrand

MAP PAGE 52, POCKET MAP C12
Rua Garrett 73.
Officially the world's oldest bookshop, founded in 1732 and once the meeting place for Lisbon's literary set. Offering novels in English and a range of foreign magazines, it's also a good place to find English translations of Portuguese writers, including Fernando Pessoa.

Luvaria Ulisses

MAP PAGE 52, POCKET MAP D11
Rua do Carmo 87a.
The superb, ornately carved wooden doorway leads into a

minuscule glove shop dating from 1925, with hand-wear to suit all tastes tucked into rows of boxes.

Manteigaria

MAP PAGE 52, POCKET MAP B12
Rua do Loreto 2.

In a former buttery dating back to 1900, this tiny shop specializes in *pastéis de nata*, those delectable custard tarts, served piping hot and some say the best in the city. It also serves coffee and, somewhat bizarrely, port.

Restaurants

26 Vegan Food Project

MAP PAGE 52, POCKET MAP B12
Rua Horta Seca 5 ☎ 967 989 184.

Classy restaurant which, unusually for Lisbon, is purely plant-based. What's more, it gives vegans the opportunity to try meat-free versions of traditional Portuguese dishes such as vegan cuttlefish, *bifanas* (pork sandwiches) and even sardines. There are also more conventional dishes such as Thai curry, mushroom steaks and tofu recipes. €€

Cantinho do Avillez

MAP PAGE 52, POCKET MAP C13
Rua dos Duques de Bragança 7
Ⓦ cantinhodoavillez.pt.

In a contemporary space, with tram #28 rattling by its door, this laid-back but classy canteen is a good place to sample food from Lisbon's top chef, José Avillez, at reasonable prices. Delectable mains include the likes of duck red curry and flaked cod with exploding olives. Starters include a superb baked Queijo de Nisa, and the house wines are equally top-notch. €€€

Cervejaria Farol

MAP PAGE 52, POCKET MAP H9
Largo Alfredo Dinis 1–3, Cacilhas
Ⓦ restaurantefarol.com.

The most high-profile seafood restaurant in Cacilhas, with fine views across the Tejo to match. If you feel extravagant, it's hard to beat the lobster, though other fish and meat dishes are better value. *Azulejos* on the wall show the old *farol* (lighthouse) that once stood here – the restaurant is located along the quayside, on the right as you leave the ferry. €€

Encanto

MAP PAGE 52, POCKET MAP C12
Largo de São Carlos 10
Ⓦ encantojoseavillez.pt.

One of a handful of dedicated vegetarian restaurants in the world to have been awarded a Michelin star, *Encanto* is proof that José Avillez triumphs at everything he turns his hand to. The sole tasting menu uses local and seasonal ingredients to produce sublime, innovative and surprising dishes that look as beautiful as they taste. Expect playful golden eggs of hummus, edible flowers created from spring greens, "scallops" made of cep mushrooms, or pearls of lime-based "caviar". The accompanying wines are from small Portuguese vineyards, and the non-alcoholic drink pairing features delicious home-made kombuchas and cordials. €€€

La Brasserie L'Entrecôte

MAP PAGE 52, POCKET MAP C12
Rua do Alecrim 117–120
Ⓦ encantojoseavillez.pt.

This upmarket restaurant has won awards for its entrecôte steak, which is just as well, as that's all it serves (though there is a vegetarian "steak" too). With a sauce said to contain 35 ingredients, it is truly delicious. Reservations are advised. €€€

Pap'Açôrda

MAP PAGE 52, POCKET MAP B14
Primeiro Piso do Mercado da Ribeira
Ⓦ papacorda.com.

Pap'Açôrda was the place to be seen when it was in the Bairro Alto, and though it's not quite as fashionable as it was, the famous old restaurant now boats a classy first-floor position above Time Out Market with fine views over the bustling square. It specializes in *açorda* dishes, served with a garlicky bread sauce. Try the *açorda de gambas* (with prawns) or the fantastic John Dory filets. €€€

Rio Grande

MAP PAGE 52, POCKET MAP B12
Rua Nova do Carvalho 55 ☎ 213 423 804.
It might be on a street full of hip bars, but *Rio Grande* is reassuringly traditional, with *azulejos* on the walls beneath a vaulted ceiling. The spacious restaurant plates up good-value Portuguese classics such as pork steaks and a good array of fresh fish. €€

Vicente

MAP PAGE 26, POCKET MAP C13
Rua das Flores 6 ☎ 936 725 384.
Fashionable café-restaurant in an old charcoal factory with a brick-vaulted ceiling and seats outside on a small square. Specialities are meaty dishes from the Alentejo, the region between Lisbon and the Algarve: the steaks and sausages are wonderful, as is its range of *petiscos*, tapas-like snacks. €€

Café a Brasileira

Cafés

Benard

MAP PAGE 52, POCKET MAP C12
Rua Garrett 104.
Often overlooked because of its proximity to *A Brasileira*, this ornate nineteenth-century café offers superb cakes, croissants and *pastéis de nata*; it also has a hugely popular outdoor terrace on Chiado's most fashionable street. €

Café a Brasileira

MAP PAGE 52, POCKET MAP C12
Rua Garrett 122.
Opened in 1905 and marked by an outdoor bronze statue of the poet Fernando Pessoa, this is the most famous of Lisbon's old-style coffee houses. The tables on the pedestrianized street get snapped up by tourists but the real appeal is in its traditional interior, where prices are considerably cheaper, especially if you stand at the long bar. At night, buskers often add a frisson as the clientele changes to a more youthful brigade, all on the beer. €€

Leitaria Académica

MAP PAGE 52, POCKET MAP C12
Largo do Carmo 1–3.
In a 1930s former dairy, this little place has outdoor tables on one of the city's leafiest squares. Besides drinks and snacks, it also does light lunches; the tasty grilled sardines are perfect in summer. €

Bars and clubs

A Tabacaria

MAP PAGE 52, POCKET MAP B13
Rua de São Paulo 75–77 ☎ 213 420 281.
In a wonderful old tobacco shop dating back to 1885 – with many of the original fittings – this cosy bar specializes in cocktails made from gin, vodka, whisky and seasonal fruits.

Palácio Chiado

Music Box

MAP PAGE 52, POCKET MAP C13
Rua Nova do Carvalho 24
Ⓦ musicboxlisboa.com.
Tucked under the arches of Rua Nova do Carvalho, this cool cultural and music venue hosts club nights, live music, films and performing arts, with an emphasis on promoting independent acts. There's a top sound and light system and usually a buzzy, happy crowd.

Palácio Chiado

MAP PAGE 52. POCKET MAP C12
Rua do Alecrim 70 Ⓦ palaciochiado.pt.
This ornate former eighteenth-century palace (whose long and fascinating history is detailed on the website) has been transformed into a hip outlet for various bars and restaurants. Head to the top floor for a stunning bar area, complete with a golden-winged lion suspended overhead, for a range of tantalizing cocktails including O Mistério, a cherry liqueur with lime and basil. The adjacent room has good views over Chiado.

Pensão Amor

MAP PAGE 52, POCKET MAP C13
Rua Nova do Carvalho 38 ☎ 213 143 399.
The "Pension of Love" is a former "house of ill-repute" that now serves tasty cocktails. It has retained its eighteenth-century burlesque fittings for its current incarnation as a trendy bar with risqué photos, frescoes and mirrors. You can browse through the small erotic bookstore, or enjoy occasional live concerts.

Povo

MAP PAGE 52, POCKET MAP C13
Rua Nova do Carvalho 32–26 Ⓦ povolisboa.com.
This fashionable tavern in the heart of "Pink Street" offers fado from up-and-coming stars (Tues–Sun), late-night DJs at weekends, plus Monday poetry readings. There's a great menu of *petiscos* and mains such as mussels with seaweed, *bacalhau* dishes and steaks.

Sol e Pesca

MAP PAGE 52, POCKET MAP C13
Rua Nova do Carvalho 44 ☎ 213 467 203.
Once a shop selling fishing equipment, this is now a hip bar. The fishing equipment is part of the decor, and you can still purchase tinned fish to enjoy with bread and wine at low stools inside, or outside on trendy Pink Street.

Bairro Alto and São Bento

The Bairro Alto, the Upper Town, sits on a hill west of the Baixa. After the 1755 earthquake, the relatively unscathed district became the favoured haunt of Lisbon's young bohemians. Home to the Institute of Art and Design and various designer boutiques, it is still the city's most fashionable district. By day, the central grid of narrow, cobbled streets feels residential. After dark, however, the area throngs with people visiting its famed fado houses, bars and restaurants, while the city's LGBTQ+ community coalesces around the clubs of neighbouring Príncipe Real. There are impressive monuments, too, including the Palácio da Assembléia, Portugal's parliamentary building in nearby São Bento. This area houses good ethnic restaurants, a legacy of the city's first Black community established by the descendants of enslaved Africans.

Elevador da Glória

MAP PAGE 60, POCKET MAP C11
From the bottom of Calçada da Glória (off Praça dos Restauradores, see page 30), the iconic **Elevador da Glória** funicular had climbed the knee-jarringly sheer street since 1885.

Igreja de São Roque

However, in September 2025, a cable snapped, and the topmost car plunged downhill and crashed into a building. The tragedy led to the death of sixteen people and a day of national mourning. At the time of going to press, the future of this *elevador* and the two other similar street lifts – Lavra and Bica – remains uncertain.

Igreja de São Roque

MAP PAGE 60, POCKET MAP C11
Largo de Trindade Coelha
Ⓦ museusaoroque.scml.pt, free.
The sixteenth-century **Igreja de São Roque** looks like the plainest church in the city, with its bleak Renaissance facade. Yet inside lies an astonishing succession of lavishly decorated side chapels. The highlight is the **Capela de São João Baptista**, for its size the most expensive chapel ever constructed. It was ordered from Rome in 1742 by Dom João V to honour his patron saint and, more dubiously, to gratify Pope Benedict XIV whom he had persuaded to confer a patriarchate on Lisbon. It was erected at the Vatican for the Pope

Convento do Carmo

to celebrate Mass in, before being dismantled and shipped to Lisbon at the then vast cost of €300,000. If you examine the four "oil paintings" of John the Baptist's life, you'll find that they are in fact intricately worked mosaics. The more valuable parts of the altar front are stashed in the adjacent **museum** (charge), which also displays sixteenth- to eighteenth-century paintings and a motley collection of church relics.

Convento do Carmo

MAP PAGE 60, POCKET MAP D12
Largo do Carmo

museuarqueologicodocarmo.pt, charge. Built between 1389 and 1423, and once the largest church in the city, the **Convento do Carmo** was partially destroyed by the 1755 earthquake, but is even more striking as a result, with its beautiful Gothic arches rising grandly into the sky. Today, it houses the splendid **Museu Arqueológico do Carmo**, home to many of the treasures from monasteries that were dissolved after the 1834 revolution. The entire nave is open to the elements, with columns and statuary scattered in all corners. Inside, on either side

of what was the main altar, are the main exhibits, centering on a series of tombs. Largest is the beautifully carved stone tomb of Ferdinand I; nearby, that of Gonçalo de Sousa, chancellor to Henry the Navigator, is topped by a statue of Gonçalo himself. There is also an Egyptian sarcophagus, whose inhabitant's feet are just visible underneath the lid; and a sixteenth-century mummified Peruvian boy.

The exit to the **Elevador de Santa Justa** (see page 29) is at the side of the Convento do Carmo – clamber onto the rampway leading to it for fine views over the city or the partly lawned terrace in front, the **Terraços do Carmo**, with its handy café.

Bairro Alto

MAP PAGE 60, POCKET MAP B11
Quiet by day, the graffitied core of the **Bairro Alto** buzzes with people after dark, especially on summer weekends when the central grid becomes a giant mass of partygoers. The liveliest area is the tight network of streets to the west of Rua da Misericórdia, particularly after midnight in Rua do Norte, Rua Diário de Notícias,

Bairro Alto and São Bento

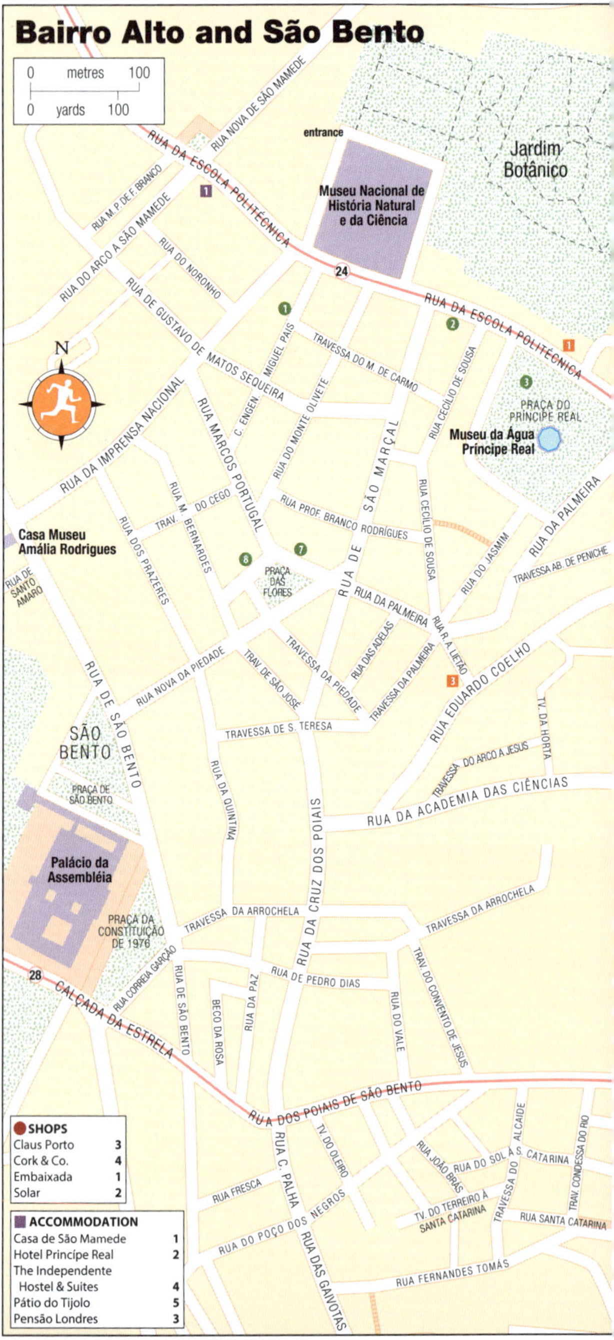

entrance

Jardim Botânico

Museu Nacional de História Natural e da Ciência

Casa Museu Amália Rodrigues

Museu da Água Príncipe Real

PRAÇA DO PRÍNCIPE REAL

PRAÇA DAS FLORES

SÃO BENTO

PRAÇA DE SÃO BENTO

Palácio da Assembléia

PRAÇA DA CONSTITUIÇÃO DE 1976

● **SHOPS**

Claus Porto	3
Cork & Co.	4
Embaixada	1
Solar	2

■ **ACCOMMODATION**

Casa de São Mamede	1
Hotel Príncipe Real	2
The Independente Hostel & Suites	4
Pátio do Tijolo	5
Pensão Londres	3

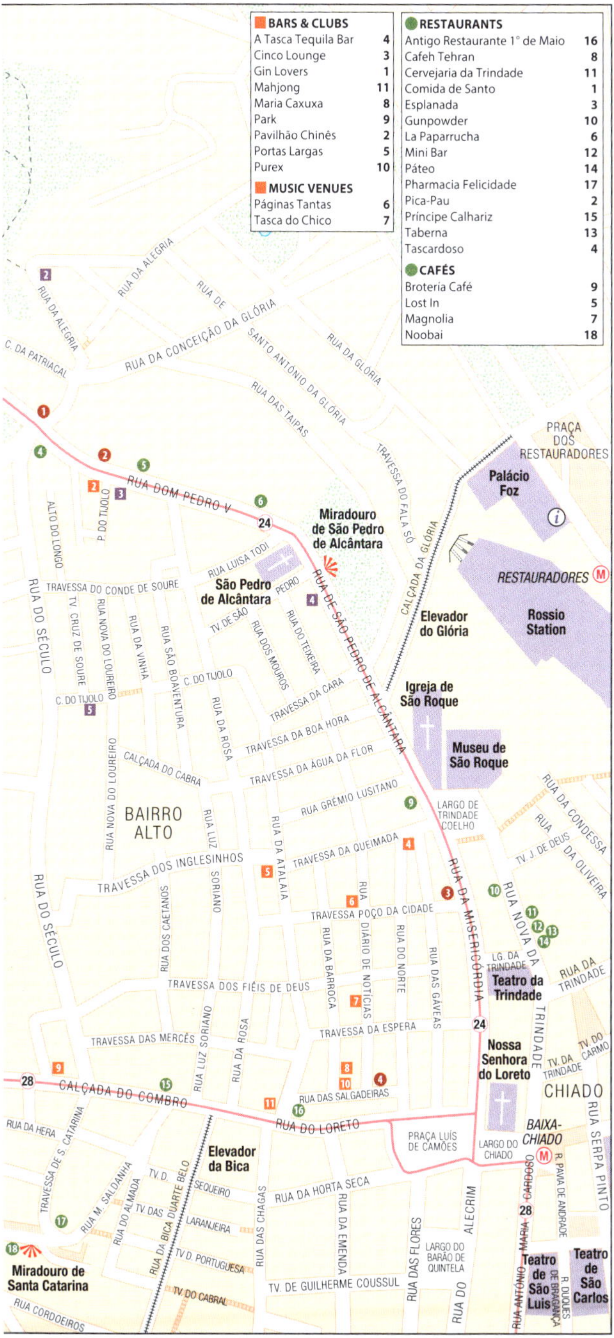

BARS & CLUBS
A Tasca Tequila Bar 4
Cinco Lounge 3
Gin Lovers 1
Mahjong 11
Maria Caxuxa 8
Park 9
Pavilhão Chinês 2
Portas Largas 5
Purex 10
MUSIC VENUES
Páginas Tantas 6
Tasca do Chico 7
RESTAURANTS
Antigo Restaurante 1° de Maio 16
Cafeh Tehran 8
Cervejaria da Trindade 11
Comida de Santo 1
Esplanada 3
Gunpowder 10
La Paparrucha 6
Mini Bar 12
Páteo 14
Pharmacia Felicidade 17
Pica-Pau 2
Príncipe Calhariz 15
Taberna 13
Tascardoso 4
CAFÉS
Brotéria Café 9
Lost In 5
Magnolia 7
Noobai 18
Miradouro de São Pedro de Alcântara
São Pedro de Alcântara
Palácio Foz
PRAÇA DOS RESTAURADORES
RESTAURADORES
Rossio Station
Elevador do Glória
Igreja de São Roque
Museu de São Roque
BAIRRO ALTO
Teatro da Trindade
Nossa Senhora do Loreto
CHIADO
BAIXA-CHIADO
Elevador da Bica
Miradouro de Santa Catarina
Teatro de São Luis
Teatro de São Carlos
RUA DOM PEDRO V
RUA DE SÃO PEDRO DE ALCÂNTARA
RUA DA MISERICÓRDIA
RUA DA CONCEIÇÃO DA GLÓRIA
RUA DA ALEGRIA
RUA DE SANTO ANTÓNIO DA GLÓRIA
RUA DA GLÓRIA
RUA DAS TAIPAS
TRAVESSA DO FALA SÓ
CALÇADA DA GLÓRIA
C. DA PATRIARCAL
RUA DO SÉCULO
TRAVESSA DO CONDE DE SOURE
CALÇADA DO COMBRO
RUA DO LORETO
PRAÇA LUÍS DE CAMÕES
LARGO DO CHIADO
LARGO DE TRINDADE COELHO
RUA NOVA DA TRINDADE
RUA DA TRINDADE
RUA SERPA PINTO
RUA DA HORTA SECA
RUA DAS FLORES
RUA DO ALECRIM
TRAVESSA DOS INGLESINHOS
TRAVESSA DA QUEIMADA
TRAVESSA POÇO DA CIDADE
TRAVESSA DOS FIÉIS DE DEUS
TRAVESSA DA ESPERA
TRAVESSA DAS MERCÊS
RUA DAS SALGADEIRAS
RUA DA ROSA
RUA DA ATALAIA
RUA DO NORTE
RUA DAS GÁVEAS
RUA DO DIÁRIO DE NOTÍCIAS
RUA DA BARROCA
RUA DA CONDESSA
RUA DA OLIVEIRA
TV. DE GUILHERME COUSSUL
RUA CORDOEIROS

Rua da Atalaia and Rua da Rosa. Running steeply downhill, Rua do Século is one of the area's most historic thoroughfares. A sign at no. 89 marks the birthplace of the Marquês de Pombal, the minister responsible for rebuilding Lisbon after the Great Earthquake.

Miradouro de Santa Catarina

MAP PAGE 60, POCKET MAP A12
Tram #28.

At the bottom end of the Bairro Alto grid, set on the cusp of a hill high above the river, the railed **Miradouro de Santa Catarina** has spectacular views. Here, in the shadow of the statue of the Adamastor – a mythical beast from Luís de Camões's *Lusiads* – an alternative crowd often collects around an alluring drinks kiosk, built in 1883, which has a few outdoor tables.

Praça do Príncipe Real

MAP PAGE 60, POCKET MAP A10
Bus #758 from Chiado.

North of the Bairro Alto, the streets open out around the leafy **Praça do Príncipe Real**, one of the city's loveliest squares. Laid out in 1860 and surrounded by the ornate homes of former aristocrats – now mostly shops or offices – the area is the focal point of Lisbon's LGBTQ+ scene, though by day it is largely populated by families or locals playing cards under the trees.

Museu da Água Príncipe Real

MAP PAGE 60, POCKET MAP A10
Praça do Príncipe Real 1. Bus #758 from Chiado W epal.pt, charge.

The **Museu da Água Príncipe Real** is accessed down steps in the centre of the square of the same name. Inside is the eerie nineteenth-century Patriarchal reservoir, where you can admire brick and vaulted ceilings, part of a network of tunnels that links up with the Aqueduto das Águas Livres (see page 94). Not for claustrophobics, the tours (book in advance) take you along one of these, a humid 410m tunnel that exits at the viewpoint of Miradouro de São Pedro.

Museu Nacional de História Natural e da Ciência

MAP PAGE 60, POCKET MAP H5
Rua Escola Politécnica 56. Bus #758 from Chiado W museus.ulisboa.pt, charge

Jardim Botânico

Lisbon graffiti

Graffiti has long been a feature of Lisbon life – in the form of political protest under the Salazar regime – and the council's heritage department has given over certain walls to be part of a Galeria de Arte Urbana (🌐 gau.cm-lisboa.pt), in which street art is encouraged. The result: a dazzling array of graffiti all over the city, but particularly around the Bairro Alto and the Alcântara docks. Lisbon's best-known graffiti artist is Alexandre Farto, aka Vhils, whose large and striking works are often chiselled into brickwork using pneumatic drills, and Bordalo II, whose street art is made from recycled rubbish.

(combined ticket includes entry to Jardim Botânico).

The nineteenth-century Neoclassical former technical college now hosts the mildly engaging museums of natural history. The **Museu da Ciência** (whose labs featured in the film *The Promise*, starring Christian Bale) has some absorbing geological exhibits and a low-tech interactive section where you can balance balls on jets of air and swing pendulums among throngs of schoolchildren.

The **Museu Nacional da História Natural** houses a rather dreary collection of stuffed animals, eggs and shells, though temporary exhibitions can be more diverting.

Jardim Botânico

MAP PAGE 60, POCKET MAP H5
Rua Escola Politécnica 58 🌐 museus. ulisboa.pt, charge (combined ticket includes Museu Nacional de História Natural e da Ciência).

The lush **Jardim Botânico** is almost invisible from the surrounding streets and provides a tranquil escape from the city bustle. Portuguese explorers introduced many plant species to Europe during the Age of Exploration and these botanical gardens, laid out between 1858 and 1878, are packed with twenty thousand neatly labelled species from around the world. Shady paths lead downhill under towering palms and luxuriant shrubs past rare cycads.

Palácio da Assembléia

MAP PAGE 60, POCKET MAP H6
Rua de São Bento, Tram #28.

Below the Bairro Alto in the district of São Bento, you can't miss the late sixteenth-century Neoclassical facade of the **Palácio da Assembléia**. Formerly a Benedictine monastery, it was taken over by the government in 1834 and today houses the Assembléia da República, Portugal's **parliament**. Since it's not open to the public (online tours are available via 🌐 parlamento.pt), most visitors make do with the view of its steep white steps from tram #28 as it rattles along Calçada da Estrela, though it is worth exploring the streets nearby. This was where Lisbon's Black community put down roots.

Casa Museu Amália Rodrigues

MAP PAGE 60, POCKET MAP G6
Rua de São Bento 193, bus #706 from Cais do Sodré, or a short walk from tram #28 🌐 amaliarodrigues.pt, charge.

The daughter of an Alfama orange-seller, **Amália Rodrigues** was the undisputed queen of fado music until her death in 1999. The house where she lived since the 1950s has been kept as it was, and guided tours take you round to admire original posters advertising her performances on stage and in the cinema, portraits by Portuguese artists and some of her prized personal possessions.

Shops

Claus Porto

MAP PAGE 60, POCKET MAP C11
Rua da Misericórdia 135.

Portugal's premium soap brand, Claus Porto has been making top-quality toiletries in Porto since 1887. You can sample its full range of beautifully packaged soaps and smellies in this Lisbon branch, housed in an old pharmacy with the original wooden medicine cabinets and tiled floors.

Cork & Co.

MAP PAGE 60, POCKET MAP B12
Rua das Salgadeiras 6
Ⓦ corkandcompany.pt.

Portugal supplies around fifty percent of the world's cork, and this stylish shop displays the versatility of the product with a range of tasteful cork goods, from bags and bracelets to umbrellas.

Embaixada

MAP PAGE 60, POCKET MAP A10
Praça do Príncipe Real 26
Ⓦ www.embaixadalx.pt.

Housed in a former pseudo-Moorish palace overlooking Praça do Príncipe Real, this beautiful upmarket shopping emporium showcases some of Portugal's leading designers. Inside you'll find sleek airy spaces selling high-end clothes, shoes and contemporary furniture. As you wander around, take in the temporary exhibits dotted about and when you need a refresh, call into the café-bar-restaurant, which is located in a wonderfully ornate room, or head outside to grab a table on the shaded terrace.

Solar

MAP PAGE 60, POCKET MAP B10
Rua Dom Pedro V 70 Ⓦ solar.com.pt.

Claiming to be the country's oldest and largest antiques store, this huge treasure trove of tiles, plates and ceramics has items dating back to the sixteenth century – many rescued and preserved for sale.

Restaurants

Antigo Restaurante 1° de Maio

MAP PAGE 60, POCKET MAP B12
Rua da Atalaia 8 ☎ 213 426 840.

This restaurant serves simple home cooking, such *as* slabs of grilled fish and meat with boiled veg and chips. You can watch the cook through a hatch at the back, adding to the theatrics of a bustling, traditional *adega* (wine cellar) with a low, arched ceiling. Arrive early to be sure of a table. €€

Cafeh Tehran

MAP PAGE 60, POCKET MAP H6
Praça das Flores 40 ☎ 210 736 530.

Facing onto the attractive Praça das Flores, with outdoor tables, this restaurant – as the name suggests – serves delicious Iranian food. As well as chicken kebabs and grilled lamb, try typical dishes such as *kookoo sabzi*, a kind of frittata cooked with bitter herbs. There are vegetarian options, too. €€

Cervejaria da Trindade

MAP PAGE 60, POCKET MAP C11
Rua Nova da Trindade 20
Ⓦ cervejariatrindade.pt.

The city's oldest beer hall dates from 1836. The restaurant is housed in the original vaulted hall, the walls of which are decorated with traditional *azulejos* depicting the elements and seasons. Shellfish and steak are the specialities here, though the *petiscaria* also serves lighter dishes such as *pregos*, cheese and charcuterie platters. €€

Esplanada

MAP PAGE 60, POCKET MAP A10
Praça do Príncipe Real ☎ 962 311 669.

A good range of burgers, salads and tapas makes this an ideal and inexpensive lunch spot. The outdoor tables beneath the trees get snapped up quickly, though the glass pavilion comes into its own when the weather turns. Service can be on the tardy side. €

Gunpowder

MAP PAGE 60, POCKET MAP C11
Rua Nova da Trindade 13 ☎ 218 227 470.
Delicious Indian small plates are the thing to go for at this lovely restaurant, where spicing and flavour are key. Sit at the counter and watch the chefs produce dishes such as delicate French bean pakoras, tasty turbot marinated in turmeric and curry leaves, and the delicious Gunpowder chaat, with potatoes, tamarind, yoghurt and chickpeas. Make sure to leave room for the seriously yummy rum bread-and-butter pudding, in a pool of custard. €€

La Paparrucha

MAP PAGE 60, POCKET MAP B10
Rua Dom Pedro V 18–20
ⓦ lapaparrucha.com.
The best feature of this Argentinian restaurant is the fantastic back room and terrace offering superb views over the Baixa. The food is recommended too, with steaks, fish and pasta dishes, and good-value lunchtime buffets. €€

Elegant Pharmacia Felicidade

Mini Bar

MAP PAGE 60, POCKET MAP C11
Bairro do Avillez, Rua Nova da Trinade 18
ⓦ minibar.pt.
There's certainly a theatrical element to the cuisine in this buzzy restaurant, set in an amazing vaulted former chapel and the centrepiece of chef José Avillez's gourmand complex, Bairro do Avillez. Various themed tasting menus feature innovative and quirky tapas-style dishes, including Algarve prawns, tuna and mackerel ceviche and beef croquettes. Some of Avillez's creations are decidedly Blumenthal-esque, including amazing "edible" cocktails and "exploding" olives. Highly recommended, there's also occasional live music. €€€€

Páteo

MAP PAGE 60, POCKET MAP C11
Bairro do Avillez, Rua Nova da Trinade 18
ⓦ bairrodoavillez.pt.
Another of the four lively restaurants in Avillez's culinary enclave in an artfully converted former monastery: *Páteo* is at the heart of the "patio", a beautiful balconied space beneath soaring roof lights. It specializes in fish and seafood, with sublime dishes such

Pharmacia Felicidade, part of the Pharmaceutical Society and Museum

as garlic prawns, fish rice and tuna *escabeche*, as well as a few meat and vegetarian dishes. €€€

Pharmacia Felicidade

MAP PAGE 60, POCKET MAP A12
Rua Santa Catarina 1 ☏ 213 462 146.
Part of the Pharmaceutical Society and Museum, this traditional building on lawns facing the Tejo is a terrific spot for the quirky café-restaurant decked out with retro pharmacy fittings. The speciality here is tapas and mains such as black pork cheek. Also good for cocktails. €€

Pica-Pau

MAP PAGE 60, POCKET MAP H6
Rua da Escola Politécnica 27 ☏ 212 698 509.
A bustling modern taverna-style restaurant, with a leafy backroom facing a garden, and an open kitchen where you can watch the chefs rustling up top-quality traditional Portuguese dishes. The food uses regional ingredients such as flatbread from Mafra, butter from the Azores and Queijo de Nisa from the Alentejo. The menu includes a delicious monkfish and prawn rice and a tasty *bacalhão a bràs*. €€

Príncipe Calhariz

MAP PAGE 60, POCKET MAP B12
Calçado do Combro 28–30 ☏ 213 420 971.
Here's a place that's reliable, good value, has plenty of tables, generous portions – and a local buzz. Recommended are the *porco Portuguesa* (fried pork cubes with potatoes) and the salmon steaks. Don't miss the chocolate mousse. €€

Taberna

MAP PAGE 60, POCKET MAP C11
Bairro do Avillez, Rua Nova da Trinade 18
ⓦ bairrodoavillez.pt.
The more affordable of José Avillez's *Bairro* restaurants, set out like an old tavern with cured hams hanging above the bar. But there is nothing downmarket about the cuisine from Lisbon's star chef: choose from an array of Portuguese cheeses, hams, sausages and cod dishes. The tuna *prego* is superb. €€

Tascardoso

MAP PAGE 60, POCKET MAP A10
Rua Dom Pedro V 137 ☏ 213 427 578.
A long-standing favourite, the tiny eating area opposite Praça do Princípe Real serves excellent and inexpensive tapas-style meats and cheeses and affordable hot dishes. €

Cafés

Brotería Café

MAP PAGE 60, POCKET MAP C11
Rua de São Pedro de Alcântara 3.
☎ 213 961 660.

Set in a historic Jesuit college, this library and cultural centre has a small café tucked at the back, with tables in a lovely patio beneath a lemon tree. There are good-value dishes of the day such as prawn kebab or steak, and the usual hot and cold drinks. €

Lost In

MAP PAGE 60, POCKET MAP B10
Rua Dom Pedro V 56
ⓦ lostinrestaurante.com.

This little Asian-inspired shop and café-restaurant has a great terrace with exhilarating views over town and occasional live jazz. The menu features curries, tuna tataki and the like, or just pop in for a drink. €€

Magnolia

MAP PAGE 60, POCKET MAP H6
Praça das Flores 43 ☎ 935 315 456.

With outdoor seating overlooking the pretty Praça das Flores, this

lovely café catches the afternoon sun. It serves an amazing array of tasty cakes, while more filling options include Turkish eggs, fish buns and roast cauliflower. In the evening it turns into more of a wine bar attracting a young, stylish crowd. €

Noobai

MAP PAGE 60, POCKET MAP A12
Miradouro do Adamastor, Rua de Catarina
ⓦ noobaicafe.com.

Modern, jazzy café-restaurant with a superb terrace situated just below Miradouro de Santa Catarina. Fabulous views complement the concise list of inexpensive fresh juices, cocktails, tapas, quiches and the like. €€

Bars and clubs

A Tasca Tequila Bar

MAP PAGE 60, POCKET MAP C11
Trav da Queimada 13–15 ☎ 915 617 805.

Colourful Mexican bar with lively Latin sounds, which caters to a good-time crowd knocking back tequilas, margaritas and punchy Brazilian *caipirinhas*.

New York-style *Cinco Lounge*

Cinco Lounge

MAP PAGE 60, POCKET MAP A11

Rua Ruben A. Leitão 17a

Ⓦ cincolounge.com.

A New York-style cocktail lounge run by Brits in the heart of Lisbon – there are over a hundred cocktails to choose from; plump for one of the wacky fruit concoctions (anyone for tequila, beetroot and lime?) while sinking into an enormous comfy sofa. It also runs cocktail workshops.

Gin Lovers

MAP PAGE 60, POCKET MAP A10

Praça do Príncipe Real 26 Ⓦ ginlovers.pt.

This amazing bar-restaurant nestles inside the indoor patio of the pseudo-Moorish Embaixada shopping emporium, an opulent setting for reasonably priced bar food such as spinach-stuffed chicken and *bacalhau à bras*. As the name implies, the speciality here is gin, with over sixty varieties, though there are plenty of other drinks too.

Mahjong

MAP PAGE 60, POCKET MAP B12

Rua da Atalaia 3 ☎ 213 421 039.

At the bottom of the Bairro Alto and traditionally a decent place to start an evening before moving on up. It's a great space, with plain white tiles and a rough wooden bar juxtaposed with modern Chinese motifs – the clientele is similarly eclectic.

Maria Caxuxa

MAP PAGE 60, POCKET MAP B12

Rua da Barroca 12 ☎ 965 039 094.

This arty lounge-bar has plenty of space for big sofas and eclectic decor – including record players and aged machinery – though these get lost in the crowds when the DJ pumps up the volume as the evening progresses.

Park

MAP PAGE 60, POCKET MAP A12

Calçada do Combro 58 ☎ 215 914 011.

Reached via a poky little entrance inside a car park, this chic rooftop bar comes as quite a surprise. There are lots of potted plants and trees, great cocktails and tasty bar snacks, and a stunning view across the river. At weekends, it often hosts top guest DJs and cool cultural events.

Bairro Alto

Leafy *Esplanada*

Pavilhão Chinês

MAP PAGE 60, POCKET MAP B10
Rua Dom Pedro V 89–91 ☎ 213 424 729.
Once a nineteenth-century tea
and coffee merchants' shop, this
quirky bar is spread across a series
of comfy spaces, including a
pool room. Most are lined with
mirrored cabinets containing a
bizarre range of four thousand
artefacts from around the world,
including a display of model trams.
There's waiter service and a long
list of cocktails.

Portas Largas

MAP PAGE 60, POCKET MAP B11
Rua da Atalaia 103–105 ☎ 218 466 379.
Not quite what it once was but
the eponymous bar's *portas largas*
(big doors) are usually thrown
wide open, inviting passersby into
a buzzy disco bar with inexpensive
drinks and pulsating sounds.

Purex

MAP PAGE 60, POCKET MAP B12
Rua das Salgadeiras 28.
Popular queer bar that attracts
a young, trendy, mixed crowd.

A small and intimate space with
a tiny dancefloor, it gets packed
pretty quickly. Expect DJs,
cocktails and theme nights.

Music venues

Páginas Tantas

MAP PAGE 60, POCKET MAP B11
Rua do Diário de Notícias 85
☎ 966 249 005.
Highly rated jazz den featuring live
music most nights from 10pm,
with bands performing in the
alcove of the exterior window. The
bar serves a good range of draft
beers and cocktails – look for the
beer tap shaped like a saxophone.

Tasca do Chico

MAP PAGE 60, POCKET MAP B12
Rua do Diário de Notícias 39
☎ 961 339 696.
Atmospheric little haunt filled with
football scarves (a fine spot for a
drink), which morphs into a very
popular fado bar most nights, when
crowds pack in to hear moving
performances from 8pm.

Estrela, Lapa and Santos

West of the Bairro Alto sits the leafy district of Estrela, best known for its gardens and enormous basilica. To the south lies opulent Lapa, Lisbon's diplomatic quarter, sheltering a clutch of top hotels. Sumptuous mansions and grand embassy buildings peer out majestically towards the Tejo. The superb Museu Nacional de Arte Antiga below here is Portugal's national gallery, while down on the riverfront, Santos is promoted as "the district of design" with some of the city's coolest shops.

Basílica and Jardim da Estrela

MAP PAGE 73, POCKET MAP G6
Largo da Estrela, Tram #28 or #25, church free, charge for roof visits.

The impressive **Basílica da Estrela** is a vast monument to late eighteenth-century Neoclassicism. Constructed by order of Queen Maria I (whose tomb lies within), and completed in 1790, its landmark white dome can be seen from much of the city. You can visit the flat roof (via 140 steep stone steps) for fine views over the western suburbs, and also walk round the inside of the dome to peer down at the church interior 25 metres below. Opposite, the **Jardim da Estrela** (free) is one of the city's most enjoyable gardens with a pond-side café and a well-equipped children's playground.

Cemitério dos Ingleses

MAP PAGE 73, POCKET MAP G6
Rua São Jorge 6, Tram #28 or #25
Ⓦ britishcemeterylisbon.com, free.

"The English Cemetery" is actually a cemetery for all Protestants, founded in 1717 on the condition that the graves

Jardim da Estrela

The English cemetery

were hidden "from the eyes of the faithful" by cypresses. Here, among the trees and tombs of various expatriates, lie the remains of author Henry Fielding. He came to Lisbon hoping the climate would improve his failing health, but his inability to recuperate may have influenced his verdict on Lisbon as "the nastiest city in the world".

Lapa

MAP PAGE 73, POCKET MAP F7
From Estrela, tram #25 skirts past **Lapa** on its way down to the waterfront. This well-heeled district is the most desired address in the city and though it contains no sights as such, it is worth wandering around to admire the stunning mansions. A good route is to follow the tram tracks from Estrela and turn right into Rua do Sacramento à Lapa, past a string of fantastic embassy buildings. Turn left into Rua do Pau da Bandeira past the *Olissippo Lapa Palace* hotel (if you have the funds, have a drink at the bar). From here, turn left into Rua do Prior and right into Rua do Conde and it's a

ten-minute walk downhill to the Museu Nacional de Arte Antiga (see page 71).

Museu Nacional de Arte Antiga

MAP PAGE 73, POCKET MAP G8
Rua das Janelas Verdes 95, bus #760 from Praça da Figueira, #727 from Belém or a short walk from tram #25
Ⓦ museudearteantiga.pt, charge.
The **Museu Nacional de Arte Antiga** features the largest collection of Portuguese fifteenth- and sixteenth-century paintings in the country, European art from the fourteenth century to the present day, and a rich display of applied art. All of this is well exhibited in a tastefully converted seventeenth-century palace once owned by the Marquês de Pombal. The museum uses "15 highlights in 60 minutes" to guide you round the collection. The main calling card is **Nuno Gonçalves's altarpiece** dedicated to St Vincent (1467–70), a brilliantly marshalled composition depicting Lisbon's patron saint receiving homage from all ranks of its citizens, their faces

Santos district

appearing remarkably modern. The other standout is Hieronymus Bosch's stunningly gruesome *Temptation of St Anthony* in room 57 (don't miss the image on the back of the painting, showing the arrest of Christ). Elsewhere, seek out the altar panel depicting the *Resurrection* by Raphael; Francisco de Zurbarán's *The Twelve Apostles;* a small statue of a nymph by Auguste Rodin; and works by Dürer, Holbein, Cranach (particularly *Salome*), Fragonard and Josefa de Óbidos, considered one of Portugal's greatest female painters.

The **Oriental art** collection shows how the Portuguese were influenced by overseas designs encountered during the sixteenth century. There is inlaid furniture from Goa; Turkish and Syrian *azulejos*; Qing Dynasty porcelain; and a fantastic series of late sixteenth-century Japanese *namban* screens (room 14), depicting the Portuguese landing at Nagasaki. The Japanese regarded the Portuguese traders as southern barbarians (*namban*) with large noses – hence their Pinocchio-like features. The museum extends over the remains of the sixteenth-century St Albert monastery, most of which was razed during the 1755 earthquake, although its beautiful chapel can still be seen today, downstairs by the main entrance. Don't miss the garden café, either (see page 75).

Museu da Marioneta

MAP PAGE 73, POCKET MAP G7
Rua da Esperança 146, tram #25 then a short walk Ⓦ museudamarioneta.pt, charge.

Contemporary and historical **puppets** from around the world are displayed and demonstrated in this former eighteenth-century convent, now a well-laid-out **museum**. Highlights include shadow puppets from Turkey and Indonesia; string marionettes; Punch and Judy-style puppets; and almost life-sized, faintly disturbing modern figures by Portuguese puppeteer Helena Vaz, which are anything but cute. There are also video displays and projections, masks from Africa and Asia, and exhibits on Wallace and Gromit-style plasticine figures, including demonstrations on how they are manipulated for films.

Santos

MAP PAGE 73, POCKET MAP G7
Santos was traditionally a run-down riverside district of factories and warehouses where people only ventured after dark because of its nightclubs. Over the years, artists and designers moved into the inexpensive and expansive warehouses, and now Santos has a reputation as the city's designer heartland. Its riverside streets are not particularly alluring, but you can see many of the country's top creative talent showcasing their products in various shops and galleries. Fashionable bars and restaurants have followed in their wake, though the area around the Museu da Marioneta retains an earthy, villagey feel to its cobblestone backstreets.

Estrela, Lapa and Santos

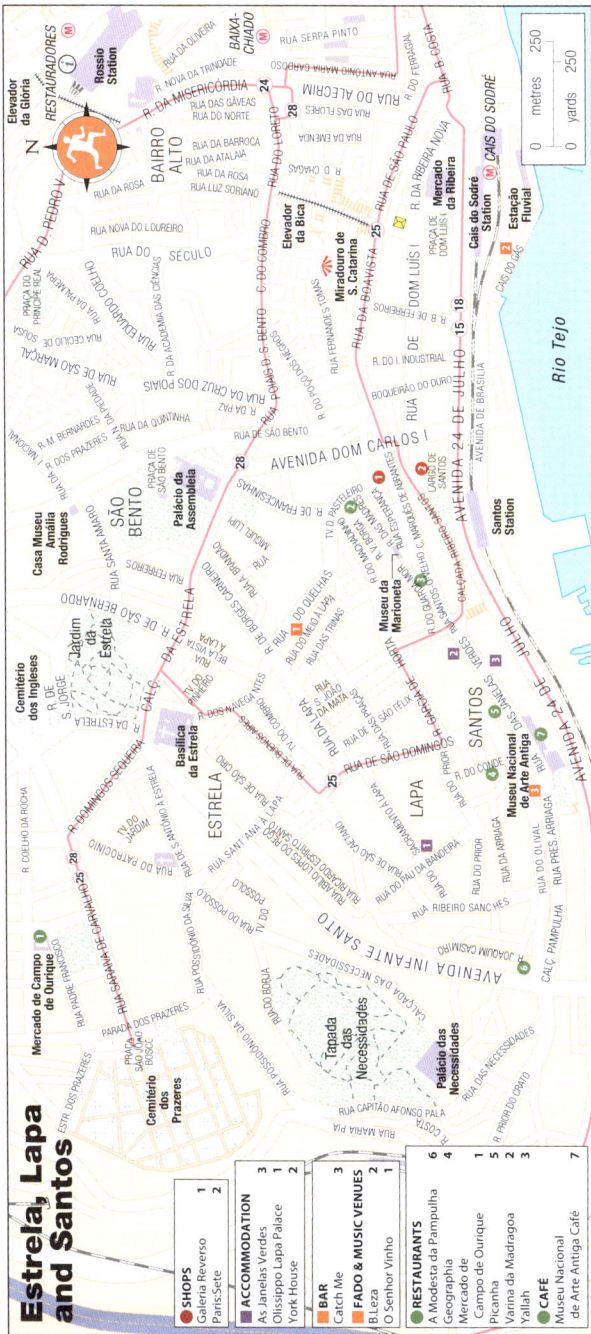

ESTRELA, LAPA AND SANTOS

SHOPS
Galeria Reverso 1
Park.Sete 2

ACCOMMODATION
As Janelas Verdes 3
Olisippo Lapa Palace 1
York House 2

BAR
Catch Me 3

FADO & MUSIC VENUES
B.Leza 1
O Senhor Vinho 2

RESTAURANTS
A Modesta da Pampulha 6
Geographia 4
Mercado de
Campo de Ourique 5
Picanha 5
Varina da Madragoa 2
Yaiiah 3

CAFÉ
Museu Nacional
de Arte Antiga Café 7

Rio Tejo

Shops

Galeria Reverso

MAP PAGE 73, POCKET MAP H7

Rua da Esperança 59–61 ☎ 919 809 131.
Jewellery workshop and gallery
managed by well-known Portuguese
designer Paula Crespo, whose large,
heavy jewellery is eye-catching.
International labels also feature,
many using unusual materials such
as rubber and wood, though to buy
anything you'll need a deep purse.

Paris:Sete

MAP PAGE 73, POCKET MAP H7

Largo Vitorino Damásio 2C
🌐 paris-sete.com.
Bright, white space selling
designer furniture and curios, with
heavyweight names such as Charles
and Ray Eames and Philippe Starck
behind some of them.

Restaurants

A Modesta da Pampulha

MAP PAGE 73, POCKET MAP F8

Rua do Olival 288 ☎ 213 963 583.
A short walk from the Museu
Nacional de Arte Antiga, this
restaurant is all the better for being
a bit off the beaten track. The
no-nonsense local, with attractive
azulejos on the walls, serves good-
value fish, seafood and grilled
meats including amazing *pasteis de
bacalhau* (dried cod cakes). Half-
portions are usually sufficient, and
the house wine is a steal. €

Geographia

MAP PAGE 73, POCKET MAP F8

Rua do Conde 1 🌐 restaurantegeographia.pt.
As you would expect from the
name, this is a travel-themed
restaurant specializing in tasty food
from Portugal's former colonies,
with a cosy, pub-like interior.
The wide range of dishes include
tuna from Cape Verde, braised
fish with okra and spinach from
Angola, black pork with saffron rice

from East Timor and caramelized
banana cake from São Tomé. There
are also recipes from Brazil and
Mozambique, not to mention
some interesting cocktails: try the
Portuguese gin with *ginginha*. €€

Mercado de Campo de Ourique

MAP PAGE 73, POCKET MAP F6

Rua Coelho da Rocha 104 ☎ 211 323 701.
This wonderful 1930s building
has been given a revamp and now
not only sells fish, fruit and veg,
but also shelters around twenty
tasquinhas (small food stalls)
serving pastries, sushi, *petiscos*,
burgers and seafood. There are
bars (gin cocktails, flavoured teas
and the like) and occasional live
entertainment in the evenings. €

Picanha

MAP PAGE 73, POCKET MAP G8

Rua das Janelas Verdes 96
🌐 picanha-janelasverdes.pt.
This ornately tiled restaurant
specializes in *picanha* (strips of
beef in garlic sauce) accompanied
by black-eyed beans, salad and
potatoes. There are also decent
pasta and fish dishes. €€

Varina da Madragoa

MAP PAGE 73, POCKET MAP G7

Rua das Madres 34 ☎ 213 965 533.
Not quite what it was in the 1970s
when it hosted the likes of former
US President Jimmy Carter and
Portuguese PM José Sócrates, but
it's easy to see why they liked it: a
lovely, traditional restaurant with
grape-motif *azulejos* on the walls
and a menu featuring dishes such as
bacalhau, trout and steaks. Desserts
include a splendid almond ice
cream with hot chocolate sauce. €€

Yallah

MAP PAGE 73, POCKET MAP G7

Rua Santos-o-Vehlo 22 ☎ 213 951 456.
With a brick-vaulted ceiling, lovely
interior decor and outdoor tables
on a lively street, this attractive
space offers a range of delicious

Mercado de Campo de Ourique

Middle-Eastern street food. Good for vegetarians, the menu includes fine falafels, hummus with flatbreads and baba ganoush as well as tajines and mezes. Tasty breakfasts, too, featuring shakshuka and organic eggs with sumac. €

Café

Museu Nacional de Arte Antiga Café

MAP PAGE 73, POCKET MAP G8
Rua das Janelas Verdes 95 ☎ 213 912 860.
There's no need to visit the museum to eat at its simple café – enter through the museum exit opposite Largo Dr J de Figueiredo and head to the basement. Lunches and drinks can be enjoyed in a superb garden studded with statues and overlooking Lisbon's docks. €

Bar

Catch Me

MAP PAGE 73, POCKET MAP F8
Jardim 9 de Abril ⓦ catch-me.pt.
A modern, glass-sided bar-restaurant adjacent to the Museu

Nacional de Arte Antiga, *Catch Me* has a terrific terrace overlooking the docks and Ponte 25 de Abril. Great at any time of the day, it's a particularly fine spot for a cocktail or sundowner, with regular DJ sets and live music.

Fado and music venues

B.Leza

MAP PAGE 73, POCKET MAP A14
Cais Gás 1 ☎ 210 106 837.
A great African club, with live music, poetry nights, *kizomba* evenings and occasional dance lessons on offer, though you'd be hard pushed to outshine the regulars.

O Senhor Vinho

MAP PAGE 73, POCKET MAP G7
Rua do Meio à Lapa 18 ⓦ srvinho.com.
In the fashionable Madragoa district, this famous 1975-founded fado club features some of the best singers in Portugal (from 9pm), hence the high prices (around €65 a head). Reservations are advised.

Alcântara and the docks

Loomed over by the enormous Ponte 25 de Abril suspension bridge, Alcântara has a decidedly industrial hue, with a tangle of flyovers and cranes from the docks dominating the skyline. The area is well known for its nightlife, thanks mainly to its dockside warehouse conversions that shelter cafés and restaurants. It also hosts a couple of fine museums, both tipping their hats to Portugal's historic links with Asia, and there's an attractive riverside promenade. To reach the docks, take a train from Cais do Sodré to Alcântara-Mar or tram #15.

Museu do Oriente

MAP PAGE 78, POCKET MAP E8
Avda de Brasília Ⓦ foriente.pt,
charge, free Fri 6–8pm.
Owned by the influential Orient Foundation, this spacious **museum** traces the cultural links that Portugal has built up with its former colonies in Macao, India, East Timor and other Asian countries. Housed in an enormous 1930s Estado Novo building, highlights of the extensive collection include valuable nineteenth-century Chinese

Treasures in the Museu do Oriente

porcelain, an amazing array of seventeenth-century Chinese snuff boxes and, from the same century, Japanese armour and entire carved pillars from Goa. The top floor is given over to displays on the Gods of Asia, featuring a bright collection of religious costumes and shrines used in Bali and Vietnam together with Taoist altars, statues of Buddha, fine Japanese Shinto masks and Indonesian shadow puppets. Vivid images of Hindu gods Shiva, Ganesh the elephant god and Kali the demon are counterbalanced by some lovely Thai amulets. There is also a decent top-floor café/restaurant with dock views.

Doca de Santo Amaro

MAP PAGE 78, POCKET MAP D9
Just west of the Doca de Alcântara lies the more intimate **Doca de Santo Amaro**, nestling right under the humming traffic and rattling trains crossing Ponte 25 de Abril. This small, almost completely enclosed marina is filled with bobbing sailing boats and lined with tastefully converted warehouses. Its international cafés and restaurants are pricier than usual for Lisbon, but the constant comings and goings of the Tejo provide plenty of free entertainment. Leaving Doca de Santo Amaro at its western side, you can pick up a pleasant riverside path

Doca de Santo Amaro

that leads all the way to Belém (see page 82), twenty minutes' walk west, or follow the slightly more urban cycle route around a half-hour walk east to Praça do Comércio.

Ponte 25 de Abril and the Pilar 7 Experience

MAP PAGE 78. POCKET MAP D9

Avenida da India Ⓦ visitlisbo.com, charge. Resembling the Golden Gate Bridge in San Francisco, the hugely impressive **Ponte 25 de Abril** was opened in 1966 as a vital link between Lisbon and the southern banks of the Tejo. Around 2.3km in length, the bridge rises to 70m above the river, though its main pillars are nearly 200m tall. It was originally named Ponte de Salazar after the dictatorial prime minister who ruled Portugal with an iron fist from 1932 to 1968, but took its present name to mark the date of the revolution that overthrew Salazar's regime in 1974. The dizzying **Pilar 7 Experience** offers the opportunity to ascend 70m up one of the bridge's pillars to a glass-encased platform for a close-up look at the thundering traffic and stunning views across the western riverfront. Inside, an exhibition space traces the history of the manufacturing marvel using models and multimedia, including a somewhat grainy projection room detailing how three thousand workers built the edifice using 55,000km of steel wire. For a small extra fee, you can experience a virtual-reality recreation of how maintenance workers carry out repairs on the central pillars, a hairy 200m above the river. Note that visitor numbers are restricted to a hundred at any one time (and only forty on the viewpoint).

Museu do Centro Científico e Cultural de Macau

MAP PAGE 78, POCKET MAP C9

Rua da Junqueira 30 Ⓦ cccm.gov.pt, charge. This attractively laid-out **museum** is dedicated to Portugal's historical **trading links** with Asia and, specifically, its former colony of Macao, which was handed back to Chinese rule in 1999. There are model boats and audio displays detailing early sea voyages, as well as various historic journals and artefacts, including a seventeenth-century portable wooden altar, used by travelling clergy. Upstairs, exhibitions of Chinese art from the sixteenth to the nineteenth centuries show off ornate collections of porcelain, silverware and applied art, most notably an impressive array of opium pipes and ivory boxes.

Museu da Carris

MAP PAGE 78, POCKET MAP D8
Rua 1° de Maio 101 Ⓦ museu.carris.pt, charge.

This engagingly quirky and ramshackle **museum** traces the history of Lisbon's **public transport**, from the earliest trams and street lifts to the development of the metro. There are three zones, the first with evocative black-and-white photos, uniforms and models. You then hop on a real tram dating from 1901 which takes you to a warehouse filled with historic trams, and then on to another with ancient buses and models of metro trains. It's especially great fun for kids, who can clamber on board and pretend to drive the vehicles. The bottom of the site also has the eye-catching **Village Underground** (Ⓦ vulisboa.com), a bizarre medley of old shipping

containers and double-decker buses now given over to workspaces for writers and artists with frequent evening events.

Berardo Museu Art Deco (B-MAD)

MAP PAGE 78, POCKET MAP D8
Rua 1 de Maio 28 Ⓦ bmad.pt.

The man behind Belém's fabulous Museu Nacional de Arte Contemporânea (see page 50), businessman Joe Berardo, has also founded this captivating museum, which will fascinate anyone interested in the art movement that influenced design and architecture in the 1920s and 30s, but which also embraces earlier Art Nouveau pieces from the late nineteenth century. Set in an ornate blue-and-white tiled eighteenth-century manor house – the former home of Nobel laureate Egas Moniz – and laid out in the style of the era, the **Berardo Museu Art Deco (B-MAD)** contains

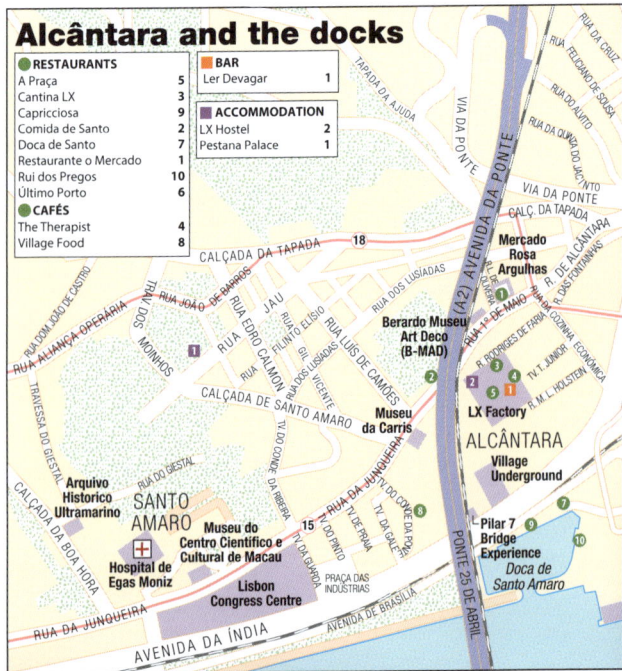

Alcântara and the docks

● RESTAURANTS	
A Praça	5
Cantina LX	3
Capricciosa	9
Comida de Santo	2
Doca de Santo	7
Restaurante o Mercado	1
Rui dos Pregos	10
Último Porto	6
● CAFÉS	
The Therapist	4
Village Food	8

■ BAR	
Ler Devagar	1

■ ACCOMMODATION	
LX Hostel	2
Pestana Palace	1

RUA DA CRUZ
RUA FELICIANO DE SOUSA
RUA DO ALTO
RUA DA QUINTA DO JACINTO
TAPADA DA AJUDA
VIA DA PONTE
CALÇ. DA TAPADA
VIA DA PONTE
RUA DOM JOÃO DE CASTRO
RUA ALIANÇA OPERÁRIA
TRAV. DOS MONHOS
RUA JOÃO DE BARROS
JAU
RUA EDRO CALMON
RUA FILINTO ELÍSIO
RUA LUÍS DE CAMÕES
RUA DOS LUSÍADAS
CALÇADA DA TAPADA
CALÇADA DE SANTO AMARO
TV. DO CONDE DA RIBEIRA
TRAVESSA DO GIESTAL
RUA DO GIESTAL
CALÇADA DA BOA HORA
SANTO AMARO
Arquivo Histórico Ultramarino
Hospital de Egas Moniz
Museu do Centro Científico e Cultural de Macau
Lisbon Congress Centre
PRAÇA DAS INDÚSTRIAS
RUA DA JUNQUEIRA
AVENIDA DA ÍNDIA
AVENIDA DE BRASÍLIA
Mercado Rosa Argulhas
R. DE ALCÂNTARA
R. DE FORTUNATA
RUA 1° DE MAIO
R. RODRIGUES DE FARIA
COZINHA ECONÓMICA
TV. T. JÚNIOR
R. M. L. HOLSTEIN
Berardo Museu Art Deco (B-MAD)
Museu da Carris
LX Factory
ALCÂNTARA
Village Underground
Pilar 7 Bridge Experience
Doca de Santo Amaro
PONTE 25 DE ABRIL
(A2) AVENIDA DA PONTE
RUA DA GUIA
TV. DE PRATA
TV. DO PINTO
RUA DA JUNQUEIRA
TV. DO CONDE DA PO

objects from some of the big names in Art Deco, including Ruhlmann, Adnet and Lalique. There is a range of sumptuous decorative ironwork, lamps, glassware, ceramics, statuettes, furniture, art and even a Picasso jar.

The tour ends with a wine tasting and the chance to buy produce from the museum wine shop.

LX Factory

MAP PAGE 78, POCKET MAP D8
Rua Rodrigues Faria 103 ⓦ lxfactory.com.
Below Ponte 25 de Abril, this former nineteenth-century industrial estate is now the place to test Lisbon's creative pulse. The factories and warehouses have turned into a mini-district of workshops and studios for the city's go-getters, along with a series of superb boutiques, shops, cafés and bars set in fashionably run-down urban spaces. Sunday afternoon is a good time to visit, with a lively flea market and many

LX Factory

places open for brunch: **LX Factory**'s Open Days take place throughout the year, featuring shows, live music and film screenings (check website for details).

Cafés

The Therapist

MAP PAGE 78, POCKET MAP D8
LX Factory, Rua Rodrigues Faria 103 H06
☎ 913 489 993.

An appealing former warehouse
space with a glass-panelled roof
and outdoor benches, this is a
good place for the morning after
the night before. A healthy "detox"
menu features an eclectic array
of dishes such as vegan risotto,
gluten-free pancakes, mushroom
bruschetta and pad Thai. There are
also all-day brunches, juices and
smoothies or, if you just need that
hair of the dog, cocktails, beers and
ciders. €

Village Food

MAP PAGE 78, POCKET MAP D9
Village Underground, Avenida da Índia 52
☎ 215 832 469.

Grab a burger, wrap, *prego* (steak in
a bun) or brunch, or just a drink,
in the eclectic Village Underground
(see page 78), where the kitchens
and seating are inside an old
double-decker bus. There are also
plenty of outdoor tables where
you can sit alongside Lisbon's cool,

creative crowd, plus there's regular
live music and entertainment at the
venue, too. €

Restaurants

A Praça

MAP PAGE 78, POCKET MAP D8
LX Factory, Edifício H, Espaço 001
☎ 210 991 792.

One of the larger restaurants in LX
Factory, a hip spot with an open
kitchen serving a range of dishes,
including pasta, steaks and seafood
and a fine brunch. It also does good
cocktails. €€

Cantina LX

MAP PAGE 78, POCKET MAP D8
LX Factory, Rua Rodrigues Faria 103
☎ 213 628 239.

Upcycled furniture and bench-
like tables in a spacious former
warehouse make this a cool
hangout. Great breakfasts, snacks
and daily specials (usually grilled
meat or fish). €

Capricciosa

MAP PAGE 78, POCKET MAP D9
Doca de Santo Amaro Armazém 8
ⓦ capricciosa.com.pt.

A bar in LX Factory

Set inside a bright former warehouse, *Capricciosa* plates up good-value "artesan" pizzas as well as pasta and salads. Next to a pedestrianized walkway around the marina, this is always popular with families; try and bag one of the alluring tables facing the bobbing boats. €€

Comida de Santo

MAP PAGE 78, POCKET MAP D8
Rua 1 de Maio 98 W comidodesanto.pt.
Formerly in the Bairro Alto, this long-established Brazilian restaurant serves classic dishes such as *feijoada a Brasileira* (bean stew) and a fantastic *ensopadinho de peixe* (fish in coconut), with good vegetarian options too. €€

Doca de Santo

MAP PAGE 78, POCKET MAP D8
Armazém CP, Doca de Santo Amaro
W https://docadesanto.com.pt.
Though it's located slightly away from the river, the first place to open in the docks has recently been renovated into a classy restaurant with an inviting outdoor dining area. Dishes include *petiscos* such as veal croquettes and fish ceviche, as well as mains of Thai prawn curry, *arroz de marisco* (seafood rice) and baked octopus. The speciality is various *pregos* (meat in a bun). €€

Restaurante o Mercado

MAP PAGE 78, POCKET MAP D8
Mercado Rosa Agulhas, Rua Leão de Oliveira, Loja 19
W restauranteomercado.pt.
On three floors by the market building – and Lisbon's markets are always worth a call – this is a great place for a hearty feast. The ingredients don't have far to travel: the fish and vegetables are day-fresh, and there's a long list of grilled meats and seafood, including a fine seafood pasta. €€

Rui dos Pregos

MAP PAGE 78, POCKET MAP D9
Passeio Doca de Santo Amaro
W ruidospregos.pt.

Bookshop-bar hybrid *Ler Devagar*

One of the less pricey options set to one side of the docks, with appealing outdoor tables. The speciality here is *pregos* (beef sandwiches), with various varieties and combinations. €

Último Porto

MAP PAGE 78, POCKET MAP F8
Estação Marítima da Rocha Conde de Óbidos T 213 979 498.
Perched at the edge of Lisbon's main container shipping docks, this earthy lunchtime restaurant ("The Last Port") is popular with the local dock workers who come here at lunchtimes for inexpensive grilled fish; the sardines are hard to beat, and portions are generous. €€

Bar

Ler Devagar

MAP PAGE 78, POCKET MAP D8
LX Factory, Rua Rodrigues Faria 103, Edifício G-03 W lerdevagar.com.
Primarily a wonderful arts bookshop, with shelves reaching an old printing press, this also has a corner café-bar – a great place to sample Portuguese wines by the glass. Plus, it hosts exhibits and occasional live music.

Belém and Ajuda

With its maritime history and attractive riverside location, Belém (pronounced ber-layng) is understandably one of Lisbon's most popular suburbs. It was from Belém that Vasco da Gama famously set sail for India in 1497. The monastery subsequently built here – the Mosteiro dos Jerónimos – stands as a testament to his triumphant discovery of a sea route to Asia, which initiated the beginning of a Portuguese golden age. Along with the monastery and the landmark Torre de Belém, the suburb boasts a group of small museums, including the fantastic Centro Cultural de Belém. Just to the northeast of Belém is Ajuda, famed for its palace and ancient botanical gardens. Higher still lies the sprawling parkland of Monsanto, Lisbon's largest green space.

Praça do Império

MAP PAGE 84, POCKET MAP C4

The formal walkways and gardens of **Praça do Império** are laid out over Belém's former beach. It's a popular spot, especially on Saturday mornings, when weddings often take place at the monastery. The seventeenth-century buildings along Rua Vieira Portuense are now mostly restaurants with outdoor seating; as a rule, the further east you head, the better value they become.

Jardim do Ultramar and Presidência da República

MAP PAGE 84, POCKET MAP C4
Garden entrance on Calçada do Galvão
☎ 213 609 660, charge.

The leafy **Jardim do Ultramar** is an oasis of hothouses, ponds and

The fabulous Praça do Império

Belém transport

You can reach Belém on tram #15 (signed Algés), which runs from Praça da Figueira via Praça do Comércio (20min). Ask at the ticket offices of the main sites about combined tickets that can save money on entry to the main attractions, which all attract long queues in the summer. You can also take a hop-on, hop-off bus tour (ⓦ yellowbustours.com, €17 valid for 48 hours) around the suburb's main sights, including the Ponte 25 Abril. Alternatively, hire bikes (ⓦ biclas.com) from the kiosk 5min east of the MAAT (see page 87).

towering palms, a lovely place for a shady walk. In the southeastern corner lies the pink **Presidência da República**, which was used as the royal's holiday home from 1726 to the birth of the Republic. Today it is the president's official residence, which opens its state rooms and gardens for guided visits on Saturdays (entrance on Praça Afonso de Albuquerque, ⓦ museu. presidencia.pt, free).

Museu de Arte Popular

MAP PAGE 84, POCKET MAP B5
Avda de Brasília
ⓦ museusmonumentos.pt, charge.
In a space which feels slightly too large for its exhibits, this charming **museum** chronicles Portugal's **folk art**, from beautiful wood and cork toys to ceramics, rugs and fascinating traditional costumes, including amazing cloaks from the Trás-os-Montes region.

Mosteiro dos Jerónimos

MAP PAGE 84, POCKET MAP C4
Praça do Império
ⓦ museusmonumentos.pt, charge.
If there's one building that symbolizes the "Golden Age of Exploration", it's the **Mosteiros dos Jerónimos**, which is also considered to be the first ever Manueline building. Now a UNESCO World Heritage Site, the monastery and its adjacent church were built to fulfill a promise that Portugal's king, Dom Manuel, made, should Vasco da Gama return safely from his inaugural voyage to India in 1498. Construction began in 1502 under the architect Diogo de Boitaca.

Appropriately, Vasco da Gama's tomb now lies just inside the fantastically embellished entrance to the church. Crowned by an elaborate medley of statues, including Henry the Navigator, the 32m-high entrance was designed by the Spaniard João de Castilho, who took over the building of the church in 1517.

The interior is even more dazzling than the exterior, displaying the elaborate maritime influences typical of Manueline architecture – the escutcheons adorning its ceiling come from the actual ships that sailed the exploratory voyages.

The church also contains the tomb of Luís de Camões (1527–1570), Portugal's greatest poet and recorder of the discoveries, alongside the tombs of former presidents and dignitaries.

Equally impressive is the adjacent monastery, gathered round sumptuously vaulted cloisters with nautical symbols carved into the honey-coloured limestone. You can still see the twelve niches where navigators stopped for confessionals before their journeys, until the Hieronymite monks were forced out during the dissolution of 1833. In 2007, the monastery was again influential in blessing future trade: the Treaty of Lisbon was signed here to cement the format of the European Union.

Museu de Arqueologia

MAP PAGE 84, POCKET MAP C4

Praça do Império

Ⓦ museuarqueologia.gov.pt, charge.
Housed in a neo-Manueline
extension to the monastery added in
1850, the **Museu de Arqueologia**
has a small section on Egyptian
antiquities dating from 6000 BC,
but concentrates on Portuguese
archeological finds. It's a sparse
collection reprieved by coins and
jewellery through the ages, and a few
fine Roman mosaics. The museum is
closed for renovations until 2026.

Museu da Marinha

MAP PAGE 84, POCKET MAP B4

Praça do Império Ⓦ cultura-marinha.pt,
charge.
In the west wing of the monastery
extension is an absorbing and
gargantuan **maritime museum**,
packed not only with models of
ships, naval uniforms and artefacts
from Portugal's Asian colonies,
but also with real vessels – fishing
boats and sumptuous state barges,
plus early seaplanes. Much of the
collection comes from King Luís I
(1861–1889), a keen oceanographer.

Centro Cultural de Belém

MAP PAGE 84, POCKET MAP B4

Praça do Império Ⓦ ccb.pt.
The stylish, modern, pink marble
Centro Cultural de Belém was built
to host Lisbon's 1992 presidency
of the EU. It's now a top cultural
centre, containing the Berardo
Collection and hosting regular
photography and art exhibitions,
concerts and shows.

Museu de Arte Contemporânea MAC/CCB

MAP PAGE 84, POCKET MAP B4

Entrance via Centro Cultural de Belém,
Praça do Império Ⓦ ccb.pt/en/macccb,
charge.
As impressive as Belém's historical
monuments is the unique **Museu**

Belém and Ajuda

de Arte Contemporânea MAC/ CCB amassed by wealthy Madeiran Joe Berardo, Portugal's answer to Charles Saatchi or François Pinault. You can enjoy some of the world's top modern artists, though not all of the vast collection is on display at the same time. The museum is organized by theme, with rooms devoted to Dadaism, Surrealism, Cubism, Abstract Expressionism and a large section on Pop Art. The artists featuring in these sections include the likes of Francis Bacon, David Hockney, Picasso, Míro, Man Ray, Bridget Riley, Roy Lichtenstein, Louise Bourgeois and Mark Rothko.

Padrão dos Descobrimentos

MAP PAGE 84, POCKET MAP C5
Avda de Brasília, reached via an underpass beneath the Avda da Índia
ⓦ padraodosdescobrimentos.pt, charge.
The **Padrão dos Descobrimentos** (Monument to the Discoveries) is

Berardo Collection, Centro Cultural de Belém

a 54m-high, caravel-shaped slab of concrete erected in 1960 to commemorate the 500th anniversary of the death of Henry the Navigator.

ALTO DA AJUDA

Palácio da Ajuda and Museu do Tesouro Real — entrance

Jardim Botânico da Ajuda

Páteo Alfacinha

Nossa Senhora da Ajuda

Igreja da Memória

AJUDA

Market   18

Jardim do Ultramar

Arquivo Histórico Ultramarino

Presidência da República

Hospital de Egas Moniz

Museu do Centro Científico e Cultural de Macau

Museu da Presidência

Lisbon Congress Centre

Museu Nacional dos Coches   15   Library

Belém Station

MAAT (Museum of Art, Architecture and Technology)

Estação Fluvial de Belém

AVENIDA DA ÍNDIA

AVENIDA DE BRASÍLIA

Rio Tejo

Ferry to Trafaria

RESTAURANTS	
A Vela	3
Portugália	4

CAFÉS	
MAAT Café and Kitchen	2
Pasteis de Belém	1

ACCOMMODATION	
Jéronimos 8	1

BAR	
Á Margem	1

0	metres	250
0	yards	250

A large and detailed statue of Henry appears at the head of a line of statues that include King Alfonso V, Luís de Camões, Vasco da Gama and other Portuguese heroes. Inside, a small exhibition space often features displays on Lisbon's history – the entrance fee also grants a ride in the lift providing fine views of the Tejo and the Torre de Belém.

Just in front of the monument, tourists pose on the marble pavement decorated with a map of the world charting the routes taken by the great Portuguese explorers.

Torre de Belém

MAP PAGE 84, POCKET MAP A5
Avda de Brasília ⓦ torrebelem.gov.com, charge.

Reached via a narrow walkway and jutting into the river, the impressive **Torre de Belém** (Tower of Belém) has become an iconic symbol of Lisbon. It is fashioned in the Manueline style that was prominent during the reign of Manuel, its windows and stairways embellished with arches and decorative symbols representing Portugal's explorations into the New World. Built as a fortress to defend the mouth of the River Tejo, it took five years to complete, though when it opened in 1520 it would have been near the centre of the river – the earthquake of 1755 shifted the waterway's course. Today, visitors are free to explore the tower's various levels, which include a terrace facing the river from where artillery would have been fired.

You can then climb a very steep spiral staircase up four levels – each with a slightly different framed vista of the Tejo – to a top terrace where you're rewarded with a blowy panorama of Belém. You can also duck into the dungeons, a low-ceilinged room used to store gunpowder; these were also used notoriously by Dom Miguel to lock up political prisoners in the nineteenth century. Closed for renovation until 2026.

Museu dos Coches

MAP PAGE 84, POCKET MAP D4
Avda Índia 136 and Praça Afonso de Albuquerque ⓦ museusmonumentos. pt, charge (combination ticket available including Royal Riding School), free Sun am.

Housed in a vast contemporary building designed by Brazilian architect Paulo Mendes e Rocha, the **Museu dos Coches** (Coach Museum) contains one of the world's largest collections of carriages and

Torre de Belém

MAAT

saddlery, including a rare sixteenth-century coach designed for King Felipe I. Heavily gilded, ornate and often beautifully painted, the royal carriages, sedan chairs and children's cabriolets dating from the sixteenth to nineteenth centuries, contrast with the stark modern building, which gives great views over Belém and the river. More are on display in the former Royal Riding School across the road, though it's only really the historic building itself that warrants the additional entrance fee.

MAAT (Museum of Art, Architecture and Technology)

MAP PAGE 84, POCKET MAP D4
Avda de Brasília ⓦ www.maat.pt, charge.
British architect Amanda Levete has masterminded a sumptuous modern building on the riverfront to house the innovative **MAAT**. It's connected to the former Museu da Electricidade next door – a disused red-brick, early-twentieth-century power station – to give eight galleries of exhibition space dedicated to contemporary designers, artists and architects. Regularly changing exhibits feature the likes of Charles and Ray Eames and French artist Dominique Gonzalez-Foerster, while the permanent art collection showcases works by around 250 contemporary Portuguese artists. But

as interesting as the exhibits can be, it is the striking architecture that's really captured people's imagination; a fluid, curving structure covered in 15,000 ceramic tiles that seems to glow at sunset. The galleries (including the giant Oval Room for the show-stopping exhibits) are sunk below street level, which means you can easily walk up onto the cantilevered roof for wonderful views across the river, and there's also a café-restaurant (see page 89).

Palácio da Ajuda

MAP PAGE 84, POCKET MAP D2
Largo da Ajuda, tram #18 from Praça do Comércio or bus #729 from Belém ⓦ palacioajuda.gov.pt, charge (combined ticket available for Royal Treasury Museum).
This massive **nineteenth-century palace** sits on a hillside above Belém. Construction began in 1802 but was left incomplete when João VI and the royal family fled to Brazil to escape Napoleon's invading army in 1807. The original plans were therefore never fulfilled, though the completed section was used as a royal residence after João returned from exile in 1821.

The crashingly tasteless decor was commissioned by the nineteenth-century royal, Dona Maria II (João's granddaughter), and gives an insight into the opulent lifestyle of royalty. The queen's bedroom comes complete with a polar bear-skin rug, while the throne and ballroom are impressive for their sheer size and extravagance. The highly ornate banqueting hall, dripping with crystal chandeliers, is also breathtaking.

Museu do Tesouro Real

MAP PAGE 84, POCKET MAP D2
Largo da Ajuda, tram #18 from Praça do Comércio or bus #729 from Belém ⓦ tesouroreal.pt, charge (combined ticket available for Palácio da Ajuda).

The west wing of the Palácio da Ajuda now hosts the strikingly modern **Museu do Tesouro Real** (Royal Treasury Museum), a bleak white concrete extension that's a suitably solid exterior for what lies inside: one of the world's largest vaults housing around a thousand pieces of royal pomp, including the Portuguese crown jewels. To enter, you need to pass through airport-style security along with sturdy entry doors before you can even reach the third-floor vault. It takes a while to adjust to the darkened interior, where you'll find a staggering volume of gold nuggets from Brazil, coins, costumery, gemstones, silverware and diamonds that once belonged to the Portuguese royal family, many plundered from the early days of colonization. Amazingly, the entire treasury was shipped to Brazil when Dom João VI fled Napoleon to South America in 1807 at great risk. The king returned to Portugal in 1821, though the collection ended up in London in 1931 and was later dispersed, only to be recently put together again for the museum. There is also a fourth-floor café with fine views over the eastern city.

Jardim Botânico da Ajuda

MAP PAGE 84, POCKET MAP C2
Entrance on Calçada da Ajuda and Calçada do Galvão ⓦ isa.ulisboa.pt, charge.

A classic example of formal Portuguese design, **Jardim**

Botânico da Ajuda is one of the city's oldest and most interesting botanical gardens, **now part of the University of Lisbon**. Commissioned by the Marquês de Pombal and laid out in 1768, it was owned by the royal family until the birth of the Republic in 1910, then substantially restored in the 1990s. The garden is divided into eight parts planted with species from around the world, arranged around terraces, statues and fountains, much of it with lovely views over the river. It also has a nice café.

Páteo Alfacinha

MAP PAGE 84, POCKET MAP D2
Rua do Guarda Jóias 44 ⓦ pateoalfacinha.com.

Just five minutes' walk from the Palácio da Ajuda, it is worth seeking out this highly picturesque *páteo* – a renovated cluster of traditional nineteenth-century Lisbon houses gathered round a central patio. These were common in the days when families lived in tight-knit communities who looked after and traded with each other. Today the houses only come alive for special events and private parties, often at weekends, though there are two decent restaurants, one which is open in summer and the other in winter.

Parque Florestal de Monsanto

MAP PAGE 84, POCKET MAP E2
Bus #729 from Ajuda or Belém.

The extensive hillside **Parque Florestal de Monsanto** – home to the city's main and well-equipped campsite (ⓦ lisboacamping.com) – is known as "Lisbon's lungs", though it used to be infamous for the sex workers here until the Mayor of Lisbon bought a house nearby in 2003.

Suddenly, the park was given a new lease of life. At weekends in summer, it's traffic-free and pop concerts are often laid on, usually free of charge.

The must-try *Pastéis de Belém*

Restaurants

A Vela
MAP PAGE 84, POCKET MAP B9
Avenida de Brasilia Doca de Recreio
☏ 213 642 711.
This bustling restaurant is tucked in to the back of a sailing school, with outdoor tables beside the river. It's far enough from the tourist sights to attract a largely local clientele enjoying fresh fish and meat dishes; try the *arroz de lagosta* (lobster rice) for two. €€

Portugália
MAP PAGE 84, POCKET MAP C4
Avda de Brasilia Edif. Espelho d'Água
ⓦ portugalia.pt.
Marooned on a little island in an artificial lake facing the Padrão dos Descobrimentos, this glass-fronted restaurant (part of a popular chain) has a serene position. Dishes include *bitoques* (small steaks) and a wonderful *gambas à brás* (prawns with stick potatoes and onions). €€

Cafés

MAAT Café & Kitchen
MAP PAGE 84, POCKET MAP B9
Museum of Art, Architecture and Technology, Avenida de Brasilia ⓦ maat.pt.
Sleek and stylish, the MAAT's café and restaurant sit below the museum's sweeping roof, superbly framing the pleasant river views. The café, with outdoor seating, serves an array of drinks and snacks (the *pastéis for nata* tartlets are superb), while the adjacent restaurant serves expensive fish and seafood. €€

Pasteis de Belém
MAP PAGE 84, POCKET MAP C4
Rua de Belém 84–92 ⓦ pasteisdebelem.pt.
No visit to Belém is complete without a coffee and hot *pastel de nata* (Portuguese custard tart) liberally sprinkled with *canela* (cinnamon) in this cavernous, tiled pastry shop and café, which has been serving them up using a secret recipe since 1837. The place positively heaves, especially at weekends, but there's usually space to sit down in its warren of rooms. €

Bar

Á Margem
MAP PAGE 84, POCKET MAP B5
Doca do Bom Sucesso ☏ 918 620 032.
Chic and minimalist café-bar with stunning views across the river – tables spill out onto the waterfront. Sandwiches plus tapas and salads, and a good list of cocktails and wines. It's near the brick-striped stumpy lighthouse.

Avenida, Parque Eduardo VII and the Gulbenkian

Lisbon's main avenue, Avenida da Liberdade (simply known as "Avenida"), links the centre with its principal park, Parque Eduardo VII, best known for its views and enormous hothouses. The busy thoroughfare, together with its side streets, was once home to statesmen and public figures. On its western side is the historic Praça das Amoreiras, the finishing point of the massive Águas Livres aqueduct. Here you'll find the Árpád Szenes-Vieira da Silva Foundation, a collection of works by two artists heavily influenced by Lisbon. Northwest of the park, the Fundação Calouste Gulbenkian is undoubtedly Portugal's premier cultural centre, featuring one of Europe's richest art collections. To the east, a further attraction awaits at the Casa Museu Dr Anastácio Gonçalves, filled with historic paintings and objects. Just north of here is the bullring at Campo Pequeno, while east lies the city's zoo.

Avenida da Liberdade

MAP PAGE 92, POCKET MAP J5

The 1.3km, palm-lined **Avenida da Liberdade** is still much as poet Fernando Pessoa described it: "the finest artery in Lisbon… full of trees… small gardens, ponds, fountains, cascades and statues". It was laid out in 1882 as the city's main north–south avenue and has several appealing outdoor cafés beneath the shade of trees that help cushion the roar of passing traffic. Some of the original nineteenth-century mansions remain, though most have been replaced by modern buildings. The upper end of the thoroughfare (Lisbon's most expensive real estate) houses designer shops and ends at the landmark roundabout of Praça Marquês de Pombal, also known as Rotunda.

Parque Mayer

MAP PAGE 92, POCKET MAP J5

Opened in 1922 as an "entertainment precinct" when theatres were all the rage, the fine Art Deco entry pillars of the little **Parque Mayer** lead to the Teatro Maria Vitória and the renovated **Teatro Capitólio** (Portugal's first great Modernist structure), both of which show various plays and shows. It also has a fine restaurant, *A Gina* (see page 99).

Casa Museu Medeiros e Almeida

MAP PAGE 92, POCKET MAP H5

Rua Rosa Araújo 41 ⓦ casa-museumedeirosealmeida.pt, charge.

This excellent **museum** was the home of the industrialist, philanthropist and art collector **António Medeiros** until his death in 1986. Today it serves as a showcase for his priceless series of artefacts. His collection of 225 Chinese porcelain items (some 2000 years old), sixteenth- to nineteenth-century watches, and English and Portuguese silverware is considered the most valuable in the world. Other highlights include glorious eighteenth-century *azulejos* in the Sala de Lago, a room complete with large water fountains; and a rare seventeenth-century clock, made for Queen Catherine of Bragança and mentioned by Samuel Pepys in his diary.

Praça das Amoreiras

MAP PAGE 92, POCKET MAP G5

One of Lisbon's most tranquil squares, **Praça das Amoreiras** – complete with kids' play area – is dominated on its western side by the Águas Livres aqueduct (see page 94), with a chapel wedged into its arches.

On the south side the **Mãe d'Água** cistern (⊚epal.pt, charge) marks the end of the line for the aqueduct. Built between 1746 and 1834, the castellated stone building contains a reservoir that once supplied the city.

The structure nowadays hosts occasional temporary art exhibitions. Head to the back where stairs lead to the roof for great views over the city. Back on the square, the little kiosk café is a popular spot for a coffee or beer, and also is the location of occasional art exhibits.

Árpád Szenes-Vieira da Silva Foundation

MAP PAGE 92, POCKET MAP G5
Praça das Amoreiras 56–58
⊚ fasvs.pt, charge.

Árpád Szenes-Vieira da Silva Foundation is a small but highly appealing gallery dedicated to the works of two painters and the artists who have been influenced by them. Árpád Szenes (1897–1985) was a Hungarian-born artist and friend of Henri Matisse and Pierre Bonnard, among others. While in Paris in 1928 he met the Portuguese artist Maria Helena Vieira da Silva (1908–92), whose work was influenced by the surrealism of Joan Miró and Max Ernst, with both of whom she was good friends. Szenes and Vieira da Silva married in 1930, and in

Mãe d'Água cistern, Praça das Amoreiras

⚠ ❶ & Estádio da Luz

Jardim
Zoológico

ESTRADA DE BENFICA

PR. MAL. HUMBERTO DELGADO

RUA DAS FURNAS

Ⓜ *JARDIM
ZOOLÓGICO*

RUA RAÚL CARAPINHA

TV. DO ESPÍRITO SANTO

AVENIDA DOS COMBATENTES

Ⓜ Bus
Station

ESTRADA DAS LARANJEIRAS

RUA FILIPE DA MATA

R. F. DE
R. R. VELOSO
RUA PORTUGAL DURÃO
RUA DA BENEFICÊNCIA
R. C. MERCIER
R. DR. ALÍA
R. F. DA MATA
R. DO DE CASTRI

Sete Rios
Station

R. DR. ANTÓNIO MARTINS

RUA PROF. LIMA BASTO

AVENIDA COLUMBANO

RUA BASÍLIO TELES

BORDALO PINHEIRO

AV.

R. DE CAMPOLIDE

AVENIDA JOSÉ MALHOA

Ⓜ PRAÇA DE
ESPANHA Ⓟ

PRAÇA
DE
ESPANHA

Jardim Amnistia
Internacional

RUA DE CAMPOLIDE

RUA RAMALHO ORTIGÃO

AV. RESSANO

RUA F. DE

Cycle path to Monsant

Campolide
Station

AVENIDA CALOUSTE GULBENKIAN

AVENIDA DE CAMPOLIDE

AVENIDA MIGUEL TORGA

RUA MARQUÊS DE FRONTEIRA

AVENIDA DA PONTE

AVENIDA CALOUSTE GULBENKIAN

RUA VITOR BASTOS

CAMPOLIDE

RUA GEN. TABORDA

R. DOM F. M. DE MELO
RUA ODETE À. VIEIRA
R. PADRE
RUA RODRIGO
R. SAMPAIO EPINA
RUA ARTILHARIA
UM

CALÇADA DA QUINTINHA

Aqueduto das
Águas Livres

R. VIERA LUSITANO

CALÇADA DAS ANTAS

RUA CONDE DAS ANTAS

RUA DE MASCARENHAS

entrance to
Aqueduto

CALÇADA DA QUINTINHA

RUA DOM

R. ALTO DO CARVALHO

CARLOS DO CARVALHO

RUA PROF.

SOUSA DA CÂMARA

AV. CON. FERNANDO SANTOS

PR. Á. VIEIRA
5

24

R. DO GARCIA

Avenida Engenheiro D. Pacheco

RUA TEMO

Amoreiras
Shopping
Center ❹

RUA CARLOS ALBERTO DA MOTA PINTO

RUA SILVA CARVALHO

GALVÃO

RUA DAS AMOREIRAS

RUA JOSÉ GOMES FERREIRA

R. DO CAMPO DE OURIQUE

PR. DAS
AMOREIRAS

AMOREIRAS

RUA DOM JOÃO V

R. DO CAMPO DE OURIQUE

RUA DO SOL AO RATO

R. PEREIRA E SOUSA

RUA FERREIRA BORGES

RUA DA ARRÁBIDA

CARVALHO

CAMPO
DE
OURIQUE

RUA DE INFANTARIA

TRAVESSA DE
CONCEIÇÃO QUARTÉIS

RUA SILVA CARVALHO

RUA DO CABO

RUA SARAIVA DE

RUA P. A. CABRAL

AV. P. A. CABRAL

● SHOPS

Amoreiras	4
Centro Colombo	1
El Corte Inglés	2
Mercado 31 de Janeiro	3

● RESTAURANTS

Animal	12
A Gina	10
Bengal Tandoori	11
Eleven	4
Forno d'Oro	5
Marisqueira Santa Marta	6
O Cantinho de São José	9
PSI	7
Ribadouro	8

● CAFÉS

A Linha d'Água	3
Galeto	1
Versailles	2

■ BAR

Red Frog Speakeasy	1

■ MUSIC VENUE

Hot Clube de Portugal	2

■ ACCOMMODATION

Double Tree Fontana Park	1
Eurostar das Letras	10
Heritage Avenida Liberdade	13
Hotel das Amoreiras	7
Hotel Avenida Park	4
Hotel Britania	9
Hotel Dom Carlos Parque	6
Hotel Hotel	14
Lisboa Plaza	12
NH Collection Lisboa Liberdade	11
PortoBay Liberdade	8
Pousada de Juventude de Lisboa	3
Sana Rex	5
Sheraton Lisboa	2

Avenida, Parque Eduardo VII
and the Gulbenkian

Estádio José Alvalade

| 0 | metres | 250 |
| 0 | yards | 250 |

Entre Campos Station

ENTRE CAMPOS

RUA SOUSA LOPES
RUA DR. E. NEVES
CHABY PINHEIRO
RUA DE ENTRECAMPOS
SERPA
AV. O. MONTEIRO TORRES

HOLANDA
SALGADO REIS
RUA TOMÁS DA COSTA
RIBEIRA
RUA DO REGO

AVENIDA DA REPÚBLICA
AVENIDA ANTÓNIO

Praça de Touros

AVENIDA JOÃO XXI

AV. MARCONI

AV. JULIO DINIS

LAURA ALVES

RUA BRITO ARANHA

M CAMPO PEQUENO

Culturgest

RUA FERNANDO PEDROSO

RUA DO ARCO DO CEGO

RUA CAETANO ALBERTO

AVENIDA BARBOSA DU BOCAGE

SANTOS DUMONT

RUA E. ESPANCA

RUA DONA ILDE DE SOUSINHA

AVENIDA MARQUÊS DE SÁ DA BANDEIRA

AVENIDA DE BERNA

M CAMPO PEQUENO

AVENIDA 5 DE OUTUBRO

AVENIDA ELIAS GARCIA

AVENIDA DOS DEFENSORES DE CHAVES

RUA XAVIER CORDEIRO

AVENIDA MARQUÊS DE TOMAR

AVENIDA VISCONDE DE VALMOR

AVENIDA ANTÓNIO JOSÉ DE ALMEIDA

RUA INTEIRA PARTICULAR

Museu Calouste Gulbenkian

AVENIDA CONDE DE VALBOM

AVENIDA FILIPA DE VILHENA

RUA ALVES

REDOL

Centro de Arte Moderna (CAM)

AVENIDA JOÃO CRISÓSTOMO 1

AVENIDA DUQUE DE ÁVILA   SALDANHA

AVENIDA ROVISCO PAIS

GARCIA

SÃO SEBASTIÃO

ALMEIDA

RUA DE BETTENCOURT

RUA DR. NICOLAU

M SALDANHA

2

PRAÇA DUQUE DE SALDANHA

AV. PRAIA DA VITÓRIA

RUA DE DONA ESTEFÂNIA

P

RUA CANDIDO

RUA ANTÓNIO ENES

R. DAS PICOAS

RUA PINHEIRO CHAGAS

AVENIDA ANTÓNIO AUGUSTO DE AGUIAR

AVENIDA LUIS BIVAR

RUA FILIPE FOLQUE

RUA TOMÁS RIBEIRO

Casa Museu Dr. A. Gonçalves

AVENIDA CASAL RIBEIRO

R. ENG. F. LOPES

R. ENG. VIEIRA DA SILVA

RUA PONTE DELGADA

R. CIDADE DA HORTA

RUA ACTOR TABORDA

LARGO DE DONA ESTEFÂNIA

P

RUA DE SÃO SEBASTIÃO DA PEDREIRA

FILIPE LATINO COELHO

2

Mercado 31 de Janeiro

RUA ALMIRANTE BARROSO

ESTEFÂNIA

1

J

PICOAS

PRAÇA JOSÉ FONTANA

SIDÓNIO PAIS

RUA VIRIATO

PEREIRA E ANDRADE

RUA SOUSA MARTINS

CORVO

RUA DA ESCOLA DE MEDICINA VETERINÁRIA

4

PARQUE

RUA PEDREIRA

RUA MARTENS FERRÃO

Estufas

Pavilhão Carlos Lopes

AV. FONTES

R. DE SANTA MARTA

RUA LUCIANO CORDEIRO

RUA DE DONA ESTEFÂNIA

ALAMEDA DO CARDEAL CEREJEIRA

RUA DUQUE DE LOULÉ

RUA DA SOCIEDADE FARMACÊUTICA

RUA GONÇALVES CRESPO

RUA J. BONIFÁCIO

RUA GOMES FREIRE

Parque Eduardo VII

RUA CASTILHO

RUA DE SANTA MARTA

R. CONDE DE REDONDO

RUA LUCIANO CORDEIRO

RUA BARATA SALGUEIRO

FONSECA

PRAÇA MARQUÊS DE POMBAL

P

M MARQUÊS DE POMBAL

RUA ENGRÁCIA QUEIRÓZ

RUA C. BRANCO

RUA RODRIGUES SAMPAIO

TV. DE SANTA MARIA

7

R. JOAQUIM ANTÓNIO DE AGUIAR

RUA BRAAMCAMP

RUA ALEXANDRE HERCULANO

RUA MOUZINHO DA SILVEIRA

6

TV. DE SANTA MARIA

5

Casa Museu Medeiros e Almeida

RUA DO PASSADIÇO

TV. LÓBREGA DOS PENTES

3

RUA R. DA FONSECA

RUA DA GLÓRIA

8

9

CAMPO DOS MÁRTIRES DA PÁTRIA

7

Árpád Szenes-Vieira da Silva Foundation

RUA DA PENHA

RUA RODRIGUES SILVA

RUA DR. ROSA ARAÚJO

AVENIDA DA LIBERDADE

RUA DE SÃO CARLOS

RUA SÃO LÁZARO

RUA DO INSTITUTO BACTERIOLÓGICO

Museu da Água & Mãe d'Água

RUA ROVISCO FONSECA

RUA CASTILHO

10

RUA DO TELHAL

RUA DE ANDRADE

LARGO DO RATO

M RATO

R. DO SALITRE

11

Jardim do Torel

RUA DE SÃO MAMEDE

1

RATO

RUA DA ESCOLA POLITÉCNICA

Jardim Botânico

Museu de História Natural & Museu da Ciência

PARQUE MAYER

12

M AVENIDA

PRAÇA DA ALEGRIA

13

TV. DA ANUNCIADA

Elevador do Lavra

RUA DE SÃO BENTO

RUA DO ARCO

10

11

TV. DA CONCEIÇÃO DA GLÓRIA

12

N

1936 both exhibited in Lisbon, where they briefly lived, before eventually settling in France. The foundation shows the development of the artists' style, with Vieira da Silva's more abstract, subdued paintings contrasting with flamboyant Szenes, some of whose works show the influence of Miró.

Aqueduto das Águas Livres

MAP PAGE 92, POCKET MAP F4
Entrance on Calçada da Quintinha 6, bus
#712/#758 from Amoreiras
🕐 218 100 215, charge.

The towering aqueduct was opened in 1748, bringing a reliable source of safe fresh water to the city for the first time. Stretching for 58km (most of it underground), the aqueduct stood firm during the 1755 earthquake, though it later gained a more notorious reputation thanks to one Diogo Alves, a nineteenth-century serial killer who threw

his victims off the top – a 70m drop. It is possible to walk across a 1km section of the aqueduct over a stone arch measuring 65m by 28m, one of the largest in the world, though you'll need a head for heights. The walkable section is accessed off a quiet residential street through a small park in Campolide, around 1km north of Praça das Amoreiras.

Fundação Calouste Gulbenkian

MAP PAGE 92, POCKET MAP H2
Avda de Berna 45a Ⓦ gulbenkian.pt.

Set in extensive grounds, the foundation was set up by the Armenian oil magnate Calouste Gulbenkian (see page 95) whose legendary art-market coups included the acquisition of works from the Hermitage in St Petersburg. Today the **Fundação Calouste Gulbenkian** has a multi-million-dollar budget sufficient to finance work in all spheres of

Lalique jewellry, Museu Calouste Gulbenkian

Calouste Gulbenkian

Calouste Sarkis Gulbenkian (1869–1955) was the Roman Abramovich of his era, making his millions from oil, but investing in the world's best art rather than footballers. Born of wealthy Armenian parents in Istanbul in 1869, he followed his father into the oil industry and eventually moved to England. After the Russian Revolution of 1917 he bought works from the Leningrad Hermitage. During World War II, his Turkish background made him unwelcome in Britain, and Gulbenkian auctioned himself to whoever would have him. Portugal bid an aristocratic palace (a marquês was asked to move out) and tax exemption, to acquire one of the most important cultural patrons of the century. From 1942 to his death in 1955, he accumulated one of the best private art curations in the world. His dying wish was that all of his collection should be displayed in one place, and this was granted in 1969 with the opening of the Museu Calouste Gulbenkian.

Portuguese cultural life. In this low-rise 1960s complex alone, it runs an orchestra, three concert halls and an open-air amphitheatre.

Museu Calouste Gulbenkian: Founders Collection

MAP PAGE 92, POCKET MAP H2
Avda de Berna 45a ⓦ gulbenkian.pt, charge (combined ticket available with Modern Art Collection), free Sun 2–6pm.

The **Museu Calouste Gulbenkian** combines the Founders Collection and the Modern Collection (Centro de Arte Moderna). The **Founders Collection** covers virtually every phase of Eastern and Western art. The small Egyptian room displays works from the Old Kingdom (c.2700 BC) up to the Roman period. Fine Roman statues, silver and glass, and gold jewellery from ancient Greece follow. The Islamic arts are magnificently represented by a variety of ornamental texts, opulently woven carpets, glassware and Turkish tiles. There is also porcelain from China, and beautiful Japanese prints and lacquerwork. European art includes work from all the major schools. The seventeenth-century collection yields Peter Paul Rubens' graphic

The Love of the Centaurs (1635) and Rembrandt's *Figure of an Old Man.* Featured eighteenth-century pieces include those by Jean-Honoré Fragonard and Thomas Gainsborough – in particular the stunning *Portrait of Mrs Lowndes-Stone.* The big names of nineteenth-to twentieth-century France – Manet, Monet, Degas, Millet and Renoir – are all represented, along with John Sargent and Turner's vivid *Wreck of a Transport Ship* (1810). Elsewhere, you'll find Sèvres porcelain and furniture from the reigns of Louis XV and Louis XVI. The last room features an amazing collection of Art Nouveau jewellery by René Lalique. Don't miss the fantastical *Peitoral-libélula* (Dragonfly breastpiece) brooch, decorated with enamelwork, gold and diamonds. Closed for renovation until 2026.

Museu Calouste Gulbenkian: Centro de Arte Moderna (CAM)

MAP PAGE 92, POCKET MAP H2
Main entrance on Rua Dr Nicolau de Bettencourt ⓦ https://gulbenkian.pt/cam, charge (combined ticket available with Founders Collection), free Sun 2–6pm.

The impressive **Centro de Arte Moderna** (CAM, Modern

Parque Eduardo VII

Art Collection), part of the Gulbenkian foundation (see page 95), features pop art, installations and sculptures – some witty, some baffling, but all thought-provoking.

Most of the big-hitting names on the twentieth-century Portuguese scene are included, including portraits and sketches by José de Almada Negreiros (1873–1970), the founder of Modernismo; the bright Futurist colours of Amadeo de Souza-Cardoso; and a scattering of works by Paula Rego, one of Portugal's leading contemporary artists, whose *Mãe* (1997) is outstanding. Pieces from major international artists such as David Hockney and Antony Gormley also feature.

The museum reopened in 2024 after several years of closure for substantial renovation. The new building was designed by Japanese architect Kengo Kuma, who worked alongside landscape architect Vladimir Djurovic to connect the design more closely to the surrounding gardens. It was inspired by the Japanese concept called *engawa*, which merges the interior with the exterior – most evident in the dramatic curved, white-tiled canopy of the roof.

Parque Eduardo VII

MAP PAGE 92, POCKET MAP H4

The steep, formally laid out **Parque Eduardo VII** was named in honour of Britain's King Edward VII when he visited the city in 1903. Its main building is the ornately tiled Pavilhão Carlos Lopes, created for the International Exhibition of Rio de Janeiro in 1922, then dismantled and rebuilt here in 1932; today, its hosts events and exhibitions such as the annual Moda Lisboa fashion week.

North of here, the main viewing platform offers commanding vistas of the city as well as a Ferris wheel during the summer months. Another highlight if you have children is the superb Parque Infantil (free), a play area built round a mock galleon.

Two huge, rambling **estufas** (Ⓦestufafria.cm-lisboa.pt, charge) can be found close by. Set in substantial former basalt quarries, both are filled with tropical plants, pools and endless varieties of palm and cactus.

Of the two, the Estufa Quente (Hothouse) has the more exotic plants; the Estufa Fria (Coldhouse) hosts concerts and exhibitions. Finally, the hilly northern reaches of the park contain an olive grove and a shallow lake which kids splash about in during the heat of the day.

Casa Museu Dr Anastácio Gonçalves

MAP PAGE 92, POCKET MAP J3
Avda 5 de Outobro 6–8, entrance on Rua Pinheiro Chagas
Ⓦ museusmonumentos.pt, charge.

This appealing neo-Romantic building with Art Nouveau touches – including a beautiful stained-glass window – was originally built for painter José Malhoa in 1904, but now holds the exquisite **private collection** of ophthalmologist Dr Anastácio Gonçalves, who bought the house in the 1930s.

Highlights include paintings by Portuguese landscape artist João Vaz and by Malhoa himself, who specialized in historical paintings – his *Dream of Infante Henriques* is a typical example of his work. You'll also find a selection of Chinese porcelain from the sixteenth-century Ming dynasty, along with furniture from England, France, Holland and Spain dating from the seventeenth century.

Praça de Touros

MAP PAGE 92, POCKET MAP J1
Campo Pequeno
Ⓦ www.sagrescampopequeno.pt.

Built in 1892 and substantially renovated in 2000 – with a retractable roof – the **Praça de Touros** at Campo Pequeno was designed as an impressive Moorish-style bullring seating nine thousand spectators. Although the Portuguese claim their bullfighting is more humane than the Spanish equivalent as the bull isn't killed in the ring, the animal is usually injured and slaughtered later in any case, and performances have become more controversial in recent years. A handful of bullfights are still held here each year, but attendance is not recommended.

Surrounded by a ring of lively cafés, bars and restaurants, the venue also hosts concerts, live acts, musicals and a range of other cultural events. Beneath the arena is a surprisingly large underground shopping and cinema complex and a parking lot.

Ethnic Lisbon

In the fifteenth century, hundreds of enslaved Africans came to Lisbon on ships during Portugal's ruthless maritime explorations. Today, over 120,000 people of African and Asian descent live in the Greater Lisbon area, most hailing originally from Portugal's former colonies – Cape Verde, Angola, Mozambique, Brazil, Goa and Macao. The 1974 revolution and subsequent independence of the former colonies saw another wave of immigrants settle in the capital. Nowadays, African and Brazilian culture permeates Lisbon life, influencing its music, food, television and street slang. Most Lisboetas are rightly proud of their cosmopolitan city, although, inevitably, racism persists and few from ethnic minorities have managed to break through the glass ceiling to the top jobs.

Jardim Zoológico

Jardim Zoológico
MAP PAGE 92, POCKET MAP E1
Praça Marechal Humberto Delgado
Ⓦ www.zoo.pt, charge.
Lisbon's **Jardim Zoológico**
opened in 1884 and makes for an
enjoyable excursion. There's a café-
lined park, which you can visit for
free and see monkeys, crocodiles
and parrots. Once inside the zoo
proper, a small cable car (free)
transports you over many of the
animals, and there's a well-stocked
reptile house and feeding sessions
for sea lions and pelicans.

Estádio da Luz
MAP PAGE 92, POCKET MAP H1
Ⓦ slbenfica.pt.
One of the most famous stadia in
the world, the **Estádio da Luz** was
built for and hosted the final of
Euro 2004, when Portugal lost in a
shock defeat to Greece. This is the
home to Benfica (officially called
Sport Lisboa e Benfica), the giant
of Portuguese football who win
(together with rivals Sporting and
Porto) most domestic trophies. It's
usually easy to buy match tickets
from the stadium ticket office (from
€25–50): expect to see the club

mascot eagle flying across the pitch
before the game starts. There is also
an impressive **museum** (charge)
with interactive exhibits tracing the
club's prestigious history, including
its two European Cup wins (1961
and 1962) and Europa League finals
in 2013 and 2014.

Estádio José Alvalade
MAP PAGE 92, POCKET MAP F1
Rua Professor Fernando da Fonseca,
Apartado 4120 Ⓦ sporting.pt.
The impressive **José Alvalade
Stadium** is home to Sporting
Clube de Portugal, better known
as Sporting Lisbon. Seating over
50,000 spectators, the stadium was
built for Euro 2004 adjacent to the
city's original football stadium. The
team boast an impressive array of
trophies: over twenty league wins
(including 2021, 2024 and 2025),
nearly twenty Portuguese Cup wins
and a European Cup Winners'
Cup in 1964. Tickets for games
(€20–45) are available at the on-
site ticket office. You can also take
a tour of the stadium and visit the
museum (charge), which features
the shirt of one of the club's best-
known sons, Cristiano Ronaldo.

Shops

Amoreiras

MAP PAGE 92, POCKET MAP F4
Avda Engenheiro Duarte Pacheco 2037, bus
#758 from Cais de Sodré ⓦ amoreiras.com.
Amoreiras, Lisbon's striking
postmodern commercial centre,
built in 1985, is a wild fantasy
of pink and blue towers – the
brainchild of adventurous
Portuguese architect Tomás Taveira.
It shelters a cinema, cafés and
restaurants, over two hundred
shops, a hotel and a roof terrace
with panoramic views over the city
(ⓦ amoreiras360view.com, charge).
Most of its stores are open daily;
Sunday sees the heaviest footfall,
with entire families descending for
an afternoon out.

Centro Colombo

MAP PAGE 92, POCKET MAP F1
Avda Lusíada ⓜ Colégio Militar/Luz
ⓦ colombo.pt.
Iberia's largest shopping centre is
almost a town in its own right, with
over 340 shops, sixty restaurants,
nine cinema screens, an IMAX
and a bowling alley. Major stores
include Benfica's official store,
Fnac, H&M and Massimo Dutti.

El Corte Inglés

MAP PAGE 92, POCKET MAP H3
Avda António Augusto de Aguiar 31
ⓦ elcorteingles.pt.
A giant Spanish department store
spread over nine floors, two of
which are underground. The
basement specializes in gourmet
food, with various delis, bakers
and a supermarket, while the
upper floors offer a range of stylish
goods, including clothes, sports
gear, books and toys. The top floor
packs in cafés and restaurants.
There's also a fourteen-screen
cinema in the basement (info on
ⓦ ucicinemas.pt).

Mercado 31 de Janeiro

MAP PAGE 92, POCKET MAP J3

Rua Enginheiro Viera da Silva ☎ 218 160
970. Tues–Sat 7am–2pm.
This bustling local market is
divided into sections; you'll find
a colourful array of fresh fruit,
vegetables, spices, fish, flowers and
a few crafts.

Restaurants

Animal

MAP PAGE 92, POCKET MAP J6
Travessa Glória 22 ⓦ hotelhotel.pt.
Classy Asian-inspired food is served
up in the restaurant (open to all) of
the boutiquey *Hotel Hotel*, which
uses locally sourced ingredients
where possible. Eat inside or on a
verdant terrace where a pool is lined
by exotic plants. Sumptuous dishes
include lime risotto with mussels,
steak with shitake mushrooms and
black pork tenderloin. Despite the
name, there are lots of vegetarian
options such as aubergine with
Japanese rice. €€€

A Gina

MAP PAGE 92, POCKET MAP J5
Parque Mayer ☎ 213 420 296.
Tucked in to the back of this
historic theatre park, this
traditional restaurant has been
serving theatregoers and actors
since the 1950s, and is well worth
a visit for its generous portions of
tasty food. There's a large outdoor
terrace, a cosy interior and a range
of meat, fish and seafood dishes.
Expect the likes of *pataniscas de
bacalhau* (cod cakes) and salmon
steaks, and don't miss the house
dessert. €€

Bengal Tandoori

MAP PAGE 92, POCKET MAP J5
Rua da Alegria 23 ⓦ bengaltandoori.pt.
This is rated as one of the best
Indian restaurants in town, set up
a steep side street. Expect all the
usual dishes – madras, biryanis
and, of course, excellent tandoori
– in an intimate space with good
service. €€

Eleven

MAP PAGE 92, POCKET MAP G3
Rua Marquês da Fronteira
Ⓦ restauranteleven.com.

At the top of Parque Eduardo VII, this Michelin-starred restaurant, under the watchful gaze of German head chef Joachim Koerper, hits the heights both literally and metaphorically. The interior is both intimate and bright, with wonderful city views. The food is expensive but not outrageous, with various tasting menus. Dishes include rack of lamb with artichokes, and blue lobster, plus there's a fine wine list. €€€€

Forno d'Oro

MAP PAGE 92, POCKET MAP H4
Rua Artilharia I 16b Ⓦ fornodoro.pt.

Some say this is one of the best pizzerias in Lisbon, and the smart modern restaurant certainly serves a delectable variety. The "Golden Oven" wood-fires Italian pizzas using Portuguese ingredients, such as *alheira* chicken sausage, *presunto* ham, black pork and regional cheeses. There are also tasty bruschetta and salads. €€

Eleven

Marisqueira Santa Marta

MAP PAGE 92, POCKET MAP J4
Trav do Enviato de Inglaterra 1 (off Rua de Santa Marta) Ⓣ 213 525 638.

Attractive and spacious *marisqueira* with bubbling tanks of crabs in one corner. Service is very attentive, and meals end with a complimentary port. €€

O Cantinho de São José

MAP PAGE 92, POCKET MAP J5
Rua São José 94 Ⓣ 213 427 866.

Friendly *tasca* serving good-value food – the menu is usually scrawled on a paper tablecloth outside. Dishes include grilled meat, salmon or other fish, with a fine house wine. €

PSI

MAP PAGE 92, POCKET MAP J4
Alameda St António Capuchos
Ⓦ restaurante-psi.com.

PSI has been serving up tasty vegetarian food to Lisboetas for more than fifteen years. It's surrounded by attractive gardens which were inaugurated by the Dalai Lama, with ponds, greenery and a children's playground. Dishes have an international twist, ranging from

laksa curries, pad Thai and ceviche to shaksuka and pasta – but all are meat-free and full of flavour. €

Ribadouro

MAP PAGE 92, POCKET MAP J5
Avda da Liberdade 155
ⓦ cervejariaribadouro.pt.
The Avenida's best *cervejaria*, specializing excellent seafood, including the superb signature prawns with garlic plus pricier lobster, crab, oysters and clams – it also does a decent *bacalhão* (salted cod) and an excellent *gambas à bras* (prawns with finely chipped potatoes). If you don't fancy a full meal, take a seat at the bar and order a beer with a plate of prawns. It's best to book for the restaurant, especially at weekends. €€€

Versailles

Cafés

A Linha d'Água

MAP PAGE 92, POCKET MAP G3
Jardim Amália Rodrigues ☏ 213 814 327.
Facing a small lake, this glass-fronted café at the northern end of the park is a tranquil spot to sip a coffee or beer. It also serves excellent-value buffet lunches, such as salted cod cakes with salad. €

Galeto

MAP PAGE 92, POCKET MAP J2
Avda da República 14 ☏ 213 544 444.
Late-opening café with striking 1960s decor and an array of snacks, pastries, beers and coffees. Drop in for a full meal at sensible prices by the bar. €€

Versailles

MAP PAGE 92, POCKET MAP J2
Avda da República 15a ☏ 213 546 340.
This traditional café, which dates back to 1922 and is full of bustling waiters, is busiest at around 4pm, when Lisbon's elderly dames gather for a chat beneath the chandeliers. Drop in for tasty cakes and pastries, coffee or a sandwich in classic surroundings. €

Bar

Red Frog Speakeasy

MAP PAGE 92, POCKET MAP J5
Praça da Alegria 66b ☏ 215 831 120.
Taking inspiration from the Prohibition era in the US, this upmarket cocktail bar has a secretive air, enhanced by the fact you have to ring a bell to enter (look for the red frog on the wall). Many of the best cocktails are made from local Portuguese brandies, *ginginha* and herbal liqueurs: try the Bamboo, with Madeira wine and tomato.

Music venue

Hot Clube de Portugal

MAP PAGE 92, POCKET MAP J5
Praça da Alegria 48 ⓦ hcp.pt.
Dating from 1948 – making it one of Europe's oldest jazz clubs – this tiny basement club hosts top names in the jazz world, along with a range of local performers. The venue was largely rebuilt after a fire in 2009 and was closed in 2023 for structural reasons, but should reopen shortly.

Parque das Nações

The Parque das Nações (pronounced "na-soysh"), or "Park of Nations", is the high-tech former site of Expo '98. Its flat, pedestrianized walkways, lined with fountains and futuristic buildings, are in complete contrast to the narrow, precipitous streets of old Lisbon, and it is packed with locals on summer weekends. The main highlight is the giant Oceanário de Lisboa, but it also features a casino, a cable car, riverside walkways, a giant park and two of Lisbon's largest concert venues. It is also impossible to miss the astonishing 17km-long Vasco da Gama bridge leaping over the Tejo. Constructed in time for the Expo in 1998, it is still the longest bridge in Western Europe.

Olivais dock and the Meo Arena

MAP PAGE 104, POCKET MAP B17–18

The central focus of the Parque das Nações is the Olivais dock, overlooked by pixie-hatted twin towers, and where boats pull in on Tejo cruises. The dock's **Marina** (☎218 949 066) offers canoeing and sailing lessons and riverboat tours. The main building facing the dock is the Pavilhão de Portugal (Portugal Pavilion), a multipurpose arena designed by Álvaro Siza Vieira, architect of the reconstructed Chiado district, featuring an enormous, sagging concrete canopy on its south side. It now hosts temporary exhibitions. Opposite – past Antony Gormley's

weird *Rhizome* sculpture, a tree of cast-iron legs – is the spaceship-like **Meo Arena** (Ⓦarena.meo.pt), Portugal's largest indoor arena and the venue for major visiting bands and musicians (including Justin Bieber, Coldplay and Madonna) and sporting events. It also hosted the 2005 MTV Europe Music Awards and the Eurovision Song Contest 2018.

Pavilhão do Conhecimento (Ciência Viva)

MAP PAGE 104, POCKET MAP B18

Alameda dos Oceanos

Ⓦpavconhecimento.pt, charge.

Run by Portugal's Ministry of Science and Technology, the **Knowledge Pavilion** (Live

Visiting the park

The best way to reach the park is to take the metro to Oriente or bus #728 from Praça do Comércio. Oriente metro station exits in the bowels of the Estação do Oriente, a cavernous glass and concrete station designed by Spanish architect Santiago Calatrava.

The park's website (Ⓦportaldasnacoes.pt) has details of the day's events, and information about the urban art dotted round the area, from murals and graffiti art to statues and sculptures, plus there is an Ask Me tourist information post on Alameda dos Oceanos (☎910 559 255).

Waterfall in the Jardins da Água, Parque das Nações

Science) hosts excellent changing exhibitions on subjects like 3D animation and the latest computer technology, and is usually bustling with school parties. The permanent interactive exhibits – allowing you to create a vortex in water or a film of detergent the size of a baby's blanket – are particularly good, and there are also children's workshops and play areas.

Jardins da Água

MAP PAGE 104, POCKET MAP B19
The **Jardins da Água** (Water Gardens), crisscrossed by waterways and ponds, are based on the stages of a river's drainage pattern, from stream to estuary. They are not huge, but linked by stepping stones, and there are enough gushing fountains, water gadgets and pumps to keep kids occupied for hours.

Oceanário

MAP PAGE 104, POCKET MAP B18
Esplanada Dom Carlos I Ⓦ oceanario.pt, charge.
Designed by Peter Chermayeff and looking like something off the set of a James Bond film, Lisbon's

Oceanário (Oceanarium) is one of Europe's largest and contains some eight thousand fish and marine animals. Its main feature is the enormous central tank which you can look into from different levels for close-up views of circling sharks down to the rays burying themselves in the sand.

Almost more impressive though, are the recreations of various ocean ecosystems, such as the Antarctic tank, containing frolicking penguins, and the Pacific tank, where otters bob around in the rockpools. On a darkened lower level, smaller tanks contain shoals of brightly coloured tropical fish and other warm-water creatures.

Find a window free of noisy school parties and the whole experience becomes the closest you'll get to deep-sea diving without getting wet.

Telecabine Lisboa and the Jardins Garcia da Orta

MAP PAGE 104, POCKET MAP B16–18
Ⓦ telecabinelisboa.pt, charge.
The ski-lift-style **telecabine** (cable car) rises up to 20m as it shuttles passengers over Olivais docks to

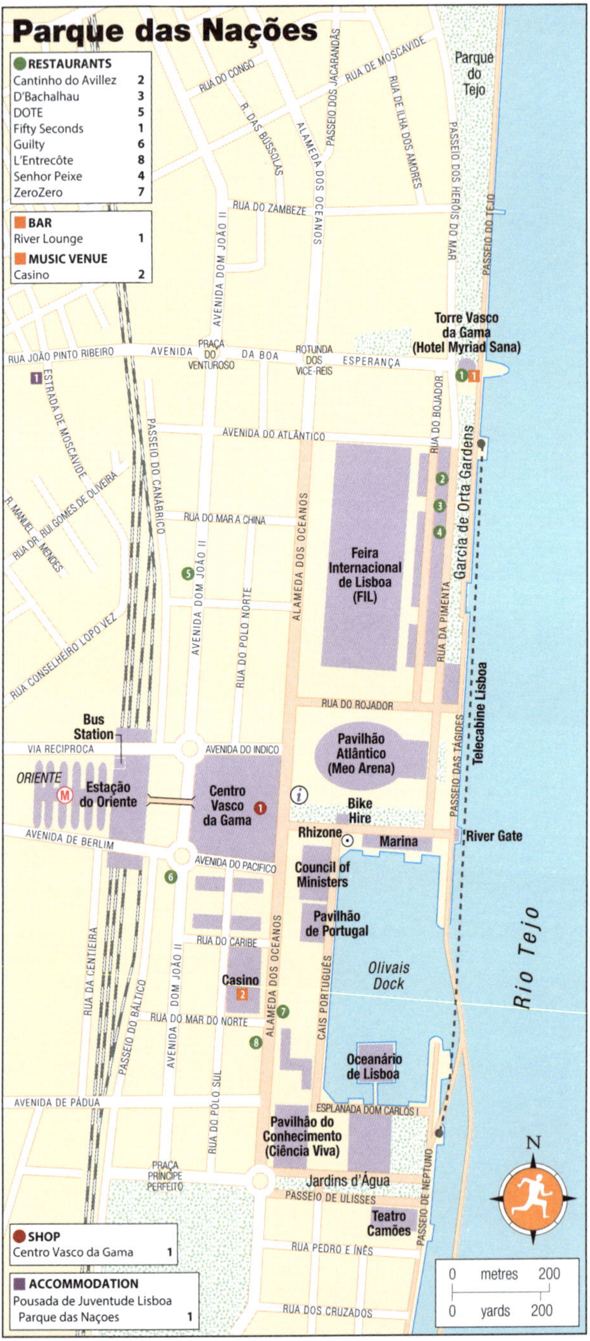

Parque das Nações

RESTAURANTS

Cantinho do Avillez	2
D'Bachalhau	3
DOTE	5
Fifty Seconds	1
Guilty	6
L'Entrecôte	8
Senhor Peixe	4
ZeroZero	7

BAR

River Lounge	1

MUSIC VENUE

Casino	2

SHOP

Centro Vasco da Gama	1

ACCOMMODATION

Pousada de Juventude Lisboa Parque das Nações	1

RUA DO CONGO
RUA DOS JACARANDÁS
RUA DE MOSCAVIDE
Parque do Tejo
R. DAS BÚSSOLAS
ALAMEDA DOS OCEANOS
RUA DE ILHA DOS AMORES
PASSEIO DOS HERÓIS DO MAR
PASSEIO DO TEJO

RUA DO ZAMBEZE
AVENIDA DOM JOÃO II

Torre Vasco da Gama
(Hotel Myriad Sana)

RUA JOÃO PINTO RIBEIRO
AVENIDA DA BOA
PRAÇA DO VENTUROSO
ROTUNDA DOS VICE-REIS
ESPERANÇA
ESTRADA DE MOSCAVIDE
RUA DO BOJADOR
Garcia de Orta Gardens

AVENIDA DO ATLÂNTICO

PASSEIO DO CANÁBRICO
RUA DO MAR A CHINA
AVENIDA DOM JOÃO II
ALAMEDA DOS OCEANOS
Feira Internacional de Lisboa (FIL)
RUA DA PIMENTA

R. MANUEL DR. RUI GOMES DE OLIVEIRA
RUA DR. MENDES
RUA CONSELHEIRO LOPO VEZ
RUA DO POLO NORTE

RUA DO ROJADOR

Bus Station
VIA RECÍPROCA
AVENIDA DO ÍNDICO
Pavilhão Atlântico (Meo Arena)
PASSEIO DAS TÁGIDES
Telecabine Lisboa

ORIENTE
Estação do Oriente
Centro Vasco da Gama
Bike Hire
River Gate

AVENIDA DE BERLIM
AVENIDA DO PACÍFICO
Rhizone
Marina
Council of Ministers

Pavilhão de Portugal
RUA DO CARIBE
Olivais Dock

RUA DA CENTIEIRA
AVENIDA DOM JOÃO II
PASSEIO DO BÁLTICO
Casino
RUA DO MAR DO NORTE
CAIS PORTUGUÊS
ALAMEDA DOS OCEANOS

Oceanário de Lisboa

AVENIDA DE PÁDUA
RUA DO POLO SUL

Rio Tejo

PRAÇA PRÍNCIPE PERFEITO
Pavilhão do Conhecimento (Ciência Viva)
ESPLANADA DOM CARLOS I
PASSEIO DE NEPTUNO

Jardins d'Água
PASSEIO DE ULISSES
Teatro Camões

RUA PEDRO E INÊS
RUA DOS CRUZADOS

N

0	metres	200
0	yards	200

the northern side of the Parque, offering commanding views over the site on the way. It drops down to the **Garcia da Orta gardens**, containing exotic trees from Portugal's former colonies. Behind the gardens, Rua Pimenta is lined with a motley collection of international restaurants, from Irish to Israeli.

Torre Vasco da Gama

MAP PAGE 104, POCKET MAP B16
Cais das Naus ⓦ vascodagamatower.com, charge.

Once an integral part of an oil refinery, the **Torre Vasco da Gama** is, at 145m high, Lisbon's tallest structure. The tower is now integrated into the five-star hotel *Myriad by Sana*, Lisbon's answer to Dubai's *Burj Al Arab*. A lift whisks you to the top for superb views across the water, and there is also a pricy bar.

Torre Vasco da Gama

Parque do Tejo

MAP PAGE 104, POCKET MAP B15
Unfurling along the waterfront for 2km right up to the Vasco da Gama bridge, **Parque do Tejo** is threaded through with bike trails and riverside walks. It's also a great spot for a picnic – supplies are available in the Vasco da Gama shopping centre.

Feira Internacional de Lisboa

MAP PAGE 104, POCKET MAP B16–17
Rua do Bojador ⓦ www.fil.pt.
Lisbon's trade fair hall, the **Feira Internacional de Lisboa** (FIL) hosts various events, including a handicrafts fair displaying ceramics and crafts from around the country (usually in July).

Vasco da Gama

The opening of Parque das Nações in 1998 celebrated the 500th anniversary of Vasco da Gama's arrival in India. One of Portugal's greatest explorers, Da Gama was born in Sines in 1460. By the 1490s he was working for João II, protecting trading stations along the African coast. This persuaded the next king, Manuel I, to commission him to find a sea route to India. He departed Lisbon in July 1497 with a fleet of four ships, reaching southern Africa in December. The following May they finally reached Calicut in southwest India, obtaining trading terms before departing in August 1498. The return voyage took a full year, by which time Da Gama had lost two of his ships and half his men. But he was richly rewarded by the king, his voyage inspiring Camões to write *Os Lusíadas*, Portugal's most famous epic poem. Da Gama returned to India twice more, the final time in 1524 when he contracted malaria and died in the town of Cochin.

Shop

Centro Vasco da Gama

MAP PAGE 104, POCKET MAP B17

Avda D. João II 40 Ⓦ centrovascodagama.pt.

Three floors of Portuguese and international stores are housed beneath a glass roof washed by permanently running water; international branches include Zara, Timberland and Mango, while local sports and bookshops also feature. There are plenty of fast-food outlets and good-value restaurants on the top floor, six cinema screens (Ⓦ cinema.nos.pt), children's areas and a Continente supermarket on the lower floor.

Restaurants

Cantinho do Avillez

MAP PAGE 104, POCKET MAP C13

Rua Bojador 55 Ⓦ cantinhodoavillez.pt.

The top place to eat in the Parque das Nações, this bright contemporary restaurant opens onto a great outdoor terrace and serves sublime food by José Avillez. The menu features his trademark

Cantinho do Avillez

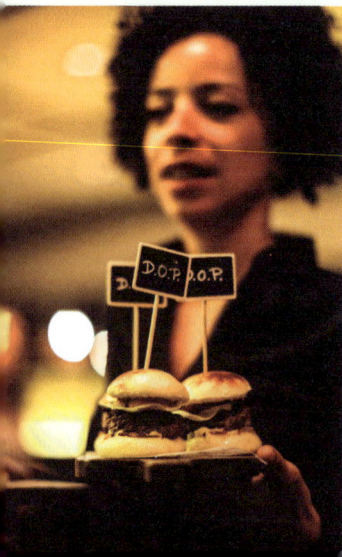

Portuguese dishes with a twist, such as cod with exploding olives and Alentejan pork with beans. €€€

D'Bacalhau

MAP PAGE 104, POCKET MAP B16

Rua do Pimenta 43–45
Ⓦ restaurantebacalhau.com.

If you want to sample one of the alleged 365 recipes for *bacalhau* – salted cod – this is a good place to come, as it serves quite a range of them: *bacalhau com natas* (with a creamy sauce) is always good. There are also other dishes, including a selection of fresh fish and meat dishes. €€

DOTE

MAP PAGE 104, POCKET MAP A17

Avenida Dom João II 43E Ⓦ dote.pt.

This modern space serves reasonably priced specialities from Portugal's second city, Porto, including its famed *francesinhas*, an OTT version of France's *croque monsieur* with additional toppings. Other dishes include steaks, *pregos* (meat in a bun), soups and salads. €€

Fifty Seconds

MAP PAGE 104, POCKET MAP B16

Cais das Naus Lote 2.21.01
Ⓦ fiftysecondsexperience.com.

This sleek hotel venue takes its name from the time it takes to ride to the top of the distinctive Torre Vasco da Gama (see page 105), whose views across the broad Tejo are as tasty as the menu of this Michelin-starred restaurant. Rui Silvestre was the youngest Portuguese chef to win the award when he was just 29, and uses his experience of cooking in France, Switzerland and Hungary to produce sublime dishes that utilize Portuguese produce, especially fish and seafood: think smoked eel with almonds, sea urchin, or octopus masala. €€€€

Guilty

MAP PAGE 104, POCKET MAP A18

Avenida Dom João II 27 77b
Ⓦ restaurantesguilty.com.

Casino

Classy and affordable comfort foods from leading chef Olivier da Costa, including giant pizzas, burgers, various pasta dishes and cocktails. There's also a special Sport TV area where you can dine and watch live events (mostly football). €€

L'Entrecôte

MAP PAGE 104, POCKET MAP B18
Alameda dos Oceanos 43a
Ⓦ brasserieentrecote.pt.
Local branch of the Lisbon restaurant famed for its fabulous steaks cooked with sublime sauces – choose from various menus. It also has an attractive outdoor terrace. €€€

Senhor Peixe

MAP PAGE 104, POCKET MAP B16
Rua da Pimenta 35–37 Ⓦ senhorpeixe.pt.
"Mr Fish" is widely thought to serve up some of the best fresh seafood in the Lisbon region – check the counter for the day's catch or choose a lobster from the bubbling tank. Most dishes are grilled in the open kitchen. There's also a little fish-themed bar and pleasant outdoor tables. €€

ZeroZero

MAP PAGE 104, POCKET MAP B18
Alameda dos Oceanos, Lote 2
Ⓦ pizzeriazerozero.pt.

This classy restaurant uses Italian ingredients for its tasty pizzas and serves a range of pastas, salads and quality antipasti. There's a bar serving prosecco and cocktails, plus an outside terrace with river views. €€

Bar

River Lounge

MAP PAGE 104, POCKET MAP B16
Myriad by Sana, Cais das Naus, Lote 2.23.01 Ⓦ myriad.pt.
Inside the deluxe *Myriad by Sana* hotel, the ultra-hip *River Lounge* juts into the Tejo so you feel as if you're right on the water. Cocktails and drinks are predictably expensive, but it's worth it for the view. Frequent live music after 7pm.

Music venue

Casino

MAP PAGE 104, POCKET MAP A18
Alameda dos Oceanos 45 Ⓦ casino-lisboa.pt.
This state-of-the-art space – with its glass-cylinder entrance hall – hosts top shows from Broadway and London as well as major concerts in the performance hall, which has a retractable roof. The usual casino attractions also feature.

Sintra

If you make just one day-trip from Lisbon, choose the beautiful hilltop town of Sintra, the former summer residence of Portuguese royalty and a UNESCO World Heritage Site since 1995. Not only does the town boast two of Portugal's most extraordinary palaces, it also contains a semitropical garden, a Moorish castle and proximity to some great beaches. Looping around a series of wooded ravines and with a climate that encourages moss and ferns to grow from every nook and cranny, Sintra consists of three districts. Sintra-Vila has most of the historical attractions; while Estefânia, a ten-minute walk to the east, is where trains from Lisbon pull in. São Pedro, to the south, is well known for its antique shops and best visited on the eve of São Pedro (June 28–29), the main saint's day, and for its market on the second and fourth Sunday of the month.

Sintra-Vila
MAP PAGE 110

The historic centre of Sintra spreads across the slopes of several steep hills, themselves loomed over by wooded heights topped by the Moorish castle and the Palácio da Pena. Dominating the centre of **Sintra-Vila** are the tapering chimneys of the Palácio Nacional, surrounded by an array of tall houses painted in the prettiest pale pink, ochre or mellow yellow tones, many with ornate turrets and decorative balconies peering out to the plains of Lisbon far below. All this is highly scenic – though, in fact, Sintra looks at its best seen on the way in from the station. Summer crowds can swamp the narrow central streets, and once you've seen the sights, you're best off heading out of town to see the surrounding attractions up in the hills.

Visiting Sintra

There are trains from Lisbon's Rossio station (every 10–30min; 45min; €5 return). A land train (6 daily; €12; ⓦ comboiodesintra. pt) runs from near Sintra station in a circuit via the Palácio Nacional, the Moorish Castle, the Pena Palace and the Quinta da Regaleira. Alternatively, bus #434 takes a circular route from Sintra station to most of the sites mentioned in this chapter (every 20–40min from 9.30am–6.20pm) and allows you to hop on and off whenever you like on the circuit. Also useful is bus #435, which runs from Sintra station to Monserrate gardens via Sintra-Vila and Quinta da Regaleira (every 45min 9.40am–6.15pm). Both buses are valid on the 24hr ticket available from Scotturb (ⓦ scotturb.com; €12.50). Ask at the tourist office about various combined tickets that can save money on entry to the main sites.

Palácio Nacional

Palácio Nacional

MAP PAGE 110
Largo da Rainha Dona Amélia
ⓦ parquesdesintra.pt, charge.
Best seen early or late in the day to
avoid the crowds, the sumptuous
Palácio Nacional was probably
already in existence at the time of
the Moors. It takes its present form
from the rebuilding of Dom João
I (1385–1433) and his successor,
Dom Manuel I, the chief royal
beneficiary of Vasco da Gama's
explorations. Its exterior style is
an amalgam of Gothic – featuring
impressive battlements – and
Manueline, tempered inside by a
good deal of Moorish influence.
Sadly, after the fall of the monarchy
in 1910, most of the surrounding
walls and medieval houses were
destroyed. Highlights on the lower
floor include the Manueline **Sala
dos Cisnes**, so-called for the swans
(*cisnes*) on its ceiling, and the Sala
das Pegas, which takes its name
from the flock of magpies (*pegas*)
painted on the frieze and ceiling –
João I, caught in the act of kissing
a lady-in-waiting by his queen,
reputedly had the room decorated
with as many magpies as there were
women at court, to imply they were
all gossips.

Best of the upper floor is the
gallery above the palace chapel.
Beyond, a succession of **state rooms**
finishes with the Sala das Brasões,
its domed and coffered ceiling
emblazoned with the arms of 72
noble families. Finally, don't miss the
kitchens, whose roofs taper into the
giant chimneys that are the palace's
distinguishing features. The palace
also hosts events for the Sintra Music
Festival (see page 142).

MU.SA – Museu das Artes de Sintra

MAP PAGE 110
Avda Heliodoro Salgado ⓦ visitsintra.
travel/en/visit/museums/mu-sa-sintra-
museum-of-the-arts, free.
Inside Sintra's beautiful
former casino, this appealing
contemporary **art museum** is
dedicated to important Portuguese
artists such as Emílio de Paula
Campos (1884–1943), who
portrays traditional rural scenes,
and innovative sculptor Dorita
Castel-Branco (1936–1996). There
is also a photography room and
temporary exhibits (charge).

SINTRA

Sintra

N

Centro Cultural O. Cadaval
RUA CÂMARA PESTANA
MU.SA

Market

RUA VEIGA DA CUNHA

AV. ADRIANO COELHO

R. GEN. A. ROCADAS

ESTR. MONTE SANTOS

AL. COMB. DA GDE GUERRA

AL. DE ALBUQUERQUE

AV. MOVIMENTO DAS FORÇAS ARMADAS

R. DR. ÁLVARO DE VASCONCELOS

AVENIDA DR. CAMBOURNAC

R. D. F. DE ALMEIDA

R. GAGO COUTINHO

RUA DA COSTA

LARGO D. MANUEL I

ESTEFÂNIA

AV. NUNES DE CARVALHO

ESTRADA DO CARVALHEIRO

AV. HELIODORO SALGADO

AV. DE BATALHA

R. DA PIACENA

RUA SOTTO MAYOR

ESTRADA DA MACIEIRA

Câmara Municipal

LARGO DR. VIRGÍLIO HORTA

Train Station

R. AFONSO

AV. DR. MIGUEL

R. JOÃO DE DEUS

R. ANDRÉ DE ALBUQUERQUE

RUA AUGUSTO O. FREIRE

LARGO FERNANDO MORAIS

RUA F. DOS SANTOS

CAMINHO CASTANHAS

RUA GUILHERME

VOLTA DO DUQUE

RUA DAS MURTAS

RUA CONDE SEIXAL

CAMINHO DA ALBA LONGA

see Sintra-Vila

SINTRA-VILA

VOLTA DO DUQUE
R. VISCONDE DE MONSERRATE
RUA MARECHAL SALDANHA

R. PEDRO A. NAVARRO

Parque da Liberdade

RUA BERNARDIM RIBEIRO

CALÇ. DOS CLÉRIGOS

CALÇADA DE S. PEDRO

Quinta da Regaleira

RUA M. EU GENIO

ESTRADA DA PENA

Santa Maria

SÃO PEDRO DE SINTRA

CALÇADA DA PENALVA

São Pedro

R. SERPA PINTO

Castelo dos Mouros

CALÇADA DA PENA

ESTRADA DA PENA

SANTA EUFÉMIA

Ticket Office

EST. R DA PENA

P

RUA RIO DA BICA

Ticket Office

P

Palácio da Pena

| 0 | metres | 250 |
| 0 | yards | 250 |

Sintra-Vila

N

RUA DO PAÇO

RUA DA RIBEIRA

PASSEIO VELHOS

RUA CONS. SEGURADO

CALÇADA DO RIO DO PORTO

CHÃO PRETO

Palácio Nacional

RUA DA PENDOA

LARGO RAINHA DONA AMÉLIA

CALÇADA DO

RUA FRESCA

PRAÇA DA REPÚBLICA

RUA BIQUINHA

PRAÇA DA REPÚBLICA

ESC. TEIXEIRA

VOLTA DO DUQUE

RUA GIL VICENTE

ESC. N. NUNES

RUA PALADARES

R. VISCONDE DE MONSERRATE

RUA CONSIGLIERI PEDROSO

R. DA FERRARIA

RUA FONTE DA PIPA

LARGO FERREIRA DE CASTRO

RUA M. EUGENIA F. NAVARRO

ESTRADA DA PENA

| 0 | metres | 50 |
| 0 | yards | 50 |

■ ACCOMMODATION

Casa do Valle	2
Chalet Relogio	6
Chalet Saudade	3
Hotel Nova Sintra	1
Hotel Sintra Jardim	5
Moon Hill Hostel	4

● RESTAURANTS

Cantinho de São Pedro	7
Harko's	6
Incomum	3
Páteo do Garrett	1
Restaurante Regional de Sintra	2
Tulhas	9

● CAFÉS

Casa Piriquita	8
Fábrica das Verdadeiras Queijadas da Sapa	5
Café Saudade	4

■ BARS

Bar Fonte da Pipa	3
Café Paris	2
O Tasco do Strauss	1

Castelo dos Mouros

Quinta da Regaleira

MAP PAGE 110

Rua Barbosa do Bocage Ⓦ regaleira.pt,
charge.

The **Quinta da Regaleira** is one of
Sintra's most elaborate estates. It was
designed at the end of the nineteenth
century by Italian architect and
theatre set designer Luigi Manini for
wealthy Brazilian merchant António
Augusto Carvalho Monteiro.
Manini's penchant for the dramatic
is obvious: the principal building,
the mock-Manueline **Palácio
dos Milhões**, sprouts turrets and
towers, while the interior boasts Art
Nouveau tiles and elaborate Rococo
wooden ceilings.

The surrounding **gardens**
shelter fountains, terraces and
grottoes, with the highlight being
the Initiation Well, inspired by
the initiation practices of the
Freemasons. Entering via a Harry
Potter-esque revolving stone door,
you walk down a moss-covered
spiral staircase to the foot of the
well and through a tunnel, which
eventually resurfaces at the edge of a
lake (though in winter you exit from
a shorter tunnel so as not to disturb
a colony of hibernating bats).

In summer, the gardens host
occasional performances of live
music, usually classical or jazz, and
light shows.

Castelo dos Mouros

MAP PAGE 110

Ⓦ parquesdesintra.pt, **charge.**

Reached on bus #434 or a steep
drive, the ruined ramparts of the
Castelo dos Mouros are truly
spectacular. It's a pleasant, if steep,
walk up (30–40min): start at the
Calçada dos Clérigos, near the
church of Santa Maria, where a
stone pathway leads all the way
up to the lower slopes, where
you can see a Moorish grain silo
and a ruined twelfth-century
church. To enter the castle itself,
you'll need to buy a ticket from
the road exit. Built in the ninth
century, the stronghold was
taken from the Moors in 1147 by
Afonso Henriques, Portugal's first
monarch: the ruins of a Moorish
mosque remain. The ancient
walls were allowed to fall into
disrepair over subsequent centuries,
though they were restored in the
mid-nineteenth century under the
orders of Ferdinand II. The fortress

Palácio da Pena

is partly built into two craggy pinnacles, and views from up here are dazzling both inland and across to the Atlantic. Recent excavations have revealed the ruins of Muslim houses, thirty medieval Christian graves, and ceramic vases dating back to the fifth century BC.

Palácio da Pena

MAP PAGE 110
Estrada da Pena ⓦ parquedesintra.pt, charge.

Bus #434 stops opposite the lower entrance to Parque da Pena, a stretch of rambling woodland with a scattering of lakes and follies. At the top of the park, about twenty minutes' walk from the entrance or a short ride on a shuttle bus (charge), looms the fabulous

Palácio da Pena, a wild fantasy of domes, towers, ramparts and walkways, approached through mock-Manueline gateways and a drawbridge that does not draw. A compelling riot of kitsch, the palace was built in the 1840s to the specifications of Ferdinand of Saxe-Coburg-Gotha, husband of Queen Maria II, with the help of the German architect Baron Eschwege. The interior is preserved exactly as it was left by the royal family when they fled Portugal in 1910.

The result is fascinating: rooms of stone decorated to look like wood, statues of turbaned Moors nonchalantly holding electric chandeliers – it's all here. Of an original convent, founded in the early sixteenth century to celebrate

Visiting Praia das Maçãs

Quaint old trams shuttle from near the Centro Cultural Olga Cadaval to the coastal resort of Praia das Maçãs via Colares (June–Sept daily 10.20am–5pm every 1–2hr; 45min; €5 single). However, check the latest routes and timetables in the Sintra tourist office on ⓦ visitsintra.travel/en/discover/sintra-tram, as there are frequent shortenings of the journey or alterations to the service.

the first sight of Vasco da Gama's returning fleet, only a beautiful, tiled chapel and Manueline cloister have been retained.

You can also look round the mock-Alpine **Chalet Condessa d'Edla**, built by Ferdinand in the 1860s as a retreat for his second wife.

Monserrate

MAP PAGE 113
Estrada da Monserrate
Ⓦ parquedesintra.pt, charge.

The name most associated with the fabulous gardens and palace of **Monserrate** is that of William Beckford, the wealthiest untitled Englishman of his age, who rented the estate from 1793 to 1799, having been forced to flee Britain after he was caught in a compromising position with a sixteen-year-old boy. Setting about improving the place, he landscaped a waterfall and even imported a flock of sheep from his estate.

Half a century later, a second immensely rich Englishman, Sir Francis Cook, bought the estate and imported the head gardener from Kew to lay out water plants, tropical ferns and palms, and just about every known conifer. For a time, Monserrate boasted the only lawn in Iberia, and it remains one of Europe's most richly stocked gardens, with over a thousand different species of subtropical tree and plant.

From the entrance, paths wend steeply down through lush undergrowth to a ruined chapel, half engulfed by a giant banyan tree. From here, lawns lead up to Cook's main legacy, a great **Victorian palace** inspired by Brighton Pavilion, with its mix of Moorish and Italian decoration – the dome is modelled on the Duomo in Florence. The interior has been restored after years of neglect, and you can now admire

Around Sintra

Azenhas do Mar

the amazingly intricate plasterwork which covers almost every wall and ceiling. The park also has a decent café for food and drink.

Azenhas do Mar

MAP PAGE 113
Bus #441 from Sintra (every 1–2hr; 40min).

A cluster of whitewashed cottages tumbles down the steep cliff-face at picturesque **Azenhas do Mar**, one of the liveliest villages along the Sintra coast. The beach is small, but there are man-made seawater pools for swimming when the ocean is too rough.

Praia das Maçãs

MAP PAGE 113
Bus #441 from Sintra (every 1–2hr; 30min); or Praia das Maças tram from Sintra.

The largest and liveliest resort on this coast, **Praia das Maçãs** is also the easiest to reach from Sintra – take the tram (see box, page 112) for the most enjoyable journey. Along with a big swath of sand, there's an array of bars and restaurants to suit all budgets.

Praia Grande

MAP PAGE 113
Bus #439 or 1254 from Sintra (every 1–2hr; 25min).

Set in a wide, sandy, cliff-backed bay, this is one of the best and safest **beaches** on the Sintra coast, though its breakers attract surfers aplenty. In August the World Bodyboarding Championships are held here, along with games such as volleyball and beach rugby. Plenty of inexpensive cafés and restaurants are strung along the beachside road, and if the waves become too rough, there are giant sea pools (May–Oct, charge) on the approach to the beach.

Praia da Adraga

MAP PAGE 113
No public transport; by car, follow the signs from the village of Almoçageme.

Praia da Adraga was flatteringly voted one of Europe's best beaches by a British newspaper; the unspoilt, cliff-backed, sandy bay with just one restaurant is certainly far quieter than the other resorts, but it takes the full brunt of the Atlantic, so you'll need to take great care when swimming.

Cabo da Roca

MAP PAGE 113

Bus #1624 from Sintra or Cascais train stations (roughly hourly; 35min).

Little more than a windswept **rocky cape** with a lighthouse, this is the most westerly point in mainland Europe, which guarantees a steady stream of visitors – arrive early to avoid the coach parties. You can soak up the views from the café-restaurant and handicraft shop, and buy a certificate to prove you've been here at the little tourist office (daily 9am–7.30pm, Oct–May until 6.30pm; ☎219 238 543).

Convento dos Capuchos

MAP PAGE 113

No public transport, a return taxi from Sintra with a 1hr stopover costs around €40 ✆ parquesdesintra.pt, charge.

If you have your own transport, don't miss a trip to the **Convento dos Capuchos**, an extraordinary hermitage with tiny, dwarf-like cells cut from the rock and lined with cork – hence its popular name of the Cork Convent. It was occupied for three hundred years until being finally abandoned in 1834 by its seven remaining monks,

who must have found the gloomy warren of rooms and corridors too much to maintain. Some rooms – the penitents' cells – can only be entered by crawling through 70cm-high doors; here, and on every other ceiling, doorframe and lintel, are attached panels of cork, taken from the surrounding woods. Elsewhere, you'll come across a washroom, kitchen, refectory, tiny chapels, and even a bread oven set apart from the main complex.

Peninha

MAP PAGE 113

With your own transport, it's worth exploring the dramatic wooded landscape between Capuchos and Cabo da Roca, much of it studded with giant moss-covered boulders. Some 3km from Capuchos lies **Peninha**, a spectacularly sited hermitage perched on a granite crag. The sixteenth-century Baroque interior is usually locked but climb up anyway for dazzling views of the Sintra coast towards Cascais. You can also take a waymarked 4.5km trail round the crag; otherwise, it's a short return walk from the woodland car park.

Convento dos Capuchos

SINTRA

Restaurants

Cantinho de São Pedro

MAP PAGE 110

Praça D. Fernando II 18, São Pedro de
Sintra Ⓦ cantinhosaopedro.com.

Large restaurant with bare stone
walls overlooking an attractive
courtyard, just off São Pedro's main
square. The traditional dishes (such
as *bacalhau com natas*) are better
than the international ones. On
cool evenings a log fire keeps things
cosy. €€

Harko's

MAP PAGE 110

Rua Serpa Pinto 4, São Pedro de Sintra
Ⓦ harkos.pt.

Perhaps unusually for village-like
São Pedro, this is a top-notch
Japanese restaurant serving a
tasty range of sushi and sashimi.
Local ingredients feature, such as
scallops and fresh tuna, and there
are also good vegetarian options.
€€€

Incomum

MAP PAGE 110

Rua Dr. Alfredo Costa 22
Ⓦ incomumbyluissantos.pt.

Close to the station, this
upmarket restaurant and wine bar
is run by chef Luís Santos. His
stints in some of Switzerland's top
restaurants are reflected in a menu
featuring the likes of scallops with
mushroom risotto, black linguini
with seafood and steak with sweet
potatoes, though the ingredients
are local and top quality. €€€

Páteo do Garrett

MAP PAGE 110

Rua Padre Amaro Teixeira de Azevedo 12,
Várzea de Sintra Ⓦ pateodogarrett.com.

You'll need a vehicle to reach this
spacious restaurant with a terrace
in the nearby village of Várzea
de Sintra. It's popular with tour
groups who admire the amazing
views across the Sintra hills, and
the excellent-value menu features

a long list of grilled meats and
fresh fish: steaks are the speciality.
€€

Restaurante Regional de Sintra

MAP PAGE 110

Trav do Município 2 Ⓦ regional.pt.

In a lovely old building next
to the Câmara Municipal, this
traditional and slightly formal
restaurant serves tasty dishes at
reasonable prices – fresh fish,
grilled meats and a very good
crêpe de marisco (seafood crêpe), as
well as some fine desserts. €€

Tulhas

MAP PAGE 110

Rua Gil Vicente 4–6 Ⓣ 962 827 777.

Imaginative cooking in a fine
building converted from old grain
silos – the original grain well takes
pride of place in the floor. The
giant mixed grills for two will
keep carnivores happy, while the
weekend specials are usually good
value, with the usual range of
grilled meat and fish. €€

Cafés

Casa Piriquita

MAP PAGE 110

Rua das Padarias 1 Ⓣ 219 230 626.

Cosy tearoom and bakery, dating
from 1862, which is often
busy with locals queueing to
buy *queijadas de Sintra* (sweet
cheesecakes), *travesseiros* (doughy
almond cakes) and other pastries.
€

Fábrica das Verdadeiras Queijadas da Sapa

MAP PAGE 110

Volta do Duche 12 Ⓣ 219 230 493.

This old-fashioned café is famed
for its traditional *queijadas*
(cheesecakes), made on the
premises for over a century. It's a
bit dingy inside, so it's best to buy
takeaways to sustain you on your
walk to the centre. €

Café Paris

Café Saudade

MAP PAGE 110
Avda Dr. Miguel Bombarda 6, Sintra ☎ 212 428 804.
This buzzy café used to be a factory selling *queijadas* (sweet tarts) and has a warren of rooms and its own art gallery, with occasional live music. As well as cakes, scones and sandwiches, it dishes up a range of salads, something-on-toasts and brunch. A long list of drinks and teas includes Gorreana tea from the Azores. €

Bars

Bar Fonte da Pipa

MAP PAGE 110
Rua Fonte da Pipa 11–13 ☎ 219 234 437.
Laid-back bar with low lighting, comfy chairs and a fine sangria. It's up the hill from *Casa Piriquita*, next to the lovely ornate fountain (*fonte*) that the street is named after.

Café Paris

MAP PAGE 110
Praçe da República 32 ☎ 219 232 375.
This attractive little blue-tiled café-bar is the highest-profile in town, which means steep prices for not especially exciting food, though it is a great place for a cocktail or a streetside coffee where you can watch the world go by.

O Tasco do Strauss

MAP PAGE 110
Largo dos Aliados 2 ☎ 939 176 351.
Sharing a building with the local philharmonic society, this friendly bar specializes in reasonably priced *petiscos* such as clams, *chorizo*, cheeses and hams, along with burgers and sandwiches. The quirky and fun decor features a jumble of vintage bottles, ceramic jugs and bric-a-brac, including old guitars and dart boards, and there are outdoor tables.

The Lisbon coast

Lisbon's most accessible beaches lie along the Cascais coast just beyond the point where the Tejo flows into the Atlantic. Famed for its casino, Estoril has the best sands, though neighbouring Cascais has more buzz. The River Tejo separates Lisbon from high-rise Caparica, to the south, on a superb stretch of wave-pounded beach, popular with surfers.

Estoril

MAP PAGE 120

With its grandiose villas, luxury hotels and health spa, **Estoril** (pronounced *é-stril*) has pretensions towards being a Portuguese Riviera. The centre is focused on the leafy **Parque do Estoril** and its enormous casino (semiformal attire required; Ⓦcasino-estoril.pt, free). During World War II, this was where exiled royalty hung out and many spies made their names. Ian Fleming was based here to keep an eye on double agents, and used his experience at the casino

as inspiration for the first James Bond novel, *Casino Royale*.

The resort's fine sandy beach, **Praia de Tamariz**, is backed by some ornate villas and a seafront promenade that stretches northwest to Cascais, a pleasant twenty-minute stroll. In summer, firework displays take place above the beach every Saturday at midnight.

Estoril is also famed for its world-class **golf courses** which lie a short distance inland (more information online at Ⓦportugalgolf.pt); it also hosts the Estoril Open tennis tournament in April or May (Ⓦmillenniumestorilopen.com).

Tamariz beach in Estoril

Transport to Estoril and Cascais

Trains from Lisbon's Cais do Sodré (every 15–30min; 35min to Estoril, 40min to Cascais; €2.90 single) wend along the shore. There are also regular buses to and from Sintra, or it's a fine drive down the corniche.

Cascais

MAP PAGE 119

Cascais (pronounced *cash-kaysh*) is a highly attractive former fishing village, liveliest round Largo Luís de Camões, at one end of Rua Frederico Arouca, the main mosaic-paved pedestrian thoroughfare.

Praia da Conceição is the ideal beach to lounge on or try out a range of watersports. The rock-fringed smaller beaches of **Praia da Rainha** and **Praia da Ribeira** are off the central stretch, while regular buses run 6km northwest to **Praia do Guincho**, a fabulous sweep of surf-beaten sands.

Cascais is at its most charming in the grid of streets north of the **Igreja da Assunção** – its *azulejos* predate the earthquake of 1755. Nearby, on Rua Júlio Pereira de Melo, the engaging **Museu do Mar** (museumar.cascais.pt, charge) relates the town's relationship with the sea, with model boats, treasure from local wrecks and stuffed fish.

Casa das Histórias

MAP PAGE 119

Avda da República 300

 casadashistoriaspaularego.com, charge.

The distinctive ochre towers of the Modernist **Casa das Histórias** mark a fantastic museum which

Cascais

Villa Shopping & Bus Station

Train Station

AVENIDA MARGINAL

★ Taxis

ALAMEDA DUQUESA PALMELA

Jardim Visconde da Luz

DR. FRANCISCO SA CARNEIRO

RUA I. DOYLE

PRAÇA

R. C. RIBEIRO

ACCOMMODATION	
Farol Hotel	4
Hotel Baía	2
The Pergola	1
Vila Bicuda	3

AV. COMB DE GRANDE GUERRA

AV. VISCONDE DA LUZ

AVENIDA VALBOM

RUA FREDERICO AROUCA

RUA MISERICÓRDIA

R. DAS FLORES

R. D. A

R. PADRARIA

RUA M. E. I. DOYLE

LARGO DA PRAIA DA RAINHA

Praia da Conceição

Praia da Rainha

RUA AFONSO SANCHES

RUA POÇO NOVO

RUA DOS NAVEGANTES

RUA DA GAMA

LARGO LUÍS DE CAMÕES

Town Hall

LARGO 5 DE OUTUBRO

ATLANTIC OCEAN

AVENIDA VASCO DA GAMA

RUA LATINO COELHO

RUA VITÓRIA

R. PROENÇA

R. ARAUJO

R. VIANA

R. L. PALMEIRIM

R. M. VALADIM

Praia da Ribeira

RUA J. ROQUETTE

R. J. P MELO

RUA C. FERREIRA

Museu do Mar

AV. DA REPÚBLICA

Igreja da Assunção

LARGO DA ASSUNÇÃO

AV. D. CARLOS I

PASSEIO DONA MARIA PIA

Casa das Histórias

Palácio da Cidadela

Pousada

RUA NICOLAU DE OLIVEIRA

R. J. P.

Parque Municipal da Gandarinha

ESTRADA DA BOCA DO INFERNO

Marina de Cascais

N

Museu Biblioteca Conde Castro Guimarães

Praia de Santa Marta

AV. REI HUMBERTO II DE ITÁLIA

Santa Marta Lighthouse

| 0 metres | 100 |
| 0 yards | 100 |

RESTAURANTS	
O Cantinho da Belinha	6
Galeria House of Wonders	4
Jardim dos Frangos	2
O Pescador	3
Restaurante Maré	8
O Solar do Bitoque	5
Taberna da Praça	7
CAFÉ	
Santini	1

is dedicated to Dame Paula Rego, who spent much of her life in the UK before she died in 2022. Designed by famous architect Eduardo Souto de Moura, the airy museum features over 120 of her disturbing but beautiful collages, pastels and engravings, as well as those by her late English husband Victor Willing, though displays change regularly. Many of her works explore themes of power: women and animals are portrayed as both powerful and sexually vulnerable; men often appear as fish or dressed in women's clothes.

Around Cascais Marina

MAP PAGE 119

The leafy **Parque Municipal da Gandarinha**, complete with picnic tables and playground, makes a welcome escape from the beach crowds. In one corner stands the mansion of the nineteenth-century Count of Guimarães, preserved complete with its fittings as the **Museu Biblioteca Conde Castro Guimarães** (Ⓦ bairrodosmuseus. cascais.pt, charge). Its most valuable exhibits are rare, illuminated sixteenth-century manuscripts.

Palácio da Cidadela

MAP PAGE 119
Avda Dom Carlos I
Ⓦ **museu.presidencia.pt, charge.**
To the east, the walls of Cascais' largely seventeenth-century **Citadela** (fortress) guard the entrance to the **Marina de Cascais**, an enclave of expensive yachts serviced by restaurants, bars and boutiques.

Originally a sea fort and then a summer retreat for Portuguese royalty, the Citadela has been used by the Portuguese president to entertain his guests ever since the declaration of the Republic in 1910. Today, you can wander around the lower-floor exhibition space, though it's worth the

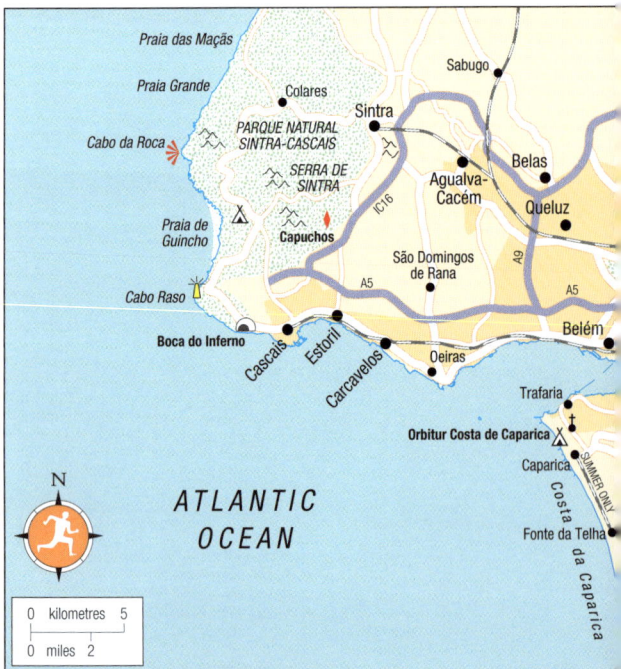

entrance fee to visit the top two floors (ask for a non-guided visit unless you understand Portuguese). There's also a lovely tearoom facing the ocean.

Caparica

MAP PAGE 120
Via Rapida express 135 (roughly hourly; 30min) or slower local buses (every 15–30min; 50min), from Cacilhas or bus #161 from Lisbon's Praça Areeiro (every 30–60min; 40–60min).
According to legend, **Caparica** was named after the discovery of a cloak (*capa*) full of golden coins. Today it is a slightly tacky, high-rise seaside resort, but don't let that put you off: it's family-friendly, has plenty of good seafood as well as several kilometres of soft, sandy beach.

From the beach, a **narrow-gauge mini-railway** (June–Sept, charge) runs south along the beach for 8km to the resort of **Fonte da Telha**. Jump off at any stop en route;

Surfers on the Costa da Caparica coastline

earlier stops tend to be family-oriented, while nudity is common in later ones.

Lisbon coast

Restaurants

O Barbas

Apoio de Praia 13, Caparica Ⓦ **obarbas.pt.**
Caparica's best-known beach restaurant with affordable fish, *caldeirada* (fish stew) and *arroz de marisco* (seafood rice) to die for. It also runs a more laid-back space next door, *Cervejaria O Barbas*, good for beer and snacks. €€

O Cantinho da Belinha

MAP PAGE 119
Avda Vasco da Gama 133, Cascais
☎ **214 822 504.**
Within the Associação de Armadores e Pescadores (Association of Shipowners and Fishermen), this cosy restaurant specializes, not surprisingly, in fresh fish. Big, tasty squid come with new potatoes and salad, while other fish depend on the day's catch: expect fresh sardines in season and sea bream, for example. Grilled meats also feature (the steak with cream and mushroom is good). There is a small terrace garden. Reservations are recommended, especially at weekends. €

The promenade in Cascais

Galeria House of Wonders

MAP PAGE 119
Largo da Misericordia 53
Ⓦ **facebook.com/houseofwonders.**
This Dutch-run veggie café-restaurant and gallery space has an appealing, alternative vibe. The street-level dining room serves amazing vegetarian meze of various sizes: expect hummus, chickpea salad and whatever fresh veg is in season. There's a separate entrance for the gallery space and laid-back café, complete with a roof terrace where you can relax for a drink on old packing cases. €€

Jardim dos Frangos

MAP PAGE 119
Avda Com. Grande Guerra 68, Cascais
☎ **214 861 717.**
Permanently buzzing with people and sizzling with the speciality, bargain grilled chicken, which is devoured by the plateful at indoor and outdoor tables. Arrive early to secure a table as it is very popular. €

O Pescador

MAP PAGE 119
Rua das Flores 10B, Cascais
Ⓦ **restaurantepescador.com.**
The best of a row of lively restaurants near the centre, offering upmarket seafood – expect superb mains such as lobster baked in salt or tuna cooked in olive oil and garlic. €€€

Restaurante Maré

MAP PAGE 119
Avda Nossa Senhora do Cabo 9000, Cascais
Ⓦ **marejoseavillez.pt.**
José Avillez' latest venture in his hometown of Cascais is a wonderful seafront restaurant with huge glass windows giving floor-to-ceiling views of the water and a large clifftop terrace. Wonderful seafood platters piled high with local clams, lobster, prawns and goose barnacles (a Portuguese delicacy), delicious chargrilled fish, seafood stew

Traditional *caldeirada*

with mint and the like are all beautifully presented and fresh from the sea. It's on the coast road to Guincho – a taxi there will cost around €10. €€€€

O Solar do Bitoque

MAP PAGE 119
Rua Regimento 19 de Infantaria Loja 11, Cascais ☎ 214 061 102.
Bitoques are thin steaks, and this lively local with outdoor seating specializes in various types, as well as burgers, salads and fresh fish. Very good value considering its position. €

Taberna da Praça

MAP PAGE 119
Cidadela de Cascais, Avda Dom Carlos I ☎ 214 814 300.
Tucked into a couple of cosy arched rooms within Cascais's impressive fortress, *Taberna da Praça* serves a range of tasty *petiscos*. You can sample regional specialities like scrambled eggs with smoked chicken chorizo, or grilled octopus with baked potatoes. There are also more substantial mains: great tuna steaks or *duel+ rice*. €€€

Café

Santini

MAP PAGE 119
Avda Valbom 28f ☎ 214 833 709.
Opened by an Italian immigrant just after World War II, *Santini*'s delicious ice creams are legendary in these parts. €

Bars and clubs

Deck Bar

Arcadas do Parque 21–22, Estoril ⓦ deckbar.pt.
Facing Estoril's park, this great little café-restaurant and bar has appealing outdoor tables. It's a good spot for a drink or snack, and also serves a range of full meals (salads, steaks, fresh fish). €€

Dr Bernard

Praia do CDS, Apoio de Praia 11, Caparica ⓦ drbernard.pt.
Jazzy seafront café-bar and also a surf school, and it's a great spot to nurse a drink or two while watching the local surfers show off their skills.

ACCOMMODATION

Hotel Avenida Palace

Accommodation

Lisbon's hotels range from sumptuous five-stars to backstreet hideaways packed with local character. The grander ones tend to be found along Avenida da Liberdade, around Parque Eduardo VII or out of the centre, though in recent years around forty have opened in the central Baixa where there is an abundance of options. Besides its hotels, Lisbon still has a few old-style guesthouses (*alojamento local* or *particular*, some of which keep the now-abandoned titles of *pensão* or *residencial*) and various good-value hostels. Over the past decade or so, a wave of boutique-style hotels and guesthouses has sprung up across the city, often in old townhouses that have been transformed into stylish accommodation – these are usually reasonably priced and make for an atmospheric and comfortable stay. The Alfama and Bairro Alto, too, are beginning to offer a greater choice, with crumbling buildings being done up into hotels or smart self-catering apartments – often with great city or river views thanks to the districts' hilltop positions. Given the surge in new accommodation, it's rarely hard to find a decent room, except in high season. Most include breakfast, anything from bread, jam and coffee to a generous spread of rolls, cereals, croissants, cold meat, cheese and fruit, but check before booking.

The Baixa and Rossio

ALMALUSA BAIXA/CHIADO MAP PAGE 26, POCKET MAP D13. Praça do Município 21, tram #28 to Praça do Município ⓦ almalusahotels.com. Beautifully positioned in the corner of a historic square, this eighteenth-century building now houses a chic boutique hotel. Most the rooms have period touches such as flagstone floors and fireplaces; some overlook the town hall and tram routes. There's also a downstairs restaurant and small outdoor terrace. **€€€**

Accommodation price codes

Each accommodation reviewed in this Guide is accompanied by a price category, based on the cost of a standard en-suite double room in high season, though as Lisbon is becoming more popular year-round, low-season rates are not much cheaper. Price ranges include breakfast, unless stated otherwise.
€ = under €100
€€ = €100–150
€€€ = €150–200
€€€€ = over €200

Booking a room

The main tourist offices (see page 141) can provide accommodation lists, but won't reserve rooms for you. Book well in advance for the best deals, or gamble on last-minute discounts. Look out, too, for deals on hotel websites, which are usually cheaper than walk-in rates.

CASA BALTHAZAR MAP PAGE 26, POCKET MAP C11. **Rua do Duque 26** Ⓜ Restauradores Ⓦ casabalthazarlisbon. com. Surely one of Lisbon's top addresses, this small luxury hotel lies hidden right in the heart of the city on a quiet side street. An old mansion has been artfully modernized to give a series of spacious and very private apartments, all with stunning views across the Baixa, the castle or the lovely central courtyard, which has its own small, heated pool. Most have big private terraces, along with kitchenettes, massive beds and fab retro furniture. Elsewhere, there's a relaxing communal lounge. €€€€

HOTEL AVENIDA PALACE MAP PAGE 26, POCKET MAP C11. **Rua 1 de Dezembro 123** Ⓜ Restauradores Ⓦ hotelavenidapalace.pt. Built at the end of the nineteenth century, and rumoured to have a secret door direct to neighbouring Rossio station, this is one of Lisbon's grandest hotels. Despite extensive modernization, the traditional feel has been maintained with chandeliers and period furniture throughout. There are 82 spacious rooms, each with high ceilings and colossal bathrooms. €€€€

HOTEL FLORESCENTE MAP PAGE 26, POCKET MAP J5. **Rua das Portas de Santo Antão 95** Ⓜ Restauradores Ⓦ hotelflorescente.com. The best option on this pedestrianized street, with a small outdoor pool. There's a large selection of air-conditioned rooms across four floors (some en suite), so if you don't like the look of the room you're shown – and some are very cramped – ask about alternatives. Street-facing rooms can be noisy. There's also a lounge plus parking. €€

HOTEL MÉTROPOLE MAP PAGE 26, POCKET MAP D11. **Rossio 30** Ⓜ Restauradores Ⓦ almeidahotels.pt. A welcoming three-star dating to the early twentieth century, with an airy lounge-bar offering superb views over Rossio and the castle. The simply furnished but spacious rooms are comfortable, though the square can be quite noisy at night. €€€

HOTEL PORTUENSE MAP PAGE 26, POCKET MAP J5. **Rua das Portas de Santo Antão 149–157** Ⓜ Restauradores Ⓦ hotelportuense.com. Singles, doubles and triples in a family-run hotel in a great position. Decently decorated, all rooms come with a/c and TV. €€

LX ROSSIO MAP PAGE 26, POCKET MAP D12. **Rua da Assunção 52** Ⓜ Rossio Ⓦ lxrossiohotel.com. One of the Baixa's most central options. With its own bar, the hotel's simple but comfortable rooms overlook relatively quiet pedestrianized streets. Triple rooms available. €€

TOREL PALACE MAP PAGE 26, POCKET MAP J5. **Rua Câmara Pestana 45** Ⓜ Avenida Ⓦ torelpalacelisbon.com. A sublime luxury retreat set in a series of historic buildings, including the home of a former royal and an erstwhile chocolate magnate, who built what was Lisbon's tallest tower. All rooms are individually decorated with oodles of character, vintage furniture and city views. The beautiful grounds contain two pools and outdoor terraces, and there are two amazing restaurants, *Black Pavilion* and the Michelin-starred *2Monkeys*. €€€€

VIP EXECUTIVE ÉDEN MAP PAGE 26, POCKET MAP C10. **Praça dos Restauradores 24** Ⓜ Restauradores Ⓦ vipedenaparthotel. com. Compact studios and apartments sleeping up to four people are available within the impressively converted Éden cinema. Book a ninth-floor apartment with a balcony and you'll have the best views and be just below the superb breakfast bar and rooftop pool. All come with dishwashers,

Self-catering

There are several fine options for self-catering in Lisbon. As well as Ⓦ airbnb.co.uk, good first points of call are Ⓦ fadoflats. pt (mostly in Chiado and Alfama) and Ⓦ castleinnlisbon.com, which has apartments right by the castle. Geared up to families is the upmarket *Martinhal Chiado* (Ⓦ martinhal.com) in the Chiado district (see page 129), while a recommended option is the tastefully furnished houses offered by *Casa Amora* (Ⓦ casaamora. com) near the attractive Praça das Amoreiras.

microwaves and satellite TV, breakfast is extra. Disabled access. **Studios, from €€**

The Sé, Castelo and Alfama

1908 LISBOA HOTELⓄ MAP PAGE 38, POCKET MAP K5. **Largo do Intendente Pina Manique 6,** Ⓜ **Intendente** Ⓦ **1908lisboahotel.com** This superb Art Nouveau hotel is the top address in fashionable Largo do Intendente. Rooms are characterful and stylish, the nicest overlooking the pedestrianized square. A generous breakfast is served in the classy *Infame* restaurant downstairs. **€€€**

ALBERGARIA SENHORA DO MONTE MAP PAGE 38, POCKET MAP L5. **Calçada do Monte 39, tram #28** Ⓦ hotelsenhoradomonte.com. Comfortable, if slightly dated, hotel in a sublime location with views of the castle and Graça convent from the south-facing rooms (avoid the north-facing ones). Breakfast on a fourth-floor terrace. Parking available. **€€€**

MEMMO ALFAMA MAP PAGE 38, POCKET MAP F12. **Trav Merceeiras 27, tram #28** Ⓦ memmoalfama.com. Hidden behind the facade of a former house, paint factory and bakery lies this sleek boutique hotel. Parts of the ground floor contain the old brick ovens, though the real appeal is the bar with terraces at the back, complete with small plunge pool, offering sumptuous views over the Alfama and the Tagus. Rooms are compact but have all mod cons and most boast fine views. **€€€**

PALACETE CHAFARIZ D'EL REI MAP PAGE 38, POCKET MAP G12. **Trav Chafariz**

d'El Rei 6, tram #25 Ⓦ chafarizdelrei. com. Luxury guesthouse built in 1909 by a wealthy Brazilian merchant and lovingly restored a century later. From the reception – flooded with light from stained-glass windows – to the mirror room and library, the house is a stunning mix of Brazilian Art Nouveau and neo-Arabic flamboyance. Huge rooms, most with river views, have chandeliers and modern bathrooms, while stonking breakfasts keep you going till dinner time. It also has its own "teahouse", serving tasty Portuguese dishes in an ornate dining room. **€€€€**

SOLAR DO CASTELO MAP PAGE 38, POCKET MAP F11. **Rua das Cozinhas 2, bus #37** Ⓦ lisbonheritagehotels.com. A tastefully renovated eighteenth-century mansion abutting the castle walls on the site of the former royal palace kitchens, parts of which remain. Its twenty rooms cluster around a tranquil inner courtyard, where you can enjoy a vast buffet breakfast. Rooms aren't enormous, but most boast balconies overlooking the castle grounds, and service is second to none. **€€€**

SOLAR DOS MOUROS MAP PAGE 38, POCKET MAP F12. **Rua do Milagre de Santo António 6, tram #28** Ⓦ solardosmouroslisboa.com. A tall Alfama townhouse done out in a contemporary style with its own bar. Each of the twelve rooms offers fantastic vistas of the river or castle. There's plenty of art to enjoy if you tire of the view. **€€**

Chiado and Cais do Sodré

HOTEL BAIRRO ALTO MAP PAGE 52, POCKET MAP C12. **Praça Luís de Camões 2** Ⓜ **Baixa-Chiado** Ⓦ **bairroaltohotel.**

com. In the middle of trendy Chiado, this grand eighteenth-century building has been modernized into a fashionable boutique hotel. Rooms and communal areas still have a period feel, but a fantastic contemporary extension by architect Eduardo Souto de Moura brings the building bang into the twenty-first century. Great views from the top-floor rooms – and from the trendy rooftop café-bar. €€€€

HOTEL BORGES MAP PAGE 52, POCKET MAP C12. **Rua Garrett 108** ⚇ **Baixa-Chiado** ⚇ **hotelborges.com.** In a prime spot on Chiado's main street, this traditional and elegantly furnished three-star is very popular, though front rooms can be noisy. Double or triple rooms come in a variety of styles, but all are good value. €€

HOTEL DO CHIADO MAP PAGE 52, POCKET MAP D12. **Rua Nova do Almada 114** ⚇ **Baixa-Chiado** ⚇ **hoteldochiado.pt.** Designed by architect Álvaro Siza Vieira, this stylish hotel has lovely communal areas – orange segment-shaped windows offer glimpses of Chiado in one direction and the whole city in the other. The cheapest rooms lack much of an outlook, but the best ones have terraces with stunning views towards the castle – a view you get from the bar terrace too. Limited parking available. €€€€

LX BOUTIQUE MAP PAGE 52, POCKET MAP C13. **Rua do Alecrim 12** ⚇ **Cais do Sodré** ⚇ **lxboutiquehotel.com.** A tasteful makeover to an old townhouse has transformed *LX Boutique* into a popular small hotel with its own chic restaurant. Themed floors are named after Portuguese poets and fado singers. Rooms are all individual, with shutters and tasteful

lighting – try to nab one with river views rather than over Rua Nova do Carvalho. €€€

MARTINHAL CHIADO MAP PAGE 52, POCKET MAP C13. **Rua Flores 44** ⚇ **Baixa-Chiado** ⚇ **chiadomartinhal.com.** Taking up an entire block on the steep Rua Flores, this welcoming hotel is geared up to making family holidays a luxurious treat. Bright, spacious apartments come with their own kitchenettes if you want to self-cater, and most have comfy bunks for kids either alongside or in a separate room from large double beds. There's a kids' club, crèche, vaulted playroom and an alluring real car to clamber into in the breakfast room. The studios are ideal for couples too. €€€€

Bairro Alto and São Bento

CASA DE SÃO MAMEDE MAP PAGE 60, POCKET MAP H5. **Rua da Escola Politécnica 159, bus #1** ⚇ **casadesaomamede.pt.** On a busy street north of Príncipe Real, this eighteenth-century former magistrate's house has period fittings, a bright breakfast room and a grand stained-glass window. Rooms are rather plain, but all have a/c. €€

HOTEL PRÍNCIPE REAL MAP PAGE 60, POCKET MAP H5. **Rua da Alegria 53, bus #1** ⚇ **hotelprincipereal.com.** This small four-star sits on a quiet street just below the Bairro Alto. Eighteen rooms come with modern decor, some with balconies and superb city views. Best of all is the top-floor suite with stunning vistas. €€

THE INDEPENDENTE HOSTEL & SUITES MAP PAGE 60, POCKET MAP B10. **Rua de São Pedro de Alcântara 81** ⚇ **theindependente. eu.** This part hostel, part boutique hotel is set

Author picks

ART NOUVEAU *Hotel Lisboa 1908* see page 128
BUDGET *Home Hostel* see page 133
CHIC *Almalusa* see page 126
RETRO CHIC *Heritage Avenida* see page 131
FAMILY *Martinhal Chiado* see page 131
FIVE-STAR COMFORTS *PortoBay Liberdade* see page 131
HISTORIC *Palacete Chafariz d'el Rei* see page 128
UPMARKET *Casa Balthazar* see page 127
BEST ALL-ROUNDER *Pátio do Tijolo* see page 130

in a fantastic old building with far-reaching views over Lisbon. Lower floors house dorms (sleeping 6–12) with towering ceilings. Upstairs are quirky double rooms in the roof spaces, the best with balconies offering river views. There's a downstairs bar and patio, and the place offers everything from bar crawls to guided walks and cycle hire. The Suites element is in the building next door, offering larger rooms, a library and a hip bar on the roof terrace. **Dorms €, doubles/suites €€**

PÁTIO DO TIJOLO MAP PAGE 60, POCKET MAP B11. **Calçada do Tijolo 41A** ⓦ **patiodotijolo.com.** Tucked into a back road, this amazing boutique hideaway has been artfully remodelled from a former carpentry workshop. Spacious, contemporary rooms come with balconies offering sublime views (shared by the communal roof terrace) or have their own little garden. There is also a communal patio garden and breakfast room with complimentary hot drinks, cakes and fruit – all within a modern building neatly secreted into the historic neighbourhood. **€€€**

PENSÃO LONDRES MAP PAGE 60, POCKET MAP B10. **Rua Dom Pedro V 53, bus #1** ⓦ **pensaolondres.com.pt.** Wonderful old building with high ceilings and pleasant enough rooms sleeping up to four. Some have tiny bathrooms, but the best (402, 409 or 411) have great views over the city. **€**

Estrela, Lapa and Santos

AS JANELAS VERDES MAP PAGE 73, POCKET MAP G8. **Rua das Janelas Verdes 47, bus #727 or tram #25** ⓦ **lisbonheritagehotels.com.** This discreet eighteenth-century townhouse, where Eça de Queirós wrote *Os Maias*, is metres from the Museu Nacional de Arte Antiga. The spacious rooms come with marble bathrooms and period furnishings, most with Tejo views. Breakfast is served in the delightful walled garden in summer, while the top-floor library and terrace command fine river views. **€€€€**

OLISSIPPO LAPA PALACE MAP PAGE 73, POCKET MAP F7. **Rua do Pau da Bandeira 4** ⓦ **lapapalace.com.** A stunning nineteenth-century mansion set in its own lush gardens, with dramatic vistas over the Tejo. Rooms are luxurious, and those

in the Palace Wing are each decorated in a different style, from Classical to Art Deco. There's also a health club, disabled access and a list of facilities as long as your arm, from babysitting to banqueting. **€€€€**

YORK HOUSE MAP PAGE 73, POCKET MAP G7. **Rua das Janelas Verdes 32, bus #727 or tram #25** ⓦ **yorkhouselisboa.com.** Located in a sixteenth-century Carmelite convent (and hidden from the main street by high walls), rooms here are chic and minimalist. The best are grouped around a beautiful interior courtyard, where drinks and meals are served in summer, and there's a highly rated restaurant. **€€**

Alcântara and Belém

JERÓNIMOS 8 MAP PAGE 84, POCKET MAP C4. **Rua das Jerónimos 8, tram #15** ⓦ **almediahotels.pt.** In a great position for Belém's attractions, this hotel is housed in an attractive stone building with boutiquey touches – crisp white decor, marble bathrooms and a modern bar area, plus a substantial buffet breakfast. **€€**

PESTANA PALACE MAP PAGE 78, POCKET MAP C8. **Rua Jau 54, Tram #18** ⓦ **pestanapalacelisbon.com.** Set in an early twentieth-century palace full of priceless works of art, most beds at this five-star hotel are in tasteful modern wings that stretch either side of lush gardens. Many have large terraces and lie a short walk from a cocktail bar, a sunken outdoor pool with a fountain to swim out to, and an indoor pool and health club. The price, which can be greatly reduced for summer offers, includes a vast breakfast in the former ballroom. **€€€€**

Avenida, Parque Eduardo VII and the Gulbenkian

DOUBLE TREE FONTANA PARK MAP PAGE 92, POCKET MAP J3. **Rua Eng. Viera da Silva 2** ⓦ **Saldanha** ⓦ **hilton.com.** This buzzy designer hotel rises sleekly behind the facade of an old steelworks. Chic rooms – the best with terraces – come with Philippe Starck chromatic baths. The communal areas include a restaurant, bar and a courtyard garden with slate walls of running water. Cocktail nights with guest DJs complete the picture. **€€€**

EUROSTAR DAS LETRAS MAP PAGE 92, POCKET MAP H5. **Rua Castilho 6–12** Ⓜ **Avenida** Ⓦ **eurostarshotels.com**. Modern hotel with its own small gym and bar in a good position between the centre and the Bairro Alto. Rooms, named after writers, come with comfy beds, a choice of pillows and a complicated array of power showers. The best have balconies with downtown views. **€€**

HERITAGE AVENIDA LIBERDADE MAP PAGE 92, POCKET MAP J5. **Avda da Liberdade 28** Ⓜ **Restauradores** Ⓦ **lisbonheritagehotels. com**. In a fine mansion – whose ground floor once sold herbal remedies (the counter still remains) – this hotel superbly blends tradition and contemporary style. Though the dining area/bar is small, the rooms more than compensate with retro fittings and great cityscapes from top-floor rooms. There's also a gym and plunge pool. **€€€€**

HOTEL DAS AMOREIRAS MAP PAGE 92, POCKET MAP G5. **Praça das Amoreiras 34** Ⓜ **Rato** Ⓦ **hoteldasamoreiras.com**. In an enviable location facing one of Lisbon's loveliest small squares, this hotel has artfully reimagined a beautifully tiled townhouse. There's a pretty terrace at the back for breakfast or drinks, while very comfortable bedrooms come with large beds and coffee machines. Some face onto the square with its distinctive arches of the aqueduct. Impeccable service. **€€€€**

HOTEL AVENIDA PARK MAP PAGE 92, POCKET MAP H4. **Avda Sidónio Pais 6** Ⓜ **Parque** Ⓦ **avenidapark.com**. Good-sized rooms – beg for one with a view over the park for no extra charge – in a friendly, if dated, hotel on a quiet street. **€€**

HOTEL BRITANIA MAP PAGE 92, POCKET MAP J5. **Rua Rodrigues Sampaio 17** Ⓜ **Avenida** Ⓦ **lisbonheritagehotels.com**. Designed in the 1940s by influential architect Cassiano Branco, this Art Deco gem features huge airy rooms, each with traditional cork flooring and marble-clad bathrooms. The hotel interior, with library and bar, has been declared of national architectural importance. **€€€**

HOTEL DOM CARLOS PARQUE MAP PAGE 92, POCKET MAP H4. **Avda Duque de Loulé 121** Ⓜ **Marquês de Pombal** Ⓦ **hoteldomcarlospark.com**. Decent three-star just off Praça Marquês de Pombal, with fair-sized rooms over eight floors, each with plasma TV. Some overlook the neighbouring police and fire stations, which can add to the noise. There's a downstairs lounge bar and garage parking. **€€€**

HOTEL HOTEL MAP PAGE 92, POCKET MAP J6. **Travessa Glória 22** Ⓜ **Avenida** Ⓦ **hotelhotel.pt**. Buzzy modern hotel with comfy rooms, mostly set around the leafy courtyard pool. There's a good in-house restaurant, *Animal*, and, intriguingly, some stunning works of contemporary art outside the lifts on each floor, including one of a crow by street artist Bordalo II. **€€€€**

LISBOA PLAZA MAP PAGE 92, POCKET MAP J5. **Trav Salitre 7** Ⓜ **Avenida** Ⓦ **lisbonheritagehotels.com**. A tasteful, understated former Portuguese family home with marble bathrooms, a bar and fashionable rooftop terrace, a short walk from the main Avenida. Welcoming staff and good for families as well as being pet friendly. Limited disabled access. **€€€**

NH COLLECTION LISBOA LIBERDADE MAP PAGE 92, POCKET MAP J5. **Avda da Liberdade 180b** Ⓜ **Avenida** Ⓦ **nh-hotels. com**. Discreetly tucked into the back of the Tivoli forum shopping centre off the main Avenida, this Spanish chain hotel offers ten floors of modern flair. The best rooms have balconies facing the traditional Lisbon houses at the back. Unusually for central Lisbon, there's a rooftop pool. There's also a bar and restaurant. **€€€€**

PORTOBAY LIBERDADE MAP PAGE 92, POCKET MAP H5. **Rua Rosa Araújo 8** Ⓜ **Avenida or Pombal** Ⓦ **portobay.com**. Lisbon's top choice for five-star comforts with a range of facilities from an indoor pool with its own garden to a gym and spa. Some of the super-comfy rooms have a balcony or terrace, and there's also a top restaurant, a wine cellar and very appealing rooftop bar, *Deck 7*, which hosts occasional live music in summer. All of this is artfully secreted behind the façade of a traditional building. **€€€€**

SANA REX MAP PAGE 92, POCKET MAP G4. **Rua Castilho 169** Ⓜ **Marquês de Pombal/ Parque** Ⓦ rex.sanahotellisboa.com. One of the less outrageously priced hotels in this neck of the woods, with small but well-equipped rooms and a bar. The best are at the front, sporting large balconies overlooking Parque Eduardo VII. €€€

SHERATON LISBOA MAP PAGE 92, POCKET MAP J3. **Rua Latino Coelho 1** Ⓜ **Picoas** Ⓦ marriott.com. This 1970s high-rise is something of an icon in this part of Lisbon and a mecca for those seeking five-star spa facilities. The dated exterior hides modern attractions, including a heated outdoor pool, swanky rooms and a top-floor bar and restaurant with dazzling city views. €€€€

Sintra

CASA DO VALLE MAP PAGE 110. **Rua da Paderna 2** Ⓦ casadovalle.com. Though steeply downhill from the historic centre, this charming guesthouse still commands unbeatable views across the wooded slopes of Sintra. Rooms range from top-floor doubles with the best views, to ground-floor rooms with terraces. All rooms access a beautiful garden with its own pool. Good for families. Breakfast is extra. €€

CHALET RELOGIO MAP PAGE 110. **Estrada da Pena 22, Sintra-Vila** Ⓦ goaway.pt/en/ hotel/chalet-relogio-guesthouse. Architect Luigi Manini, who worked on the Quinta da Regaleira (see page 111), designed this mansion with a distinctive clock tower. Rooms are simply furnished but enormous, with big windows and high ceilings, and there's a garden too, though it's a long walk to town and you'll need a car. €

CHALET SAUDADE MAP PAGE 110. **Rua Dr. Alfredo Costa 21** Ⓦ saudade.pt. This tall eighteenth-century chalet has been superbly renovated by a Portuguese couple

who have retained many of the quirky but charming original fittings. The interior is all parquet flooring, swirling stairways, stained glass and beautiful *azulejos*. Stairs lead down three floors to rooms of varying sizes: if possible, pay extra to bag the one opening onto the garden. Breakfast is offered at *Saudade Café* (see page 117). €€€

HOTEL ARRIBAS MAP PAGE 113. **Avda A Coelho 28, Praia Grande** Ⓦ hotelarribas. pt. This three-star is plonked ungraciously above the beach. Large rooms come with minibars and satellite TV – those with a sea view are hard to fault – while family rooms sleep up to four. There's also a massive seawater swimming pool, a restaurant and café terrace, and disabled access. €€€

HOTEL NOVA SINTRA MAP PAGE 110. **Largo Afonso de Albuquerque 25, Estefânia** Ⓦ novasintra.com. A friendly hotel in a big mansion, whose elevated terrace-café overlooks a busy street. The modern rooms all have cable TV and shiny marble floors, and there's a decent restaurant. Two-night minimum stay in high season. €€€

HOTEL SINTRA JARDIM MAP PAGE 110. **Trav dos Avelares 12, São Pedro** Ⓦ hotelsintrajardim.pt. The best mid-range option in the area, this rambling old hotel has soaring ceilings, wooden floors and oodles of character. In winter there's a log fire in the communal lounge. A large garden shelters a swimming pool, and the giant rooms can easily accommodate extra beds, so it's great for families. €€

Lisbon coast

FAROL HOTEL MAP PAGE 120. **Avda Rei Humberto II de Italia 7, Cascais** Ⓦ farol.com. pt. Right on the seafront, this is one of the area's most fashionable hideaways, neatly combining traditional and contemporary architecture. A new designer wing has been

Lisbon hostels

Lisbon and its surroundings have some of Europe's best independent hostels. A youth hostel card is required for the official Portuguese hostels (*pousadas de juventude*), but you can buy one on your first night's stay. Unless stated, prices do not include breakfast.

welded onto a sixteenth-century villa, and the best rooms have sea views and terraces. There's also a restaurant, fairy-lit outside bar and seapool facing a fine rocky foreshore. €€€€

HOTEL BAÍA MAP PAGE 120. Avda Marginal, Cascais ⓦ hotelbaia.com. Large seafront hotel with 113 a/c rooms; the front ones have balconies overlooking the beach. There's a great rooftop terrace with a covered pool, and a good restaurant. Parking is extra. €€€€

THE PERGOLA MAP PAGE 120. Avda Valbom 13, Cascais ⓦ thepergola.pt. Sumptuous century-old mansion in the centre of town, with its own garden, stucco ceilings and ornate tiled dining room. Each room has its own character, some with balconies. €€€

REAL CAPARICA HOTEL Rua Mestre Manuel 18, Caparica ⓦ hoteisdirect.com. Friendly and reasonably priced central hotel, a few minutes' walk from the beach, just off Rua dos Pescadores. Small but pleasant rooms come with TVs and baths. Ask for one of the rooms with a balcony and sea views. €€

VILA BICUDA MAP PAGE 120. Rua dos Faisões, Cascais ⓦ vilabicuda.com. A very well-run, upmarket villa complex set in its own grounds, with two large swimming pools. Excellent for families, the modern villas are well equipped, and the complex has its own great café, shop and (pricey) Italian restaurant. But you'll need a car – it's around 3km from central Cascais towards Guincho. Studios €€€

Hostels

HOME HOSTEL MAP PAGE 26, POCKET MAP E12. Rua de São Nicolau 13–2 ⓦ homelisbonhostel.com. In the heart of the Baixa, this highly rated hostel comes with four-, six- or eight-bed dorms, double rooms, fantastic home cooking, a buzzy communal lounge and the opportunity to sign up to walking tours and pub nights. Dorms €, doubles €€€

LISBON LOUNGE HOSTEL MAP PAGE 26, POCKET MAP D12. Rua de São Nicolau 41 Ⓜ Rossio ⓦ lisbonlounge.com. A popular independent hostel in a Baixa townhouse full of stripped floorboards, comfy sofas and books. Meals on request. €

LOST INN MAP PAGE 52, POCKET MAP C13. Beco dos Apóstolos 6 Ⓜ Baixa-Chiado ⓦ lostinnlisbon.eu. In a great old building on a quiet side street a short walk from Chiado or Cais do Sodré, this hostel has six-to ten-bed mixed or single-sex dorms and cosy doubles. There's also a bar, dining area and communal kitchen. €

LX HOSTEL MAP PAGE 78, POCKET MAP D8. Rua Rodrigues de Faria 103 ⓦ lxhostel.pt. Expect a laidback vibe at this first-floor hostel in one of the hip LX Factory's converted warehouses, which uses upcycled furniture in its spacious common

room and kitchenette. There are two private rooms with shared bathroom, along with three cubicle-style dorms (one women only) sleeping six to twelve: curtains across the front offer an extra layer of privacy. There's a great rooftop bar, and LX Factory's restaurants are on your doorstep. €

POUSADA DE JUVENTUDE DE OEIRAS MAP PAGE 110. Estrada Marginal, Oeiras ⓦ pousadasjuventude.pt. This hostel is set in an eighteenth-century sea-fort overlooking the sea pools in Oeiras, a suburb on the train line to Cascais. Parking is available. Dorms/twins €

POUSADA DE JUVENTUDE DE LISBOA MAP PAGE 92, POCKET MAP H3. Rua Andrade Corvo 46 Ⓜ Picoas ⓦ pousadasjuventude. pt. The main city hostel, spread across a rambling old building, with a small bar, canteen, TV room and disabled access. There are thirty dorms sleeping four to six, as well as en-suite rooms. €

POUSADA DE JUVENTUDE LISBOA PARQUE DAS NAÇÕES MAP PAGE 104, POCKET MAP A16. Rua de Moscavide 47–101, Parque das Nações Ⓜ Oriente ⓦ pousadasjuventude.pt. A 5min walk from the Torre Vasco da Gama, this smart hostel has a pool table and disabled access. €

ESSENTIALS

Make time for a coffee and a *pastéis de nata*

Arrival

Lisbon airport is right on the edge of the city and is well served by buses and taxis. The train stations are all centrally located and connected to the metro; the main bus station is also close to metro and train stops.

By plane

Humberto Delgado Airport, or Lisbon Airport (Ⓦ aeroportolisboa.pt), is north of the city centre and has a tourist office (☏ 218 450 660; daily 7am–10pm), a 24hr exchange bureau and left-luggage facilities.

The easiest way into the city is by **taxi**; a journey to Rossio should cost around €15. The airport is also on the red Oriente line of the **metro** (see page 136), although you'll need to change at Alameda for the centre. **Local bus** #744 runs to Praça Marquês de Pombal (every 10–15min; €2.20) but is less convenient if you have a lot of luggage.

By train

Long-distance **trains** are run by CP (Comboios de Portugal, Ⓦ cp.pt). You'll arrive at Oriente station (on the red Oriente line) at Parque das Nações. There are regular connections to the more central Santa Apolónia station, from where you can access the blue Gaivota metro line or take a bus west to Praça do Comércio. Some trains also stop at Entrecampos (on the yellow Amarela line).

By bus

The national **bus** carrier is Rede Expressos (Ⓦ rede-expressos.pt). Most services terminate at Sete Rios, next to the Jardim Zoológico metro stop (for the centre) and Sete Rios train line (for Sintra and the northern suburbs). Some bus services, such as FlixBus, also stop at the Oriente station at Parque das Nações on the red Oriente metro line.

By car

Apart from weekends, when the city is quiet, **driving** round Lisbon is best avoided, though it is useful to hire a car to see the outlying sights. Parking is difficult in central Lisbon; pay-and-display spots are snapped up quickly. It may be easier to head for an official car park, for which you pay around €3–4 an hour or €30 a day. Do not leave valuables inside your car.

Getting around

Central Lisbon is compact enough to explore on **foot**, but don't be fooled by the apparent closeness of sights as they appear on maps. There are some very steep hills to negotiate, although the city's quirky *elevadores* (funicular railways) will save you the steepest climbs. Tram, bus and *elevador* stops are indicated by a sign marked "paragem", which carries route details.

Metro stations (Ⓜ) are located close to most of the main sights. Suburban trains run from Rossio and Sete Rios stations to Sintra and from Cais do Sodré station to Belém, Estoril and Cascais, while ferries (Ⓦ transtejo.pt) link Lisbon's Cais do Sodré to Cacilhas, for the resort of Caparica.

The metro

Lisbon's efficient **metro** (Metropolitano, daily 6.30am–1am, Ⓦ metrolisboa. pt) is the quickest way of reaching the city's main sights, with trains every few minutes. Tickets cost €1.85 per journey, or €1.66 with a Navegante card (see page 137) – sold at all stations (see the inside cover and pull-out map for the network diagram). The metro also accepts contactless card payments.

Buses and trams

City trams and buses (daily 6.30am–midnight) are operated by Carris (🖥 carris.pt). **Buses** (*autocarros*) run just about everywhere in the Lisbon area – the most useful ones are outlined in the box on page 137.

Trams (*eléctricos*) run on six routes, which are marked on the chapter maps. Ascending some of the steepest urban gradients in the world, most are worth taking for the ride alone, especially the cross-city tram #28 (see page 45). Another picturesque route is #12, which circles the castle area via Largo Martim Moniz. Other useful routes are "supertram" #15 from Praça da Figueira to Belém (signed Algés), and #18, which runs from Cais do Sodré via Praça do Comércio to the Palácio da Ajuda. Tram #25 trundles from near the Praça da Figueira to Campo Ourique via Santos, Lapa and Estrela. The remaining route, #24, connects Praça Luis Camões in Chiado to Compolide, via the Bairro Alto.

Elevadores

There are also several **elevadores**. These consist of two funicular railways offering quick access to the heights of the Bairro Alto (though the future of these is uncertain following the 2025 tragedy at Elevador da Glória; see pages 58 and 59) and to the eastern side of Avenida da Liberdade (see page 90); and one giant lift,

the Elevador da Santa Justa (see page 29) which climbs up to the foot of the Bairro Alto near Chiado. There are also free street lifts offering access to the lower edges of the Castelo de São Jorge (see map page 38).

Tickets and passes

On board **tickets** cost €2.20 (buses), €3.20 (trams), €4.20 for *elevadores* (valid for two trips) and €6.10 for the Elevador da Santa Justa. You need to buy a separate card for train lines to Sintra or Cascais. Note that the modern tram #15 has an automatic ticket machine on board and does not issue change.

It's possible just to buy a ticket each time you ride, but **passes**, available from any main metro station, can save you money. First, buy a rechargeable Navegante card (€0.50), which you can load up with up with credit (€3–€40), after which €1.66 is deducted for each bus or metro journey. Buses also accept contactless card payments.

You can also buy a one-day Bilhete 1dia pass (€7, or €11 including trains to Sintra and Cascais), which allows unlimited travel on buses, trams, the metro and *elevadores* for 24 hours after it is first used.

If you're planning intensive sightseeing, the Cartão Lisboa (🖥 www.lisboacard.org; €31 for one day, €51 for two, €62 for three) is a good buy. The card entitles you to unlimited

Useful bus routes

#22b A useful circular route from Cais do Sodré, passing round most of the Bairro Alto.
#201 Night bus from Cais do Sodré to the docks via Santos; until 5am.
#728 Belém to Parque das Nações via Santa Apolónia station.
#737 Praça da Figueira to Castelo de São Jorge via the Sé and Alfama.
#744 Outside the airport to Marquês de Pombal via Saldanha and Picoas (for the youth hostel).
#727 Marquês de Pombal to Belém via Santos and Alcântara.
#773 Rato to Alcântara via Príncipe Real, Estrela and Lapa.

Sightseeing tours

Bus, tram and river tours Yellow Buses (ⓦyellowbustours. com) offers tours around various parts of the city, including the Hills Tram route on a historic tram; a bus and tram tour, which includes rides to Belém and Parque das Naçoes; and river cruises on the Tejo.

River cruises Various boat tours take in the sights of Lisbon from the river, most leaving from the Sul Sueste ferry terminal (see map page 26) by Praça do Comércio. Expect to pay €15–25 for a 1hr 30min tour. A fun option is a 1hr 30min land and river tour offered by Hippotrip (ⓦhippotrip.com; €30) on an amphibious vehicle, with departures from Doca de Santo Amaro.

Walks Recommended themed two- to three-hour guided walks are offered by Lisbon Walker (ⓦlisbonwalker.com; €25), departing daily from Praça do Comércio at 10am, giving expert insight into the quirkier aspects of the city's sites, including secret histories and spies.

Segway and cycle tours Lisbon Segway Tours (ⓦlisbonsegway tours.pt) runs various Segway tours of the city from around €55 for two hours; it also offers e-bike tours (€55 for three hours).

Tuk-tuk tours Various companies offer tours in three-wheeled tuk-tuks that can negotiate Lisbon's steepest and narrow streets around the Alfama. Prices start at around €75 an hour and depart from outside the Sé cathedral and also Sintra train station.

rides on buses, trams, *elevadores* and the metro as well as free entry to, or discounts for, around 25 museums. It's available online and from all the main tourist offices. The same website also has discount passes for Sintra.

Taxis

Lisbon's cream **taxis** have a minimum charge of €3.25; an average ride across town is €10–15. Fares are twenty percent higher from 9pm to 6am, at weekends and on public holidays. Bags in the boot incur a €1.60 fee. Meters should be switched on, and tips are not expected. Outside the rush hour,

taxis can be flagged down quite easily, or head for one of the ranks such as those outside the main train stations. At night, it's best to phone a taxi (attracts an extra charge of €0.80): try Teletaxis (☏218 111 100 ⓦteletaxis. pt). Alternatively, Uber operates throughout the city (ⓦuber.com).

Car rental

Rental agents include: Avis ⓦavis. com.pt; Budget ⓦbudget.com.pt; Europcar ⓦeuropcar.com; Hertz airport ⓦhertz.com. For more information on driving in Lisbon see page 136.

Directory A–Z

Accessible travel

Lisbon airport offers a service for **wheelchair-users** if advance notice is given to your airline (details on ⓦaeroportolisboa.pt), while the

Orange Badge symbol is recognized for disabled car parking. The main public transport company, Carris, offers an inexpensive dial-a-ride minibus service, O Serviço Mobilidade

Emergencies

For police, fire and ambulance services, dial ☎112

Reduzida especial, (€2 per trip; Mon–Fri 6.30am–9.30pm, Sat & Sun 8am–noon & 2–6pm; ☎213 613 141 ⓦbit.ly/CarrisServices), though two days' advance notice and a medical certificate are required.

Addresses

Addresses are written in the form "Rua do Crucifixo 50–4°", meaning the fourth storey of no. 50, Rua do Crucifixo. The addition of e, d or r/c at the end means the entrance is on the left (*esquerda*), right (*direita*) or on the ground floor (*rés-do-chão*).

Bike hire

Most of Lisbon is very hilly, but the riverfront is flat and good for cycling. There are bike-hire outlets at Belém (see page 83) and near Cais de Sodré station (ⓦlisbonbikerentals. com). Expect to pay around €5 an hour.

Children

Portugal is very child-friendly, and kids are welcome in most restaurants and cafés. While dedicated children's menus are rare, most restaurants will serve a half-portion (*meia dose*) of dishes from the menu. Beware that many of the streets are narrow, cobbled and steep, so can be awkward for pushchairs.

Cinemas

Mainstream **films** are shown at various multiplexes around the city, usually with Portuguese subtitles. Listings can be found on ⓦagendalx.pt. The Instituto da Cinemateca Portuguesa (Rua Barata Salgueiro 39 ⓜAvenida ⓦcinemateca.pt), the national film theatre, has twice-daily shows and contains its own cinema museum. In summer, check out The Black Cat

Cinema (ⓦtheblackcatcinema.com), which shows open-air films in eye-catching locations such as the Igreja da Graça and the beach at Caparica.

Crime

Violent crime is very rare, but pickpocketing is common, especially on public transport.

Electricity

Portugal uses two-pin plugs (220/240v). UK appliances will work with a continental adaptor.

Embassies and consulates

Australia, Avenida da Liberdade 2002 ⓜAvenida ☎213 101 500; Canada, Avenida da Liberdade 198–200-3° ⓜAvenida ☎213 164 600; Ireland, Avenida da Liberdade 200–4° ⓜAvenida ☎213 308 200; South Africa, Avda Luís Bivar 10 ⓜPicoas ☎213 192 200; UK, Rua de São Bernardo 33 ⓜRato ☎213 924 000 ⓦgov.uk/ world/portugal; US, Avenida das Forças Armadas ⓜJardim Zoológico ☎217 273 300 ⓦpt.usembassy.gov.

Event listings

The best listings magazine is the free monthly *Agenda Cultural* (ⓦagendalx. pt), produced by the town hall (in Portuguese). *Follow me Lisboa* is an English-language version published by the local tourist office. Both are available from the tourist offices and larger hotels and can be downloaded from ⓦvisitlisboa.com.

Health

EU citizens with a **European Health Insurance Card** (EHIC; available online in Ireland from http://hse ie) have access to Portuguese state public-health services under reciprocal agreements. Show the card and your passport at a health centre or hospital for treatment. While the EHIC guarantees free or reduced-cost medical care in the event of minor injuries and emergencies, it won't cover every eventuality – you'll have to pay for X-rays, lab tests and the like, so proper a travel insurance policy with full health coverage is essential. If you don't have an EHIC card, you'll have to pay upfront and claim it back via your insurance, so obtain receipts.

UK residents who still have an EHIC can use that until it expires, at which point they can apply for a **Global Health Insurance Card** (GHIC; apply online at http://bit.ly/GHICCard), which entitles them to reciprocal free or reduced-cost medical treatment. Despite the reciprocal arrangement afforded by this system, private medical insurance is recommended.

Pharmacies are open Mon–Fri 9am–1pm & 3–7pm, Sat 9am–1pm. Details of **24hr pharmacies** are posted on every pharmacy door, or call ☎ 118. The most central hospital is Hospital de Santa Maria (Avenida Prof. Egas Moniz Ⓜ Entre Campos ☎ 217 805 000 Ⓦ www.chln.pt), which is part of the North Lisbon University Hospital Center (CHULN). There are various other public hospitals around the city.

Internet
Most hotels, cafés, bars and restaurants offer free wi-fi.

Left luggage
There are 24hr lockers at the airport, main train and bus station, charging around €5 per day (up to €20 at the airport); for alternative venues around the city, check Ⓦ radicalstorage.com.

LGBTQ+ travellers
The Centro LGBTI+ (Rua dos Fanqueieros 40 Ⓜ Martim Moniz ☎ 218 873 918; Thurs–Fri 7–10pm, Sat 3–11pm;) is the main LGBTQ+ community centre, run by ILGA, whose website (Ⓦ ilga-portugal.pt) is in Portuguese.

Lost property
Report any loss to the **tourist police** station in the Foz Cultura building in Palácio Foz, Praça dos Restauradores (daily 24hr ☎ 213 421 634 Ⓦ safe communitiesportugal.com/psp-lisbon-tourism-support). For items left on public transport, contact Ⓦ carris.pt.

Money
Portugal uses the **euro** (€). Banks open Monday to Friday 8.30am–3pm. Most central branches have automatic exchange machines for various currencies. You can withdraw up to €300 per day from ATMs ("Multibanco") with a maximum €200 per transaction – check fees with your home bank. Credit/debit cards are widely accepted, as are contactless payments.

Opening hours
Most **shops** open Monday to Saturday 9am–7pm; smaller shops close for lunch (around 1–3pm) and on Saturday afternoons; shopping centres are open daily until 10pm or later. Most **museums** and **monuments** open Tuesday to Sunday 10am–6pm.

Opera
Lisbon's main opera house is the Rococo Teatro Nacional São Carlos (Rua Serpa Pinto 9; Ⓦ tnsc.pt).

Phones
Most European-subscribed **mobile phones** will work in Lisbon, and those with mobiles from EU countries will pay no additional roaming charges. For other nationalities, including UK citizens, check with your provider whether there are extra charges for using roaming minutes and data while in Portugal before you travel.

Eating out price codes

Each restaurant and café reviewed in this Guide is accompanied by a price category, based on the cost of a two-course meal (or similar) for one, including a drink.

€ = under €20
€€ = €21–35
€€€ = €36–50
€€€€ = over €50

Sports

Lisbon boasts two of Europe's top **football** teams (see page 98): Benfica (Ⓦslbenfica.pt) and Sporting (Ⓦsporting.pt). Fixtures and news on Ⓦligaportugal.pt. The area also contains some of Europe's best **golf courses**, especially around Cascais and Estoril (Ⓦportugalgolf. pt). The Atlantic beaches at Caparica and Guincho are ideal for **surfing** and windsurfing, and international competitions are frequently held there (Ⓦsurfingportugal.com). **Horseriding** is superb in the Sintra hills. The Estoril Open in April/May draws **tennis** fans to the city (Ⓦmillenniumestorilopen. com), and thousands of runners hit the streets for the **Lisbon Marathon** (Ⓦmaratonaclubedeportugal.com), held in September/October.

Tickets

You can **buy tickets** for Lisbon's theatres and concerts from the desk in FNAC (Ⓦbilheteira.fnac.pt) in the Armazéns do Chiado shopping centre (see page 54), as well as the venues. Buy online tickets at Ⓦticketline.sapo. pt or Ⓦblueticket.meo.pt.

Time

Portuguese **time** is the same as Greenwich Mean Time (GMT). Clocks go forward an hour in late March and back to GMT in late October.

Tipping

Service charges are included in hotel and restaurant bills. A ten percent tip is usual for restaurant bills, and hotel porters and toilet attendants expect at least €0.50.

Toilets

There are few **public toilets** in the streets, although they can be found in nearly all main tourist sights (signed variously as *casa de banho*, *retrete*, *banheiro*, *lavabos* or "WC"), or sneak into a café or restaurant if need be. Gents are usually marked "H" (*homens*) or "C" (*cabalheiros*), and ladies "M" (*mulheres*) or "S" (*senhoras*).

Tourist information

Lisbon's main **tourist office** is the useful **Ask Me** centre located at Praça do Comércio Loja 1 (see map page 26; daily 10am–7pm; ☎ 210 312 810, Ⓦvisitlisboa.com), which can supply accommodation lists, bus timetables and local maps. There is another large tourist office situated at Palácio Foz, Praça dos Restauradores (daily 10am–7pm; ☎ 213 463 314).

Tourist offices at the airport (see page 136) and at Santa Apolónia station (Tues–Sat 10am–7pm; ☎ 910 517 982) can help you find accommodation, as can a few smaller "Ask Me" kiosks dotted around town, like the one opposite Belém's Torre de Belém (all daily 10am–7pm).

There are also Ask Me tourist offices in all the main **day-trip destinations**: Sintra Turismo (see map page 110; daily 10am–6pm, until 7pm in August; ☎ 219 231 157, Ⓦsintraromantica.not); Cascais Turismo (Praça 5 de Outubro;

daily 9am–6pm; until 8pm in summer; ☎ 214 666 230, ⓦ visitcascais.com); and Caparica Turismo (Frente Urbana de Praias; Mon–Sat 9.30am–1pm & 2–5.30pm, Oct–March closed Sat; ☎ 212 900 071, ⓦ cm-almada.pt).

Travel agents
The well-informed Top Atlântico, located at Rua do Ouro 109

(ⓦ topatlantico.pt), Baixa, also acts as an American Express agent.

Water
Lisbon's **water** is safe to drink, though you may prefer bottled water, which is sold in any supermarket, though tourist shops and restaurants charge considerably more.

Festivals and events

Carnival
February–March
Brazilian-style parades and costumes, mainly at Parque das Nações.

Peixe em Lisboa
March–April
ⓦ **tasteatlas.com/peixemlisboa**
Lisbon's annual fish festival takes place in Parque Eduardo VII and includes masterclasses by top chefs.

Sintra Music Festival
May or June ⓦ **festivaldesintra.pt**
Performances by international orchestras and dance groups in and around Sintra, Estoril and Cascais, often in historic buildings.

Rock in Rio Lisboa
May or June (even years)
ⓦ **rockinriolisboa.sapo.pt**
Five-day mega rock festival in Parque Bela Vista, in the north of the city.

Santos Populares
June
A series of city-wide events loosely based around three saints' days. Lisbon's main festival is for its adopted saint, Santo António. On June 12 a parade down Avenida da Liberdade is followed by a giant street party in the Alfama, and the whole city is decked out in coloured ribbons with pots of lucky basil placed on windowsills.

Lisboa Pride
June/July ⓦ **ilga-portugal.pt**
Lisbon's popular LGBTQ+ Pride changes venues, but in recent years has been held at Praça do Comércio.

Superbock Superrock
July ⓦ **superbocksuperrock.pt**
One of the country's largest rock festivals, at Praia do Meco, though the 2025 event was cancelled as the organizers seek a new promoter.

NOS Alive
July ⓦ **nosalive.com**
Another big-time rock festival at the Passeio Marítimo de Algés, on the riverfront west of Belém.

Jazz em Augusto
August ⓦ **gulbenkian.pt/jazzemagosto**
Big annual (Jazz in August) festival at the Gulbenkian's open-air amphitheatre.

Christmas (natal)
The main Christmas celebration is midnight Mass on December 24, followed by a meal of *bacalhau*.

New Year's Eve (ano novo)
The best place for New Year's Eve is Praça do Comércio, where fireworks light up the riverfront, while the New Year's Day swim at Carcavelos Beach is a popular hangover cure.

Public holidays

In addition to Christmas (Dec 24–25) and New Year's Day, public holidays include Shrove Tuesday (Feb/March); Good Friday (March/April); April 25 (Liberty Day); May 1 (Labour Day); Corpus Christi (late May/early June); June 10 (Portugal/Camões Day); June 12 (Santo António); Feast of the Assumption (Aug 15); Republic Day (Oct 5); All Saint's Day (Nov 1); Independence Day (Dec 1); Immaculate Conception (Dec 8).

Chronology

60 BC Julius Caesar establishes Olisipo as the capital of the Roman Empire's western colony.

711 Moors from North Africa conquer Iberia, building a fortress by the *alhama* (hot springs), now known as Alfama.

1147 Afonso Henriques, the first king of the newly established Portuguese state, retakes Lisbon from the Moors and builds a cathedral on the site of the former mosque.

1495–1521 The reign of Dom Manuel I coincides with the golden age of Portuguese exploration. So-called "Manueline" architecture celebrates the new sea routes. The 1494 Treaty of Tordesillas gives Spain and Portugal trading rights to much of the globe.

1498 Vasco da Gama returns to Belém with spices from India, which helps fund the monastery of Jerónimos.

1581 Victorious after the battle of Alcántara, Philip II of Spain becomes Filipe I of Portugal, and Portugal loses its independence.

1640 Portuguese conspirators storm the palace in Lisbon and install the Duke of Bragança as João IV, ending Spanish rule.

1706–50 Under João V, gold and diamonds from Brazil kickstart a second golden age; lavish building programmes include the Aqueduto das Águas Livres.

1755 The Great Earthquake flattens much of Lisbon. The Baixa is rebuilt in "Pombaline" style, named after the Marquês de Pombal.

1800s Maria II (1843–53) rules with German consort, Fernando II, and establishes the palaces at Ajuda and Pena in Sintra. Fado becomes popular in the Alfama. Avenida da Liberdade is laid out.

1900–10 Carlos I is assassinated in Lisbon in 1908, while two years later, the exile of Manuel II marks the end of the monarchy and birth of the Republic.

1932–68 Salazar's dictatorship sees development stagnate. Despite massive rural poverty, elaborate "New State" architecture includes the Ponte 25 de Abril, originally named Ponte de Salazar.

1974 April 25 marks a largely peaceful Revolution. Former Portuguese colonies are granted independence, leading to large-scale immigration.

1986 Entry to the European Community enables a rapid redevelopment of Lisbon.

1990s Lisbon's role as Capital of Culture (1994) and host of Expo '98 helps fund a metro extension, the Ponte Vasco da Gama and the Parque das Nações.

2000–05 In 2004 Lisbon hosts the European Football Championships. Fado star Mariza brings the music to an international audience.

2005–2015 EU leaders sign the Lisbon Treaty on Dec 13, 2007, agreeing a draft constitution. Ten new upmarket hotels open in 2014, adding to Lisbon's burgeoning hotel scene.

2016 Socialist António Costa wins a controversial election with the support of the Communist party, vowing to "turn the page on austerity".

2018 Lisbon's Altice (now Meo) Arena hosts the Eurovision Song Contest, boosting an already record-high number of visitors to the city.

2020–2021 Lisbon suffers a series of lockdowns during the Covid pandemic, though rates in Portugal remained well below the EU average.

2022–2023 Tourist numbers bounce back to almost record numbers as Lisbon establishes itself as one of the most popular – and least expensive – city-break destinations.

2024 During the year when Lisbon celebrates the 50th anniversary of the revolution that threw out the right-wing regime, the centre-right Democratic Alliance forms a minority government under Luís Montenegro, with the populist Chega party coming third.

Portuguese

English is widely spoken in most of Lisbon's hotels and tourist restaurants, but you will find a few words of Portuguese extremely useful. Written Portuguese is similar to Spanish, though pronunciation is very different. Vowels are often nasal or ignored altogether. The consonants are, at least, consistent:

Consonants

c is soft before e and i, hard otherwise unless it has a cedilla – *açucar* (sugar) is pronounced "assookar".
ch is somewhat softer than in English; *chá* (tea) sounds like Shah.
j is like the "s" in pleasure, as is g except when it comes before a "hard" vowel (a, o and u).
lh sounds like "lyuh".
q is always pronounced as a "k".
s before a consonant or at the end of a word becomes "sh", otherwise it's as in English – Cascais is pronounced "Kashkaish".
x is also pronounced "sh"– Baixa is pronounced "Baisha".

Vowels

e/é: e at the end of a word is silent unless it has an accent, so that *carne* (meat) is pronounced "karn", while *café* is "caf-ay".
ã or õ: the tilde renders the pronunciation much like the French -an and -on endings, only more nasal.
ão: this sounds something like a strangled "Ow!" cut off in midstream (as in *pão*, bread – *são*, saint – *limão*, lemon).
ei: this sounds like "ay" (as in *feito* – finished)
ou: sounds like "oh" (as in *roupa* – clothes)

Words and phrases

Basics

sim yes
não no
olá hello
bom dia good morning
boa tarde/noite good afternoon/night
adeus goodbye
até logo see you later
hoje today
amanhã tomorrow
por favor/se faz favor please

tudo bem? everything all right?
está bem it's all right/OK
obrigado/a thank you (male/ female speaker)
onde where
que what
quando when
porquê why
como how
quanto how much
não sei I don't know
sabe...? do you know...?
pode...? could you...?
há...? (silent "h") is there...? there is
tem...? (pron. "taying") do you have...?
queria... I'd like...
desculpe sorry
com licença excuse me
fala Inglês? do you speak English?
não compreendo I don't understand
este/a this
esse/a that
agora now
mais tarde later
mais more
menos less
grande big
pequeno little
aberto open
fechado closed
senhoras women
homens men
lavabo/quarto de banho toilet/bathroom

Getting around

esquerda left
direita right
sempre em frente straight ahead
aqui here
ali there
perto near
longe far
Onde é... Where is ...
 a estação de camionetas? the bus station?
 a paragem de autocarro para... the bus
stop for...
Donde parte o autocarro para...? Where
does the bus to...leave from?
A que horas parte? (chega a...?) What time
does it leave? (arrive at...?)
Pare aqui por favor Stop here please

bilhete (para) ticket (to)
ida e volta round trip

Common signs

aberto open
fechado closed
entrada entrance
saída exit
puxe pull
empurre push
elevador lift
pré-pagamento pay in advance
perigo/perigoso danger/ous
proibido estacionar no parking
obras (road) works

Accommodation

Queria um quarto I'd like a room
É para uma noite (semana) It's for one
night (week)
É para uma pessoa (duas pessoas) It's for
one person/two people
Quanto custa? How much is it?
Posso ver? May I see/ look?
Há um quarto mais barato? Is there a
cheaper room?
com duche with a shower

Shopping

Quanto é? How much is it?
banco; câmbio bank; change
correios post office
(dois) selos (two) stamps
Como se diz isto em Português? What's this
called in Portuguese?
O que é isso? What's that?
saldo sale
esgotado sold out

Days of the week

Domingo Sunday
Segunda-feira Monday
Terça-feira Tuesday
Quarta-feira Wednesday
Quinta-feira Thursday
Sexta-feira Friday
Sábado Saturday

Months

Janeiro January

Fevereiro February
Março March
Abril April
Maio May
Junho June
Julho July
Agosto August
Aetembro September
Outubro October
Novembro November
Dezembro December

Useful words

azulejo glazed, painted tile
cais quay
casa house
centro comercial shopping centre
estação station
estrada/rua street/road
feira fair or market
igreja church
jardim garden
miradouro viewpoint/belvedere
praça/largo square

Numbers

um/uma 1
dois/duas 2
três 3
quatro 4
cinco 5
seis 6
sete 7
oito 8
nove 9
dez 10
onze 11
doze 12
treze 13
catorze 14
quinze 15
dezasseis 16
dezassete 17
dezoito 18
dezanove 19
vinte 20
vinte e um 21
trinta 30
quarenta 40
cinquenta 50

sessenta 60
setenta 70
oitenta 80
noventa 90
cem 100
cento e um 101
duzentos 200
quinhentos 500
mil 1000

Food and drink terms

Basics

assado roasted
colher spoon
conta bill
cozido boiled
estrelado/frito fried
faca knife
garfo fork
grelhado grilled

Menu terms

pequeno almoço breakfast
almoço lunch
jantar dinner
ementa turística set menu
prato do dia dish of the day
especialidades speciality
lista de vinhos wine list
entradas starters
petiscos snacks
sobremesa dessert

Soups, salad and staples

açucár sugar
arroz rice
azeitonas olives
batatas fritas chips/french fries
caldo verde cabbage soup
fruta fruit
legumes vegetables
manteiga butter
massa pasta
molho (de tomate/piri-piri) tomato/chilli sauce
omeleta omelette
ovos eggs
pão bread
pimenta pepper

piri-piri chilli sauce
queijo cheese
sal salt
salada salad
sopa de legumes vegetable soup
sopa de marisco shellfish soup
sopa de peixe fish soup

Fish and shellfish

atum tuna
camarões shrimp
carapau mackerel
cherne stone bass
dourada bream
espada scabbard fish
espadarte swordfish
gambas prawns
lagosta lobster
lulas (grelhadas) squid (grilled)
mexilhões mussels
pescada hake
polvo octopus
robalo sea bass
salmão salmon
salmonete red mullet
santola spider crab
sapateira crab
sardinhas sardines
tamboril monkfish
truta trout
viera scallop

Meat

alheira chicken sausage
borrego lamb
chanfana lamb or goat casserole
chouriço spicy sausage
coelho rabbit
cordeiro lamb
dobrada/tripa tripe
espetada mista mixed meat kebab
febras pork steaks
fiambre ham
fígado liver
frango no churrasco barbecued chicken
leitão roast suckling pig
pato duck
perdiz partridge
perú turkey
picanha strips of beef in garlic sauce

presunto smoked ham
rim kidney
rodizio barbecued meats
rojões cubed pork cooked in blood with potatoes
vitela veal

Portuguese specialities

açorda bread-based stew (often seafood)
arroz de marisco seafood rice
bacalhau à brás salted cod with egg and potatoes
bacalhau a Gomes Sá dried cod baked with potatoes
bacalhau na brasa dried cod roasted with potatoes egg and olives
bife à portuguesa steak with a fried egg
caldeirada fish stew
cataplana fish, shellfish or meat stew
cozido à portuguesa boiled casserole of meat and beans, served with rice and vegetables
feijoada bean stew with meat and vegetables
migas meat or fish in a bready garlic sauce
porco à alentejana pork cooked withclams

snacks and desserts

arroz doce rice pudding
bifana steak sandwich
bolo cake
gelado ice cream
pastéis de bacalhau dried cod cakes
pastel de nata custard tart
prego steak sandwich
pudim crème caramel

Drinks

um copo/uma garrafa de/da... a glass/bottle of...
vinho branco/tinto white/red wine
cerveja beer
água (sem/com gás) (still/sparkling) mineral water
fresca/natural chilled/room temperature
sumo de laranja/maçã orange/apple juice
chá tea
café coffee
sem/com leite without/with milk

SMALL PRINT

Publishing Information
Seventh edition 2026

MIX
Paper from responsible sources
FSC® C014138
FSC
www.fsc.org

Distribution
UK, Ireland and Europe
Apa Publications (UK) Ltd; mail@roughguides.com
United States and Canada
Two Rivers; ips@ingramcontent.com
Australia and New Zealand
Woodslane; info@woodslane.com.au
Worldwide
Apa Publications (UK) Ltd; mail@roughguides.com

Special Sales, Content Licensing and CoPublishing
Rough Guides can be purchased in bulk quantities at discounted prices. We can create special editions, personalized jackets and corporate imprints tailored to your needs. mail@roughguides.com.
roughguides.com

EU Representative
LOGOS EUROPE, 9 rue Nicolas Poussin, 17000, LA ROCHELLE, France; Contact@logoseurope.eu; +33 (0) 667937378
Printed by Finidr in Czech Republic
ISBN: 9781835294123
This book was produced using **Typefi** automated publishing software.
A catalogue record for this book is available from the British Library.

Rough Guide Credits
Editor: Joanna Reeves
Cartography: Katie Bennett
Picture manager: Tom Smyth
Layout: Pradeep Thapliyal
Original design: Richard Czapnik
Publishing technology manager: Rebeka Davies
Production operations manager: Katie Bennett
Head of Publishing: Sarah Clark

Acknowledgements

Thanks for everyone who helped with the update, especially Vitor Carriço at Visit Lisbon, Vera Fonseca, Ines Graça, Carla de Flavlis and Amelia Bird, and to everyone at Rough Guides, especially Joanna Reeves.

About the author

Matthew Hancock has worked as a teacher and writer in Lisbon and has visited every corner of the country as co-author of the Portugal Rough Guide. Now living in Dorset, he is also co-author of the Rough Guide to Dorset, Hampshire and the Isle of Wight.

Amanda Tomlin is a travel writer and editor who has worked on scores of Rough Guides as well as writing for travel websites and blogs. She has lived in Lisbon and visits the city regularly, having watched it change and grow for more than 35 years.

Help us update

We've gone to a lot of effort to ensure that this edition of the **Pocket Rough Guide Lisbon** is accurate and up-to-date. However, things change – places get "discovered", restaurants and rooms raise prices or lower standards, and businesses cease trading. If you feel we've got it wrong or left something out, we'd like to know, and if you can direct us to the web address, so much the better.

Please send your comments with the subject line "**Pocket Rough Guide Lisbon Update**" to mail@roughguides.com. We'll send a copy of the next edition (or any other Rough Guide if you prefer) for the very best emails.

Photo Credits

Index

CW01424876

THE
TWO FOOT GAUGE
ENIGMA

BEIRA RAILWAY
1890-1900

BY

ANTONY BAXTER, C.St.J., F.I.C.E.

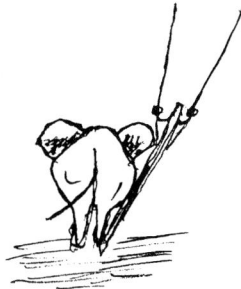

PLATEWAY PRESS 1998

First published 1998

ISBN 1 871980 34 8

Published by
PLATEWAY PRESS
Taverner House, Harling Road
East Harling, Norfolk, England

Printed by
Postprint, East Harling, Norfolk, England

Front cover illustration: Beira Railway large Falcon 4-4-0 No. 16 at Umtali in 1898, shortly after the opening of the 2ft gauge line through from Beira. *(National Archives of Zimbabwe)*

Frontispiece: Cartoon in Punch, January 1898.

CONTENTS

DEDICATION

*To my wife, a reluctant Ferroequinologist
who later became a narrow gauge steam engine driver,
and who gave me the inspiration
and encouragement to write this book*

FOREWORD

When Tony Baxter asked me to write a few words about the Beira Railway, I had my doubts because I have never actually travelled on it; however, I do happen to own an engine that worked on it, so I can claim to have had considerable involvement over many years with that part of the world.

It was many years ago when the two passions in my life, wildlife conservation, and the love of steam locomotives, came together in a tangible way, in both the United States and Zambia. I had managed to raise, with many others, enough money through the auction of my wildlife paintings to buy a Bell Jet Ranger helicopter to help the government of Zambia to catch wildlife poachers. It was as a result of this that the then President of Zambia, Dr. Kenneth Kaunda, presented me with a British built locomotive dating from 1896, together with a railway coach of slightly later vintage. These were ending their days on the Zambezi Sawmills Railway which, in many ways like the Beira Railway, was a monument to early British railway engineering of the last century. It took courageous men – indeed many "larger than life" – to tackle the incredible difficulties of Africa at the turn of the century, blazing a railway trail through impenetrable bush, but that is exactly what they did.

The locomotive presented to me was sent out in the reign of Queen Victoria, working originally on the Cape Government Railway. She was the last Class 7 in South African Railways service and then she went up to Zambia to work on the Sawmills Railway. She is now, therefore, more than 100 years old and basically still in working order. Together with the coach, she would have been typical of the rolling stock used on the Beira Railway. Tony Baxter played a major part in the return of the locomotive and coach to the United Kingdom in 1971, but that is another story; however, I was very pleased when Tony asked me to write a few words about this exciting tale of adventure, telling of the efforts of those true railway pioneers who blazed railway trails for those of us who come after, and perhaps take everything just a little too much for granted.

David Shepherd, O.B.E., F.R.S.A., F.R.G.S.

INTRODUCTION

In the latter half of this century Mozambique has featured in the world's media for its breakaway from Portugal and its subsequent civil war. Similarly, Rhodesia (Zimbabwe) has featured for its civil war and separation from Britain.

However, a hundred years ago it was a very different story, with Queen Victoria's government negotiating with the Queen's cousin, the King of Portugal, to establish their respective spheres of influence in Africa and, in Britain's case, to establish a route from what was to become Rhodesia to a port in Mozambique on the Indian Ocean.

All this resulted in the building of the two foot gauge Beira Railway between the years 1890 and 1900. The full story has not previously been told but so fascinating and unusual is the tale that this needs to be done.

The pages ahead reveal the saga that drove governments to quarrel and men to die in large numbers as the ten years of this enigma found their way into Railway history.

R.A.H.B.

ACKNOWLEDGEMENTS

The author would like to express his thanks to the following organisations and people who have given him considerable help:–

The National Railways of Zimbabwe Historical Committee for the loan of documents; The National Archives of Zimbabwe for photographs; Pauling and Company for photographs from the Commemorative Album presented to A. L. Lawley; The Leicestershire Record Office for builders photographs; Michael Whitehouse and Mrs J. Lawrence for copying photographs; Roy Laverick, George Toms, and John Buckland for research into Brush records, and the Revd Ted Hamer for photographs of Cam and Motor Mine. In particular I must thank Graeme Gilmour for all his work in committing the whole book to paper ready for publishing. Finally, I am most grateful to Anthony Lambert for all his assistance.

MASHONALAND RAILWAY.

["Sir Charles Metcalfe, the engineer, is now busy at Umtali arranging for the station at that place." – *Daily Telegraph*.]

Umtali Station in the near Future.   The Boo-Boola Express Just due

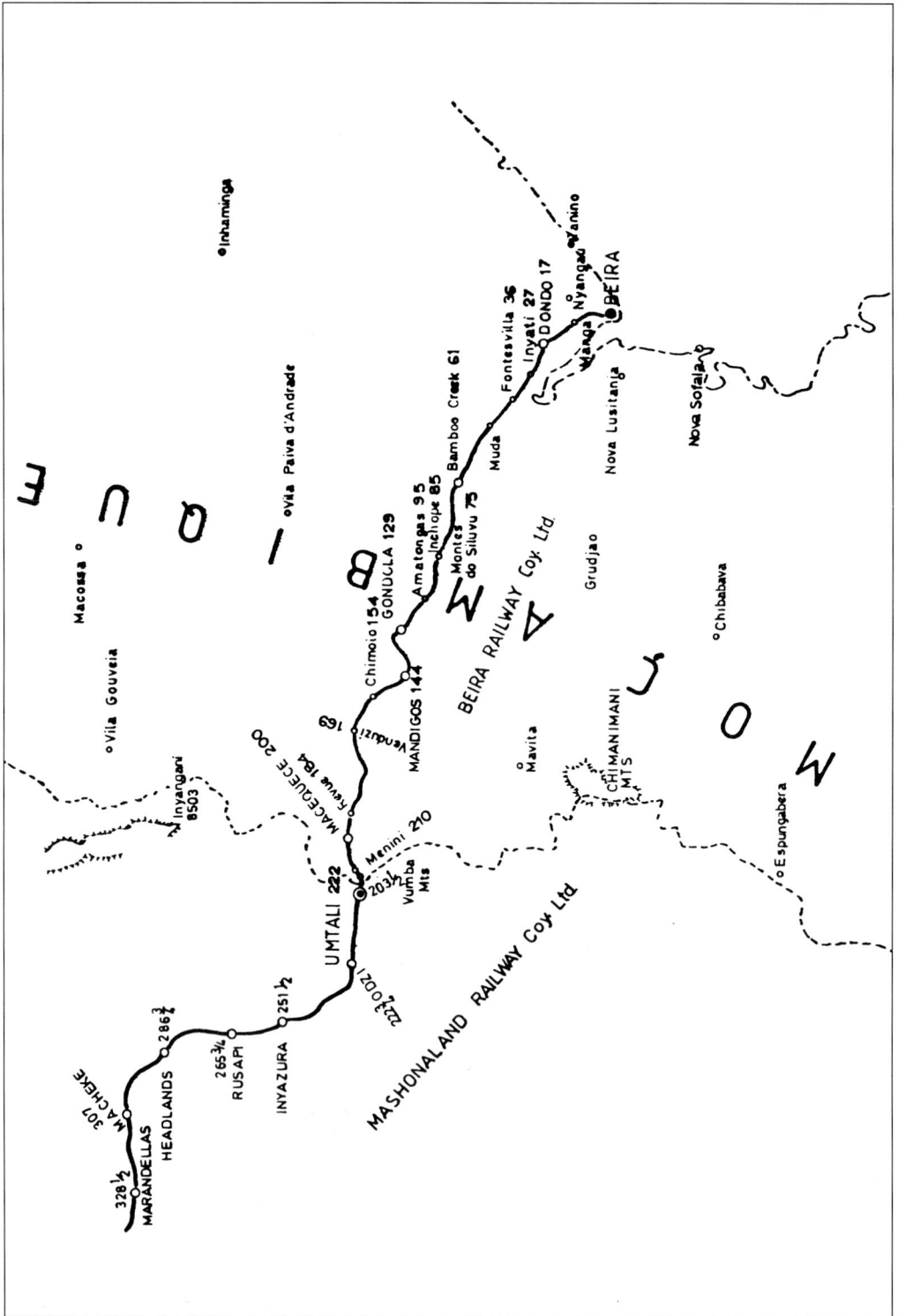

Chapter 1
PROLOGUE

Development of railways in Southern Africa had begun at Capetown in 1863 with the standard gauge Capetown to Wellington line just fifty-eight miles long. Six years later, with the arrival of the great entrepreneur from England, Cecil John Rhodes, everything changed dramatically. Construction of the railway northward was started but proved to be very difficult because of the geographical features encountered. It took eleven years to reach Kimberley by which time Rhodes controlled all the diamond rights and had become a member of the Cape Parliament.

In 1886 gold was discovered on the Witwatersrand, where Johannesburg now stands, and Rhodes quickly acquired the mining rights to this as well. This gave him the incentive to extend the railway north-east to that region, but because of the hostility of the President of the Republic of the Transvaal, Paul Kruger, the line had to stop at Bloemfontein in the Orange Free State. As a result of this hostility, Rhodes turned his attention to the possibility that gold might be found further north in what is now the Republic of Zimbabwe. In this enterprise he could extend the railway all through British Territory without opposition. In the meantime he planned to send a pioneer column of settlers and prospectors, escorted by troops, to that part of Zimbabwe known as Mashonaland. In 1890 Mashonaland was added to the British Empire which led to much dramatic negotiation between the governments of Britain and Portugal as to the boundaries of their respective spheres of influence in South Central Africa, particularly as Rhodes had upset Queen Victoria's cousin, the King of Portugal, by planning to take Pungwe Bay (later to be known as Beira) and establish a corridor to Mashonaland from the Indian Ocean.

Many heated letters and telegrams were exchanged between Lisbon and London until finally on August the 20th 1890 a Convention was signed between the two governments. This laid down the extent of what was to become Mozambique, and the laws governing trade and mineral concessions which included equal rights in the use of ports on the coast. In Article XIV of this Convention it was agreed that the Portuguese would grant freedom of passage between the British sphere of influence and Beira. In this connection they would undertake to build a railway to serve the area, and that after the survey the line would be completed with the least possible delay. An engineer to be named by the British government was to form part of the survey team which should have commenced work within four months of the signing of the Convention. If these terms were not carried out a concession was to be issued to a joint company with an equal number of British and Portuguese directors. At the same time provision was made for the construction of a telegraph line under the same conditions as the railway and alongside it.

The Convention was finally signed by the Marquess of Salisbury for Britain and by Beijon de Freitas, the Portuguese Ambassador in London on behalf of Portugal. It was subsequently agreed also that the railway rates should be on a par with those of the Cape Government Railway, and that materials for the Beira Railway should be carried free of charge.

After the Convention was signed the republican press in Portugal criticised it very strongly, one paper going as far as to say that it was 'a supreme act of spoliation' and that it would be better to dispose of Mozambique altogether than to keep it in terms of the Convention. On the other hand the pro-government press declared it an honourable solution to a long-running conflict between the two governments.

When the Convention was published finally in September the row blew up again and this time the point that seemed to raise the strongest objection was the building of the railway which, it was said, was entirely for the benefit of Britain. A second source of considerable anger was the provision that Portugal should not cede any part of Mozambique to another power without British consent. As a result of all this the commercial sector in Portugal was urged to oppose the ratification of the Convention in their Parliament (the Cortes).

Ultimately the British Government agreed to the nomination of a neutral engineer in place of a British one for the survey, in an effort to pacify the objectors and to allow the project to proceed.

More drama followed. In the middle of September, after the modification and subsequent re-signing of the Convention, the Portuguese Foreign Minister resigned when he was given a riotous reception in the Cortes. Not unnaturally this cancelled the ratification of the Convention and the negotiations had to start again.

A few weeks later, the Portuguese Parliament sat again with considerable precautions being taken to prevent rioting. Even so, conflict broke out between the police and the public around the Cortes building. This resulted in one man being killed and about a dozen others being seriously injured. To make a strange situation even stranger, some of the army men sided with the people against the police. It was evident that the concessions made by the British Government had had little effect on the strong opposition in Portugal, even to the extent that a number of Portuguese Ministers threatened to resign. These threats were put into effect when the matter was presented once more to the Cortes. A very stormy meeting took place and the whole Portuguese Cabinet resigned.

A new Cabinet was formed in October and they promptly closed Parliament without having ratified the Convention of August 20th. The outcome was that the British Government declared it null and void. The Portuguese Government then proposed the negotiation of a completely new treaty but as this was liable to take a considerable time they suggested that legal authority should be sought to build the railway and to establish freedom of navigation on the Zambezi River. This suggestion resulted in the

British South Africa Company under Cecil Rhodes being given permission to build the telegraph line, but without mention of the railway. Further discussion followed between the two governments and the result was a concession given to the Mozambique Company to build the railway in conjunction with the building of the telegraph line by the British South Africa Company.

Cecil John Rhodes, founder of Rhodesia and member of parliament for the Cape Colony in South Africa. *(National Archives of Zimbabwe)*

At last in November an agreement was signed which, for six months, would give the go ahead for these arrangements, during which time a permanent Convention would be negotiated. This was done and the Anglo-Portuguese treaty was signed on June 11th 1891 in Lisbon. In terms of Article IV of that Treaty the Portuguese agreed to construct a railway from the coast to the British boundary near Umtali. It was stipulated also that the survey of the line should be completed within six months, after which time the Governments would decide when the construction should start and finish. If all this was not done the Portuguese Government would grant a contract to a firm nominated by a neutral power. As before, a telegraph line was to be constructed on the same terms and at the same time.

THE BEIRA RAILWAY COMPANY,
LIMITED.

Incorporated under the Companies Acts, 1862 to 1890, as a Company limited by guarantee, and not having a Capital divided into Shares.

The Memorandum of Association declares that every Member of the Company undertakes to contribute to the assets of the Company, in the event of the same being wound up during the time that he is a Member, or within one year afterwards, for payment of the debts and liabilities of the Company contracted before the time at which he ceases to be a Member, and the costs, charges and expenses of winding-up the same and for the adjustment of the rights of the contributories amongst themselves, such amount as may be required, not exceeding £1 sterling.

The total liability of each Shareholder in any event is thus limited to £1 whatever the number of Shares he holds.

Issue of £250,000 FIRST MORTGAGE DEBENTURES (Series A), bearing Interest at 6 per cent. per annum, payable half-yearly on 30th June and 31st December, and repayable at par on 30th June, 1922, but redeemable by the Company at a premium of 10 per cent. at any time after 30th June, 1897.

Of the above issue, £110,000 have already been subscribed for at par and allotted. The Contractors for the construction of the Railway take £43,500, other part of the issue at par.

The Balance, £96,500, is now offered by the Company for public subscription at par.

The Debentures will be issued in sums of £20, £50, £100 and £1,000, to suit the convenience of Subscribers, and will be made payable to bearer (with Coupons attached) or registered at the option of Subscribers.

Trustees for the Debenture Holders:
ROBERT BENSON, Esq., 66, New Broad Street, E.C.
CARL MEYER, Esq., New Court, St. Swithin's Lane, E.C.

Directors:
ALFRED BEIT, Esq., Director of the British South Africa Company.
MARQUIS DE FONTES PEREIRA DE MELLO, Director of the Mozambique Company.
R. HINRICHSEN, Esq.
ROCHFORT MAGUIRE, Esq., M.P.
C. ALGERNON MOREING, Esq., Director of the Mozambique Company.
HENRY T. VAN LAUN, Esq.

Bankers:
Messrs. SIR SAMUEL SCOTT, BART., & CO., 1, Cavendish Square, W.

Brokers:
Messrs. CAZENOVE & AKROYDS, 52, Threadneedle Street, E.C.

Engineers:
SIR GEORGE B. BRUCE, Past President Inst. C.E., 3, Victoria Street, S.W.
SIR CHARLES METCALFE, Bart., Assoc. M. Inst., C.E., 28, Victoria Street, S.W.

Solicitors:
Messrs. HOLLAMS, SONS, COWARD & HAWKSLEY, Mincing Lane, E.C.

Secretary:
Mr. JOHN CLULOW.

Offices:
19, ST. SWITHIN'S LANE, E.C., LONDON.

Messrs. Sir SAMUEL SCOTT, BART., & CO., the Bankers of the Company, will receive Subscriptions at par for the above £96,500, payable as follows :—

On APPLICATION	-	-	-	10 per cent.
„ ALLOTMENT	-	-	-	20 „
„ 15th JANUARY, 1893	-	-	-	30 „
„ 15th FEBRUARY, 1893	-	-	-	20 „
„ 15th MARCH, 1893	-	-	-	20 „

Subscribers can prepay in full on Allotment or at any subsequent time.

Interest will commence on all payments as from the date they are made.

Scrip will be issued in exchange for Letters of Allotment, and will be exchangeable for Debentures when fully paid.

Subscribers will receive, by way of Bonus, in addition to their Debentures, Shares in the Railway Company, at the rate of 10 Shares for every £10 of Debentures subscribed, as explained in the Prospectus.

1. The Beira Railway Company has been formed for the purpose of procuring the construction and equipment of a Railway, with Landing Places, Quays, Wharves, and Docks, starting from or near Beira, on Pungwe Bay, in the Province of Manica and Sofala, on the south-east coast of Africa, and terminating at the eastern frontier of the British sphere of influence, whereby the Manica

First Issue of Shares for The Beira Railway Company.

4

The treaty stipulated also that the Portuguese Government would retain the right to acquire all public works, and that the railway was to revert to the state in ninety-nine years. However this matter could be reviewed after fifty years, and every twenty years after that.

In the event, the Portuguese issued a Royal Decree nominating the Mozambique Company to carry out the work. In their turn the Company appointed H. T. Van Laun of London to be their Concessionaire and this was agreed by all concerned in September 1891. Van Laun was a Company Secretary of two companies, one of which was the Union Debenture Company which was interested in capital investment, and it was on their behalf that Van Laun signed the Concession. The Mozambique Company then allocated blocks of land to the Railway. These were five kilometres square on alternate sides of the line in addition to the land required for the railway itself. It was laid down also that no competing railway could be constructed within a hundred kilometres on either side of the proposed line, although branch lines could be constructed, but only by Van Laun. As a result of all this Van Laun was to form a Railway Company to build and operate the line within six months of the signing of the agreement. But at this time finance for investment on the London stock market was very scarce, so the Mozambique Company allowed an extension of three months to the original six months required.

In the meantime Van Laun felt that as he was not himself an engineer he could not organise the construction of the railway on his own. At the end of 1891 and under pressure brought by Rhodes he signed an agreement with the British South Africa Company for them to make the necessary arrangements and applied to the Mozambique Company to amend the original agreement accordingly. This was done.

One year later The Beira Railway Company was formed and the British South Africa Company transferred all its rights to the new Company. Some time later, Van Laun also assigned his own rights to the Railway Company for £10,000, but insisted on keeping his directorship.

The new Company settled down and began plans for the railway. It was decided that as from the beginning of 1893 meetings should be held annually and that at these there must be six directors from the British South Africa Company, two from the Mozambique Company, and two to be nominated by Van Laun. The duties of these Directors were very onerous as they not only had to act as diplomats between the British and Portuguese governments but also between the British South Africa and Mozambique Companies. Alfred Beit was the Chairman and he was most skilful at keeping everything under control – especially Rhodes. In sharp contrast to business today, the Directors received very little compensation for the work they undertook as it was only after much argument and discussion that the shareholders finally agreed that they could receive £3,000 for their first five years of service.

Thus, at last, after much negotiation and drama the Beira Railway Company was established to build and run a railway from Beira to the boundary of British territory near Umtali.

Alfred Beit, Financial Advisor to Rhodes who became Chairman of The Beira Railway Company.

Chapter 2
DRAMATIC CONSTRUCTION

The Beira Railway Company had been established to build and operate 180 miles of 2ft gauge line to the British border, with all the necessary quays, docks, stations etc. Ultimately the line was 222 miles long by the time it reached Umtali.

It was estimated that the provision of the railway from Beira would save over a thousand miles compared to the distance from Capetown to Mashonaland. Furthermore it was taking three months to carry goods by the latter route through Mafeking, and then only in the dry season, whereas the Beira Railway could be used almost all the time, apart from flooding and at only a third of the cost including the shipping rates from Capetown to Beira.

The finance for the first phase was raised by the financier Baron Frederic Emile d'Erlanger who was the head of the London banking firm of D'Erlangers. Shares of limited guarantee were issued to the Mozambique Company and the British South Africa Company. Some of the latter were later sold to private individuals provided that, when required, they voted with the Company. As mentioned previously the financial situation at that time was very tight and thus the Baron was able to raise only enough money for the first seventy-five miles.

In 1877 the brothers George and Harry Pauling had formed the civil engineering contracting business of Pauling and Company in London, a firm which is still in existence today. George Pauling was basically in charge of the construction of railways in Southern Africa and because of his interest in the area he was later to become the Commissioner of Works and Mines and the Postmaster General of Southern Rhodesia.

In the year before the formation of the Railway Company, the Pauling brothers had offered to build the first seventy-five miles for £70,000, which only goes to show that by accepting this, the Chartered Company was ready to start almost before the ink was dry on the various political agreements. However in 1892, Alfred Beit, the Chairman of the British South Africa Company, formalised matters by calling for tenders from Paulings and A. L. Lawley, two civil engineering contractors working in Southern Africa at that time. George Pauling himself was a very eccentric character known at a later date to have carried a donkey round the dining room at the Victoria Falls Hotel and to have accomplished several other hilarious feats of strength. Also, he had a fantastic appetite for both liquids and solids; for example, it is said that he and two friends sat down to breakfast in Port Elizabeth and consumed eight bottles of champagne and a thousand oysters between them!

In view of their previous offer, a conditional contract was let to Pauling & Coy for the first seventy-five miles with an option for extension, and a completion date of December 30th 1892. Feeling that Lawley would be the best man for the job, George

L to R: A. L. Lawley, George Pauling, Harold Pauling.

P. St G. Mansergh, Surveyor of the Beira Railway.

Pauling asked him to become the Engineering Manager. Harold Pauling, George's cousin, then went out with Lawley to start the survey. When it was well under way Harold went home and Lawley then organised the construction so that the actual survey was taken over by a very competent Consulting Surveyor named E.Mansergh who went out from England. In the meantime, the British South Africa Company had appointed one of its directors, Sir Charles Metcalfe, to be the overall Consulting Engineer in London. So was born one of the longest, but shortest-lived, 2ft gauge railways in the world.

Beira Railway Co.
0-4-2 No. 1. Shunting at Fontesvilla. Converted from Brush/Falcon
0-6-0- No. 214/93. Ordered by Kerr Stuart. *(Pauling & Co.)*

At that time Beira was more or less non-existent, being merely a few huts on the sandbanks at the mouth of the River Pungwe. So it was decided that the complications were too great to build a railway from that point. Instead, they started in September 1892, with Lawley in charge, to build from a place called Fontesvilla (Ponte do Pungwe) which was about thirty-five miles up the Pungwe from Beira. Harold Pauling then returned to help generally and he and a man named Neumeyer arranged shooting parties so that the labour force could have enough meat. This was quite a problem because there were several thousand African labourers to feed. Unfortunately Harold died of blackwater fever in 1895. He was greatly missed because of the high esteem in which he was held.

Initially Pauling imported a large number of Indians and Chinese to carry out the construction work but the death rate was so high that he had to employ local Africans who, though slower workers, were much more resistant to fever.

0-6-0 No. 2 Falcon No. 215/93 crossing the flats near Fontesvilla in 1894.
(National Archives of Zimbabwe)

The decision to start the construction at Fontesvilla meant that the contractors had to transfer all the freight from ocean-going ships to lighters which then carried it up the Pungwe river – a very lengthy and difficult process.

A depot was built at Fontesvilla and a large amount of equipment and materials was landed and stored there; but this was an appalling place, no better really than Beira. It lay in the middle of the swamps of the Pungwe delta and because of frequent flooding the buildings had to be raised above ground. Again, because of the humid climate and thick grass, mosquitos swarmed almost literally in clouds. An additional hazard was the presence of great numbers of wild animals. Lions and elephants abounded, to say nothing of crocodiles in the swamps. It was a saying of George Pauling that the only Europeans worth employing under such conditions were men who were not teetotallers, for non-drinkers would die of fever! At one time, while they were building the first seventy-five miles of line across the flats, sixty percent of the white staff died and of these, fifty-five percent were teetotallers or only light drinkers. At the same time it was said that "one of the imported Indians or Chinese men died for every sleeper laid."

Pauling proved the point himself when, some time later, he with two other men, of whom Lawley was one and Moore, the Resident Engineer of the Mashonaland Railway, was the other, went on a tour of the Beira Railway with a view to widening the gauge. The trip lasted three days and two nights during which time the three men consumed around three hundred pints of beer. Obviously they were determined not to die of fever! The only possible cure for malaria at that time was quinine taken in large revolting flakes.

Cutting at 70 miles under construction. (Pauling & Co.)

In view of the shortage of money everything had to be built as economically as possible. So, to start with, only 20lbs per yard rail was used. Steel sleepers were employed to avoid attack by white ants, and the track was all laid on "muck" ballast as there were no supplies of stone locally. It was unusual that all this equipment, including three or four small locomotives, were supplied by one firm, Kerr Stuart and Company of Kilmarnock in Scotland. The track was appalling as it was just thrown down where the bush had been cleared, and it was recorded that most of the time there were more derailments than smooth running!

The survey was being pushed ahead by Mansergh but was proving very difficult in view of the fact that it lay through thick bush and later forest where nobody had ventured before. Lawley accompanied him for much of the time but later developed fever and had to be sent up the coast to recover. That he did recover was fortunate as there could not have been a better choice of Resident Engineer in view of the engineering and climatic difficulties. Without his tenacity and personality it is probable that the line would never have been completed.

Work progressed very slowly for the first twenty-five miles over the flats and it was in this area that they had considerable difficulty with the large number of wild animals. Pauling related how he and Lawley were heading back to Fontesvilla on a locomotive which had derailed several times, when they came upon a pride of forty-two lions. This was a considerable problem as the driver felt that they could not move at more than four miles per hour or they would derail again. The problem was compounded by the fact that they had no gun among the three of them; so they climbed on to the side of the locomotive away from the lions. The driver sounded the whistle and opened the cylinder drain cocks while they all held their breath. Luckily the lions moved away and the party arrived home safely.

As mentioned previously all goods and passengers from ocean-going ships had to be ferried up the Pungwe by steam lighter. It was here that the question of liquor arose again because it became the habit to run the boats lightly aground on a sandbank until the liquor dried up, at which point they were miraculously refloated! During one flood

Beira Jetty 1898 with
Falcon "Midge" type 0-4-2T.
(Croxton Collection)

season a lighter named AGNES was duly run aground for the 'liquor break', but somebody had miscalculated, for the sandbank on which the lighter had grounded was no less than seven miles from the normal course of the river. In consequence, it was three years before the wretched boat could be rescued and pressed back into regular service again. The AGNES was no small rowing boat but quite a large steamer! The whole progress across the flats was a marvellous example of 'do or die' British endeavour in building sixty miles of railway across fever and crocodile infested swamps.

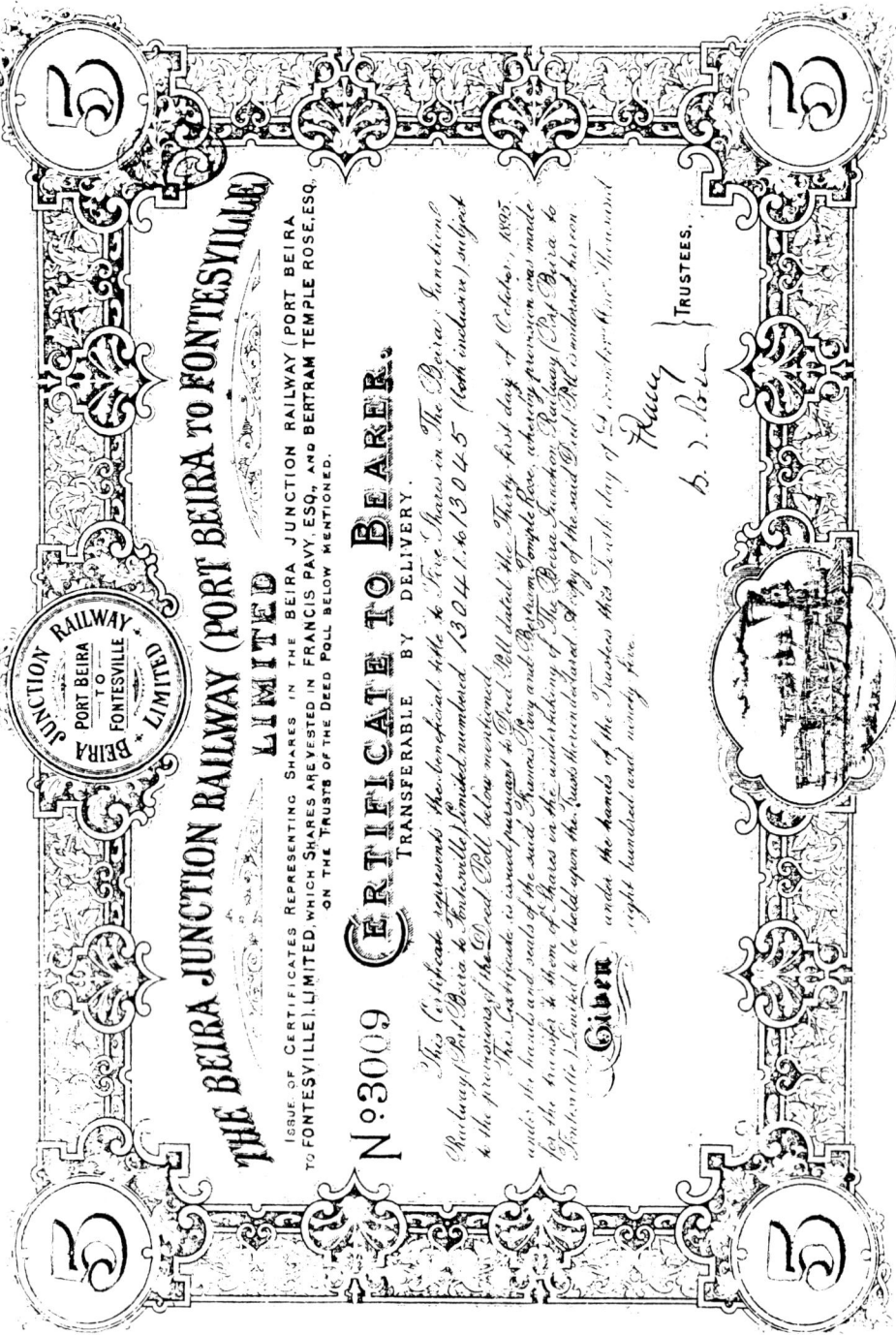

Share Certificate for the Beira Junction Railway

Beira Station in 1896 with three F2 type locomotives visible. The goods office is on the left, and beyond the station building on the right can be seen the harbour offices.
(National Archives of Zimbabwe)

By the spring of 1894 the energetic Baron d'Erlanger had managed to raise some more money and so authorisation was given to extend the railway another forty miles to Chimoio. At the same time, the Beira Junction Railway Company was formed to fill the gap between Fontesvilla and Beira. This was a subsidiary company to the London and Paris Exploitation Company which had been formed by the Baron and Paulings to give them access to more finance. The Baron tried to persuade George Pauling not to be involved in the Chimoio extension but the latter pressed on regardless. The first seventy-five miles had been completed in just over a year which was a marvellous achievement in view of the fact that much of it had been done in the rainy season. The last twenty-five miles involved a climb of 1380 feet and included a series of reverses which later were to prove a great hindrance to the operation of the trains. This section lay through the Amatongas Forest which was very thick, with trees up to 250 feet high, including a plentiful supply of mahogany. Work started on the Chimoio extension in June 1894 and this proved considerably easier as the work force was now in action above the tsetse fly belt and Pauling had already made his change to local labour, though there was still a considerable problem with lions in this area.

It was during this period that Rhodes, who oversaw the construction of railways in southern Africa, paid a visit to the railway to see how the construction was progressing towards Chimoio. He asked for a train to be made ready at the seventy-five mile peg (Gondola) to carry him and his party to Fontesvilla. Lawley made the necessary arrangements and waited for the great man to arrive, which he ultimately did three days late and in a very bad mood. Pauling related how Rhodes started swearing at Lawley in his high-pitched voice and in front of the staff. Lawley had enough of this and asked Rhodes who the hell he thought he was and to stop squealing like a damned rabbit. Rhodes, astounded by Lawley's daring, stalked off, but returned to join the train at the last moment. Later, at a water stop, Rhodes sent Dr Jamieson to ask Lawley to come to his compartment, whereupon he shook hands and apologised for his outburst. From then on they became the best of friends.

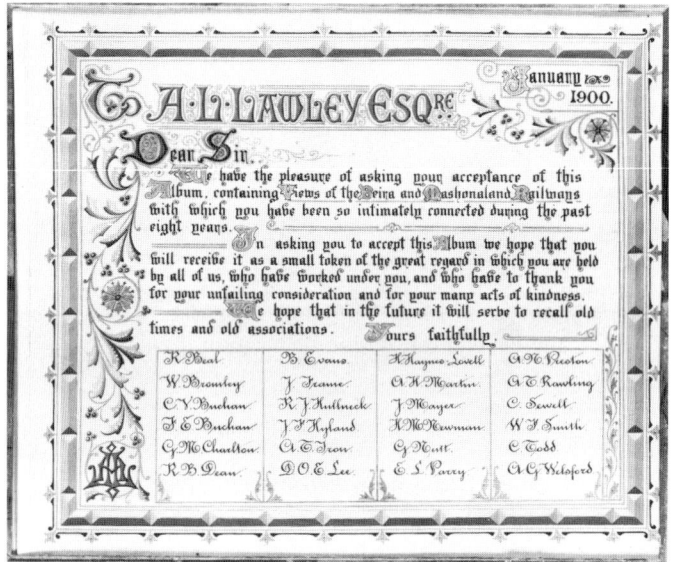

Illuminated address in the front of a photograph album presented to A. L. Lawley by the senior staff (of the Beira Railway Co.).
(Pauling & Co.)

All the bridges and culverts on the first section were built of wood, including a bridge of very light construction over the wide Pungwe river. This meant that for the first eighteen months or so the heavier locomotives were not allowed to cross the bridge with a load attached. One locomotive, therefore, would haul a train from Beira and when it arrived at the bridge over the Pungwe it would 'fly shunt' one coach or wagon at a time across at high speed, to be picked up by another locomotive on the other side. For passengers on these trains it must have been a hair-raising experience as the coaches overhung the bridge by eighteen inches on either side. It must have seemed as if they were airborne! During the construction of one of the bridges seven engineers were lost through fever and, to quote Lawley, "I then completed the damn thing myself using mahogany, as by then we had run out of steel and engineers!"

Ten miles short of Chimoio, at Mandegos (Vila Pery), sufficient suitable space was found to construct workshops and running sheds which sufficed until much larger facilities were built by the Mashonaland Railways at Umtali in 1898. These latter facilities are still in use today.

4-4-0 F2 No. 6. at Mandegos in 1896. Falcon works No. 232/95. *(Croxton Collection)*

Having reached Chimoio in November 1894, the arrival of the first train was celebrated with a somewhat riotous party during which two platelayers competed in firing at beer bottles. The Portuguese Commandant ordered them to be arrested and when they resisted, firing broke out, during which one of the platelayers was shot dead. Shortly afterwards the Commandant himself was arrested and sent to Angola to serve a prison sentence.

At this point there was a considerable pause of two years because Rhodes had turned his attention to his Cape-to-Cairo railway dream. This gave the contractors the opportunity to move their camp from Fontesvilla to Chimoio which was not so fever-infested. In consequence, the death rate dropped appreciably. In the middle of the year 1895 work started on building the line back from Fontesvilla to Beira. Because of the marshy ground and many small streams, it took fifteen months to complete this thirty-five mile section. Lawley was away for part of this time, having taken part in the notorious Jamieson Raid on the Transvaal.

In 1896 the Matabele Rebellion broke out in the west of Southern Rhodesia making it even more urgent that the Beira railway be completed in order to give Mashonaland access to the sea. Thus, work started again in May 1896 to complete the last sixty-eight miles to the border. This section was very difficult, even for a 2ft gauge line, as the area was very mountainous, with magnificent scenery, necessitating curves of 4 chains radius and a ruling gradient of 1 in 50. Earthworks were heavy and included such features as a 43 ft high bank taking four months to build, and deep cuttings in hard rock involving considerable blasting. Finally the line reached the border in October 1897; but only after one more major problem had been solved did the railway reach Umtali, seventeen miles further on. When the survey was in the area of Umtali it was found that the town was almost inaccessible by rail because of the surrounding mountains.

4-4-0 No. 8. at Macequece in 1898. Falcon No. 234/95 with a mixed train from Beira.
(National Archives of Zimbabwe)

The only possible route would have involved a lengthy tunnel. As a result of this Rhodes and Pauling decided to meet the residents and propose to them that the whole town should be moved twenty miles to the east. Ultimately, after Rhodes and Pauling had offered to bear all the costs of erecting new but similar shops and houses on the new site, the residents finally agreed that the move should take place.

Work went ahead under Tom Gilbert, a young man from England who travelled by train to Chimoio and then walked the sixty-eight miles to Umtali through the wild and mountainous bush country. He was appointed District Commissioner by Cecil Rhodes personally with the specific job of moving the town. Later he became the Railway's first paymaster and was interviewed by the author when he was ninety-three years old. The tapes of this interview are held in the Railway Museum at Bulawayo. It is interesting to note that all payments were made in British gold sovereigns.

Luckily the new town of Umtali was completed just in time for the arrival of the first train on February 4th 1898.

4-4-0 No. 9. FE 255/95 on an Umtali bound train at Macequece 1898.
Note the small tender and bogie rolling stock. (*National Archives of Zimbabwe*)

Replacement bridge on the Menini River with F4 No. 11 crossing it in 1899. *(National Railway Archives)*

Chapter 3

DEVELOPMENT

By the time the railway was completed to Umtali the freight traffic had increased to such an extent that major improvements were urgently required. Work started almost immediately on replacing all the small wooden bridges with larger steel ones, and the makeshift culverts with earthenware pipes. The Pungwe river bridge was replaced by a much longer steel girder bridge made to suit 3' 6" gauge for the future. This was pre-fabricated by William Arrol in Glasgow and shipped out in sections. Thus the Company was able to cut out the dreadful 'fly shunting' and save at least two hours in the running time to Fontesvilla.

Another factor making these bridge replacements very necessary was a succession of bad rainy seasons, particularly that of 1894/95 in which only seven miles of line on the flats were open to traffic and during which time one locomotive, probably No. 5, fell off a bridge. It was out of service for a month and had to be provided with a new tender. In October 1897 it was decided to put in a deviation through the Amatongas Forest in order to do away with the section that had reverses causing long delays, so that, when completed, there was a saving of about three hours in the running time. At the same time as all this other work was in progress, it was decided to replace as much as possible of the very light rail used previously with new rail weighing 30lbs per yard, and to install larger 5,000 gallon water tanks fitted with high pressure pumps.

The third major development was to move all the workshops and offices from places like Fontesvilla, Chimoio and Mandegos to Umtali. The engine shed from Mandegos

Group photographed at Beira in 1898. Seated left to right: A. L. Lawley, A. T. Iron, Sir Charles Metcalfe and George Pauling.
(National Archives of Zimbabwe)

21

later became the dining room of the Victoria Falls Hotel in 1905. This move caused somewhat of a row between the railway and its customers as all the rolling stock was used for the best part of a week to carry it out, causing a complete hold up of all other traffic. At the same time, in order to conform to Portuguese law, the railway had to establish a General Manager's office in Mozambique. This was done at Beira with A.L.Lawley installed as General Manager, G.Brand as Traffic Manager and A.E.Wainwright as Mechanical Superintendent. At the same time a hospital was built on the outskirts of the town and staffed with a doctor and nurses.

Because of the deep sand formation of the streets and the consequent absence of wheeled vehicles it was very difficult to move about in the town, so narrow gauge rails were laid and an effective means of transport for both passengers and goods was established with hand-pushed trolleys. Everybody who was anybody owned one of these trolleys which were fitted with garden seats and canopies. Motive power was provided by two 'trolley boys'.

Amusing incidents took place, such as arguments about who had the right of way on single track. If one met a lady on a trolley coming in the opposite direction, one removed one's helmet from ones' head and one's trolley from the track. There was an exchange of courtesies and then everyone proceeded with mutual respect. Sometimes it also led to heated arguments with the 'trolley boys' taking part. This form of transport lasted for thirty years.

Beira main street with the
Savoy Hotel on the left.
(Baxter Collection)

During this period of development the telegraph line had been completed using iron poles on the lower section to obviate the problems caused by white ants. This did not, however, get over the trouble caused by elephants who found the poles to be excellent back scratchers!

In July 1898 it had been agreed between the Mozambique Company and the Beira Railway Company that when the railway had carried 5000 tons of freight per month

Beira Railway Co.'s Head Offices at Beira. *(Pauling & Co.)*

Beira Railway Hospital. *(Pauling & Co.)*

for twelve consecutive months, the gauge should be widened to 3' 6" (Cape gauge). As a result of this decision a contract was let to Paulings to carry out the work, and the gauge widening started at Umtali in mid-1899. The first forty miles to Revue were opened for traffic by November of that year with the Mashonaland Railway having provided half the finance. In return, the Beira Railway agreed to pay the Mashonaland Railway £35,000 per annum as a rent. Finally the companies were amalgamated from 1930 until 1948, at which time the Beira Railway was taken over by the Mozambique government. As was usual for the Beira Railway, however, nothing went smoothly, and no sooner had the gauge widening started than the Boer War broke out.

Following the outbreak of war the British Government took the decision to protect

Mandegos workshops and running shed showing from left to right:
locomotives Nos 36. 33. not known and 11. *(Pauling & Co.)*

Southern Rhodesia (as it had become named in 1898) by sending 5000 Australian and New Zealand troops into the country through Beira, accompanied by a large number of horses and all the necessary stores and equipment. The assembly point for all these was at Bamboo Creek (Vila Machado). This was a serious mistake. The area was rampant with fever and surrounded by thick tropical vegetation which proved ideal shelter for the great number of marauding wild animals which caused havoc amongst the horses.

The situation was not helped by Rhodes himself who had become disenchanted with the war and had decided to charter a steamship which he loaded with prize pigs, cattle, sheep and poultry for his farms in Rhodesia. When all these arrived at Beira he chartered two special trains on the narrow gauge and one on the Cape gauge to carry the livestock inland. The trains departed after much ceremony and champagne-

4-4-0 No. 12 at Beira Goods Station. Note the small tender. *(Baxter Collection)*

drinking and eventually reached the change of gauge where chaos followed the attempts made to tranship the animals, some of which broke free. When the transhipment was eventually accomplished and Rhodes, together with his party and his livestock were able to continue on their way, they came across a troop train in a siding. The locomotive had broken down and the train was stranded. It did not occur to Rhodes to lend the troop train his locomotive. Instead, he gave his own train priority and merely agreed to tow away the dead engine. When the gradients eventually became too steep, his train crew decided to abandon it in the bush. It seems very doubtful that these troops ever reached Mafeking before it was relieved!

Two trains crossing at Amatongas Station in 1898. Five locomotives can be see of which No.13 FE 245/96 is the nearest. *(Pauling & Co.)*

Umtali Station in 1898 with a Drummond 4-4-0 on a mixed train and
"Midge" type locomotive shunting. *(National Archives of Zimbabwe)*

Despite all this drama Lawley succeeded in moving the 5000 troops, 1000 horses, and 14,000 tons of stores up to Southern Rhodesia (Mashonaland) between March and July 1900 – an operation which involved transhipping all this from the narrow gauge to the Cape gauge in the middle and at a 75% abatement of the normal freight rates.

The conversion work continued apace and the last sixty miles were divided into three equal sections. Amazingly, these sections were relaid, even if somewhat roughly, in only four days, which allowed for the arrival of the first train of a wagon and a coach hauled by the famous JACK TAR on August 1st 1900. This was followed by a two-coach train of V.I.Ps hauled by a Cape 6th Class 4-6-0 belonging to the Mashonaland Railways. Needless to say, liquid celebrations continued for several days afterwards.

On the completion of the widening of the gauge the whole railway and Beira port were handed over to the Mashonaland Railway, so becoming the B & M Rly. Thus, with all the narrow gauge rolling stock stored at Bamboo Creek, the very short but amazingly eventful life of the 2ft gauge enigma came to its end.

Chapter 4
OPERATIONS

Prior to the building of the railway, passengers and goods had been conveyed from Beira to Umtali by road twice a month and then only in the dry season between April and September. The oxen employed to draw the wagons died in large numbers owing to the area being infested by tsetse flies which caused sleeping sickness. To remedy this problem, the oxen were replaced by mules imported from Argentina which seemed to have a greater immunity to the disease. This situation was made worse by the fact that everything had to be brought ashore by lighters, then weighed and loaded into the wagons by a very small force of the local Shangaans, as even they did not want to work in somewhat desolate Beira. As soon as the railway reached Chimoio things eased a little as the weighing and handling took place at that point where labour was much more plentiful. From Umtali, a man named Jenner sent down a steam traction engine to ease the situation, but all that this accomplished was to make the appalling roads even worse. As a result the engine disappeared without trace!

When the railway was completed for the first seventy-five miles, at a cost of £169,200, Paulings undertook to work it for the Railway Company's account on a twelve months basis, and this resulted in a loss of £8,220. The second section to Chimoio having been completed in 1894 at a cost of £188,178, the Railway Company decided to operate the line themselves. After the previously mentioned two year pause, however, and when the extension to Umtali had begun, Paulings entered into an

4-4-0 No. 5 at Beira Station, with a mixed train for Umtali. Note the Fowler bogie tender.
(National Archives of Zimbabwe)

Brush F4 type locomotive No. 24 at Mandegos in 1898. Note Brunswick Green and Darker Green can be seen clearly.
(National Archives of Zimbabwe)

No. 30 FE No. 268/97 at Siluvu in 1898. Note the wood fuel on the tender
(Baxter Collection)

agreement with the Railway Company to work the line once more. This was followed by yet another agreement signed in December 1896 which laid down that the Beira Railway Company and the Beira Junction Railway Company would complete the railway to Umtali and build a better pier at Beira in order to get the port properly established. This pier was 250ft long with three small steam cranes on it. Later, two much larger piers were built and the cranes were moved onto them.

From this point onward the two companies were responsible for maintaining the railway and the pier for a period of thirty years. Jointly the companies would supply all rolling stock and staff to work the two railways and pier as one organisation. In this connection it is another strange feature of this railway that until about 1930 there were virtually no members of the staff who were Portuguese. The revenue from the whole operation was split between the companies on a pro rata mileage basis with the pier counting as ten miles. On August 4th 1897 a further agreement was signed to lease the whole railway and pier to Pauling & Co. at a rental of £60,000 per annum for two years beginning on October 1st of that year, at which time all staff and stores would be

Freight train with two
locomotives awaiting a
crossing at Amatongas
in 1899.
(Pauling & Co.)

transferred. This agreement was very detailed and named all the staff. Every piece of equipment was itemised, from locomotives down to the smallest paint brush. At the same time that this agreement came into force, a special toll of five shillings per ton was levied on all freight. This money was required over and above the normal revenue to pay for the rebuilding of the Pungwe bridge, despite the fact that the Mashonaland Railway Company met half the cost.

As far as freight was concerned trains had started running, as and when required, as soon as the railway had reached Gondola (75 miles). If any passengers wanted to travel at that time they had to ride in open wagons; but as described by Kingsley Fairbridge, of Fairbridge Schools fame, the journey was really very hazardous bearing in mind the clouds of mosquitos, the hot sun and the sparks from the wood-burning locomotives. By September 1894 sufficient coaches had arrived to allow a passenger service to start between Fontesvilla and Gondola every Wednesday. If one was lucky and there were no derailments, the journey took nine-and-a-half hours for the seventy five miles.

The speed of trains was limited to 20 mph, although this could rarely be achieved because of the many sharp curves of four chains radius and an extremely steep ruling gradient of 1 in 50. This speed was further reduced by the fact that all facing points had to be approached at 4 mph! Passenger fares were quite expensive at sixpence per mile first class, threepence per mile third class, and a penny per mile for local Africans. But if you were dead, it would cost you twice as much!

By January 1895 freight trains were running regularly to Chimoio with two or three a day in each direction. In addition, a mixed passenger and goods train had started running daily, leaving Fontesvilla at 6.30 am and arriving at Chimoio early next morning. A vivid account of this journey was given by Edith Campbell, one of the first woman passengers, who wrote in her diary in December 1895:

"Landed at Beira and joined the tug "Kimberley" which steamed four miles up the Pungwe, and then anchored for the night. Next morning we went on but came bang on a sandbank where we stuck. Breakfast on the tug cost three shillings with eggs, bacon, curry and bread with beer or cold water. Later we went on to Fontesvilla, which is on the right bank and almost part of the river itself with a few houses about three feet above ground level.

Beira Railway Drummond 4-4-0 No. 40, enjoying a new lease of life on the Lomagunda (Ayreshire) Railway, Rhodesia, in 1905. *(National Archives of Zimbabwe)*

Well we started with ten of us in the carriage. The Beira railway is a queer looking concern, very narrow, with only a couple of carriages and about three engines. The carriages are long and narrow things with hard seats on each side, like garden seats and ten inches wide.

The train conveniently slackened off for hunters to shoot at each herd of game. Mr Jansen shot a Hartebeeste, cut it up and put it on the train. Then on to the forty mile peg where we had to wait an hour for the down train from Chimoio, so a fire was lit, steaks were cooked, and we picnicked under a big tree. After beer and canned pears for dessert we went on again through lovely forest. At the sixty mile peg we came to a dead stop. The engine and first truck had run off the line, and were lying gracefully on their side against some rocks. Fortunately our carriage stood up. The engine driver jumped off in time and dragged the stoker with him. Then help was sent for up and down the line. Next morning a man came along on a trolley with a basket of meat, some gin and beer. We had to wait for another engine. From the sixty two mile peg the line is comical as it is a zig zag on the side of a hill, and the train is pushed backwards and forwards to get to the top. I lived in a funk all along the line!"

In June 1898 a Rules and Regulations Book consisting of forty-eight pages was issued by Lawley. This had to be signed for by all members of the running staff in the presence of a witness. It laid down some pretty strict rules, starting with:

"Every person employed by this Company must devote himself exclusively to its work; reside at whatever place may be appointed; attend at such hours as may be required; and pay prompt obedience to all persons placed in authority over him; and conform to all the rules and regulations of the Company."

Macequece Station in 1899, during Pauling's lease shown by the name of the company on the cab side.
(National Archives of Zimbabwe)

Obviously there were no Unions in Mozambique at that time!

It must be assumed that a telegraph order system of trains operating was in use, since the rules required all drivers to have an order before starting from a station. As the locomotives had small tenders, the trains had to stop every hour or so to take on more water and wood. In view of the many possible causes of delay and, therefore, a complete lack of punctuality of trains, it is surprising that the Rules and Regulations laid down that uniform time had to be kept along the whole route of the railway. If, therefore, the telegraph had broken down, which must frequently have been the case, the guard of the first passenger train from Beira each week had to make sure that all the clocks at the stations were showing the same time as his watch which he had set at Beira.

A derailment near Siluvu in 1898 illustrating the uncertainty of uneventful journeys.
(National Archives of Zimbabwe)

Another strange regulation was that when trains approached the Beira hospital, the driver had to sound the whistle twice if there was anybody or anything on his train for the hospital, and once if not.

Umtali bound train approaching a wood and water stop. *(Pauling & Co.)*

Bamboo Creek station in 1899. *(Pauling & Co.)*

Passenger trains were not allowed to run through the night because of the many hazards on the way, such as big game, fallen trees, broken rails and floods. Most trains stopped for the night at Mandegos where there was a locomotive depot and which was about half-way in time. There was also a hotel of sorts managed by J.Lawson who later ran the first dining car services on Rhodesia Railways.

If we are to judge by press reports it would seem that derailments were fairly frequent. In the case of passenger trains, however, the first priority was always to save the whisky stocks even though the wagons might be thrown into the bush after they had been off-loaded. Passengers were advised to take their own provisions on these journeys since there were no stores en route where these could be purchased. But this was not the only inconvenience of travelling on the Beira Railway. Kingsley Fairbridge reported that although he had travelled first class, this had to be in an open wagon, with some

Group at Umtali in 1899. Left standing: C. J. Rhodes, and right Sir Charles Metcalfe.
Seated middle and right: Mr & Mrs J. Kloppers (author's son in law's great grandparents).
(National Archives of Zimbabwe)

companions who shot continually at game on the way, causing the train to stop each time. Apparently they were also kept well occupied trying to stop their clothes catching fire from the sparks from the the wood-burning locomotive.

The extension to Beira was completed in October 1896 and a weekly passenger train was then started which left the port at 5 am. All being well, this train arrived at Mandegos at 10.30 pm. After the railway reached Macequece (Vila de Manica) the passenger service was increased to two trains a week in each direction which justified the opening of a refreshment room at that point. This was a major step forward.

A 1920 view of an Umtali tram in Main Street.
(National Archives of Zimbabwe)

There were still a number of strange incidents such as a day in December 1897 when the passenger train stopped suddenly and everyone was told to get out as the locomotive boiler was about to explode. Luckily, it changed its mind and no explosion occurred; however, because of the steep gradient, it then required three following goods trains to push the stranded passenger train into the next siding. Much drama followed as the trains tried to sort themselves out in order to continue their journeys.

The town of Umtali having been moved at the end of 1897, as mentioned earlier, the first construction train arrived there on February 4th 1898. It was hauled by Pauling & Company's small tank engine, RHODES, which was decorated with flowers and flags and with a banner across the front reading, "Now we shan't be long to Cairo." Immediately after this the first mail train arrived, carrying seventeen passengers, and the whole event was celebrated by a week of festivities with banquets, fancy dress balls, cricket matches and athletic sports. No doubt a good time was had by all concerned. The occasion was marked by a cartoon in *Punch* on January 29th 1898 showing a rondavel station with the name-board reading, "Umtali, change for Rum Tum Tali." Unfortunately, because of the many delays during construction, the Beira Railway was three months too late to claim to be the first line into Southern Rhodesia as the first train from Mafeking had arrived in Bulawayo at the end of October, 1897.

Chapter 5
LOCOMOTIVES

Initially Pauling & Coy ordered two 'Wasp' type 0-4-2 saddle tank engines from John Fowler of Leeds. They were numbered 5946 and 6523 by the builders and used by Paulings for construction purposes on the Beira Railway. Once the construction of the railway had started and the Railway Company had been formed in 1892 Messrs Kerr Stuart of Kilmarnock were appointed as agents for the supply of equipment including

Pauling's construction tank locomotive built by Fowler of Leeds in 1892.
(Baxter Collection)

all track and rolling stock. It was recorded in their London Register that they ordered five locomotives from the Brush Electrical Engineering Company at the Falcon Engineering and Car Works in Loughborough in July. The first two of these locomotives were of the Brush 'Midge' type and were 0-4-2 side tank engines which

Brush "Midge" type
0-4-2T "RHODES" of 1892.
(National Archives of Zimbabwe)

37

never received running numbers on the Beira Railway though one of them was named RHODES and pulled the first construction train into Umtali.

The other three were 0-6-0 tender locomotives, also built by Brush, and delivered in 1893. They received the running numbers 1, 2 and 3, and their dimensions are given at the end of this chapter. They had Salter spring safety valves on the domes, spark

Brush 0-6-0 No. 3 FE 216. *(Engineering, October 1893)*

arresting funnels, double roofed cabs and twin slide bars. Because of their long fixed wheelbase these locomotives proved very unstable on the rough track and so at least one of them (No. 1) was modified to 0-4-2 wheel arrangement. Whether this experiment was successful is not recorded but certainly no further engines of this type were ordered and all the remainder were 4-4-0s of Brush types F2 and F4. Each of these first five locomotives carried Kerr Stuart builder's plates and were delivered in 1895.

The first Brush 4-4-0 was No. 4 and it differed from the subsequent members of its class by having a cab similar to the 0-6-0s with square louvred windows all round. This design, known as F2, evidently proved successful and so an order was given directly to

Brush F2 type 4-4-0 No. 4 FE 230.
(Leicestershire Archives)

Brush in 1895 for a further five locomotives of this class, ending with No. 9 (FE. No. 235). The principal dimensions of these engines are given at the end of the chapter. In general, apart from the wheel arrangement, the sanding equipment and the cabs, they were very similar to the 0-6-0s.

In 1896 a further six were ordered but this time the design was altered to type F4 which was larger than the F2 and had a tractive effort of 3987 lbs against the 3000 lbs of the earlier type. They had slightly larger boilers, stepped footplates, single slidebars, straight lipped funnels and conventional pop safety valves over the fireboxes.

The arrival of these locomotives meant that when Paulings took on the lease of the railway that year they had the use of seventeen of them. Subsequently, as traffic grew,

Brush F4 type 4-4-0
No. 15 FE 247.
(Leicestershire Archives)

twenty-eight more of type F4 were delivered in three batches. The first four of these, Nos. 16-19 (FE. Nos. 254-257) were delivered at the end of 1896 and the remaining sixteen of the Brush engines were delivered in 1897, ending with No. 35 (FE.No. 273). All these locomotives were the same as the previous batches except that they had bigger six-wheel tenders to carry 600 gallons of water. These F4 type engines could pull 180 tons up the ruling gradients compared to the 160 tons of the F2s.

Brush F4 type 4-4-0 No. 38
built by the Glasgow
Engineering Co. in 1898.
(Baxter Collection)

The last batch of ten locomotives was subcontracted by Brush to the Glasgow Engineering Company owned by Dugald Drummond of London South Western Railway fame. They were built in 1898 and differed from the previous batches in having wasp-waisted safety valves and oval running number plates in place of the previous individual brass numbers on the sandboxes. In addition, they were fitted with vacuum brakes in view of the fact that it had been decided at the 1898 Annual General Meeting to fit all rolling stock with this equipment. Like the cowcatchers with which all locomotives were fitted when built, the vacuum brakes were never used and those on the Drummond engines were blanked off.

The locomotives were fitted with three types of headlamp. The Brush type was smallish and cube-shaped with a large ventilator on top. These were gradually replaced by a much smaller and thinner type with no ornamentation. The third type was fitted only to the 0-6-0s and was a very large ornamental type of lamp which was not replaced during the lifetime of these locomotives.

In most cases the livery would seem to have been a mid- or Brunswick green with the paint supplied by the Torbay Paint Company. This was bordered or banded in a darker green with gold or yellow bands separating the two greens. The letters 'B.R.' appeared

SAR NG 6 type locomotive No. 105 showing Brush F2 type frames, Glasgow Engineering Co. boiler, and Fowler bogie tender. *(Croxton Collection)*

on all the tenders and from No. 11 onwards the engines had their numbers painted on the buffer beams with, in some cases, a gold or yellow edging line.

In addition to the forty-five engines and tenders delivered, there were two large bogie tenders ordered from John Fowler of Leeds and one of these was attached to engine No. 5 after its tender was wrecked in an accident. What happened to the other tender is not known but both of them turned up later on the South African Railways attached to engines No. 105 and 106.

Beira Railway locomotive at Igusi Saw Mills in 1953, which when the photo was taken by the author surprisingly was in steam. *(Baxter Collection)*

When the gauge was altered to 3'6" the 2ft gauge locomotives were stored at Bamboo Creek, with the exception of those required for the Ayrshire Railway which was then under construction. This railway used much of the Beira Railway equipment until it, too, was converted to 3'6" gauge in 1914 and became the Sinoia branch of the Beira, Mashonaland and Rhodesia Railways.

Beira Railway locomotive No. 40 and third class coach on the Cam & Motor Mine Railway at Gatooma, Zimbabwe in 1945.
(Hamer Collection)

South African Railway's NG6 type locomotive No. 104 (previously of Beira Railway) at Selukwe
Chrome Mines, Zimbabwe, in 1925. The other locomotive is "Hans Sauer" built by
Hunslet in 1905. Both from the Ayreshire Railway.
(Zimbabwe Chrome Mines Ltd.)

Six Beira Railway locomotives are known to have gone to the Ayrshire Railway and
these were Nos. 30, 40, 41, 42, 43 and 44. With the exception of No. 30, all were
Drummond engines. Two others went to Lupani Forest Estates in Rhodesia and were

Beira Railway locomotive on
the Zebedeila Sugar Estates
in Northern Transvaal,
South Africa.
(Croxton Collection)

South African Railway's NG6 type locomotive No. 104 shunting at Selukwe in 1931.
(Zimbabwe Chrome Mines Ltd.)

transferred later to Igusi Sawmills. These two were recovered later. No. 19 was restored, using parts from both of them, and then placed in the Railway Museum in Bulawayo. The remains of the other were assembled and placed in the children's playground in Bulawayo's Centenary Park. Nos. 21 and 42 finished up going to the Cam and Motor Mine at Gatooma whilst another Drummond engine went to Arcturus Mine east of Harare.

Beira Railway locomotive preserved on the Busi Sugar Estates in Mocambique.
(Baxter Collection)

Falcon F4 4-4-0 No. 19 (not 27 as shown) preserved in the National Railways of Zimbabwe Museum in Bulawayo, taken by the author. *(Baxter Collection)*

In 1916, because the South African Railways were short of 2ft gauge locomotives, having sent some to South West Africa, they bought thirteen Beira Railway locomotives from Bamboo Creek. Subsequently these were overhauled in the railway's workshops and nine of them were returned to service as Class NG6, numbered 96 to 98 and 101 to 106, and worked on various branch lines in South Africa. Unfortunately the original identities of these locomotives were lost following the overhauls because much exchanging of frames, boilers and tenders took place and no record was kept of their previous running numbers.

One of these locomotives, No. 104, was later returned to Rhodesia to work at Selukwe Chrome Mines. Another, No. 96, was also returned and became 'Cement No. 1' at the Portland Cement Company's works in Harare. Nos. 97, 98 and 106 went to the Zebedeila Sugar Estates in the Northern Transvaal.

As far as is known there are still seven survivors. Two of these are in Bulawayo, three at Busi in Mozambique, and two in Johannesburg at the James Hall Transport Museum and at Milner Park. It is unfortunate that none of these locomotives was kept in running condition as they had very little use during their two years on the Beira Railway and six on the South African Railways.

BEIRA RAILWAY COMPANY LOCOMOTIVES
SUPPLIED BY
BRUSH ELECTRICAL ENGINEERING COMPANY LIMITED

PRINCIPAL DIMENSIONS

Batch	0-6-0s	F2 Class	F4 Class
Wheel base (Engine)	9ft 6ins	13ft 9ins	14ft
Wheel base (Tender)	4ft 6ins	4ft 6ins	4ft 9ins
Cylinder Diameter	8ins	8ins	9ins
Cylinder Stroke	15ins	15ins	15ins
Wheel Diameter (driving)	32ins	32ins	36ins
Wheel Diameter (carrying)		–	24ins 24ins
Heating Surface (Tubes)	246 sq ft	200 sq ft	246 sq ft
Heating Surface (Firebox)	30 sq ft	25 sq ft	30 sq ft
Grate Area	4.75 sq ft	4.5 sq ft	5.25 sq ft
Weight of Engine (i.w.o.)	11 tons	11.25 tons	13 tons
Weight of Tender (i.w.o.)	6.5 tons	6.5 tons	7.5 tons
Width over Running Plates	6ft 3ins	6ft 3ins	6ft 3 ins

Chapter 6

ROLLING STOCK

A s with the locomotives the majority of the rolling stock was supplied by the Falcon Engine and Car Works at Loughborough. Initially, Kerr Stuart and Company ordered a number of timber bolsters and platform wagons from Robert Hudsons of Leeds. These were six feet long over the buffer beams and 5ft 6 ins wide, running on two axles three feet apart. They were fitted with Norwegian-style couplings but no braking equipment was provided.

By the time the railway had reached Chimoio the Brush Electrical Engineering Company at the Falcon works had supplied six passenger bogie coaches, which were open saloons with longitudinal seating on each side with a total capacity of thirty-eight passengers. They had open platforms at the ends for access and the total length of the body was 29ft 6ins with a width of 6ft 3ins. The height was 6ft 6ins from the floor to the highest part of the ceiling. These bodies were of varnished teak and rested on steel underframes having four-wheel bogies with a three-foot wheelbase. Like the rest of the rolling stock they had only hand-operated screw brakes.

Brush Third Class type coach delivered in 1893. *(National Archives of Zimbabwe)*

In late 1893 Brush supplied two first-class coaches with four compartments, each seating six passengers. Like the previous coaches they had teak bodies on steel underframes and double roofs appropriate to the climate. Inside, they were much more luxurious, with leather padded seats and Lincrusta ceilings. It is surprising, in view of the steep gradients on the Beira Railway, that these coaches were not fitted with

Brush First Class type coach delivered in 1894. *(National Archives of Zimbabwe)*

continuous brakes although they had been planned at one stage. On the arrival of these new coaches the original ones were down-graded to third-class, and after the gauge was widened they went to the Ayrshire Railway in Mashonaland.

As the result of a resolution at the 1898 Annual General Meeting, equipment for fitting all the locomotives and coaches with vacuum brakes was sent out to Beira, but there is no evidence to show that this equipment was ever used.

A large number of freight vehicles were supplied by Brush so that by the end of 1898 there were eighteen pairs of timber bolsters, ninety goods wagons of which about half were covered, eleven horse boxes, nine platform wagons and nine brake vans. There were also one hundred and fifty wagons of varying types, all open and four-wheeled. All vehicles were wooden-bodied and the covered ones had corrugated iron roofs. It had been found that wooden roofs were liable to catch fire from sparks from the wood-burning locomotives.

Subsequently, a further twenty timber bolsters were supplied as there was a great deal of use for these in carrying large baulks of timber from the forests, and sections of pipe for constructing culverts. Some of the more unusual loads must have been the parts for the 3ft 6ins gauge locomotives for the Mashonaland Railway which were assembled at Umtali.

When the gauge had been widened most of the larger freight rolling stock and the third-class coaches went to the Ayrshire Railway. What became of the two first-class coaches is unknown but it seems likely that they rotted away at Bamboo Creek.

Builders' plates of locomotives No. 21 and 40. *(Hamer Collection)*

Chapter 7

EPILOGUE

After the widening of the gauge of the Beira Railway in 1900, Lawley continued to work for Paulings on the development of the railways in Rhodesia and Nyasaland (Malawi). He lived in Beira and established its first brick-built hotel, to which he gave the ludicrous title of THE SAVOY. There he presided with a rod of iron over the welfare of the many visitors. Eventually he retired to England where he died in 1930. The hotel was then bought by the Rhodesia Railways Ltd. which had come into existence in 1927.

Some of the Beira Railway narrow gauge track was used to build a horse tramway along the main street of Umtali and it survived as the only town tram system in Rhodesia until 1920. A further eighty-three miles of the track was used to build the narrow gauge branch line from Salisbury to Ayrshire. This line was opened as the Lomagunda Railway in 1902 and it lasted until 1913 when it, too, was converted to Cape gauge and became the Sinoia branch of the Rhodesia Railways. Finally, some of

Beira Railway locomotive and rolling stock on an Ayreshire Railway train at Salisbury A Station in 1910. *(National Archives of Zimbabwe)*

Beira Railway locomotives Nos. 44, 40 and 42 at Mount Hampden, Zimbabwe in 1912.
(National Archives of Zimbabwe)

this track material was taken to Victoria Falls to provide two trolley lines linking the Victoria Falls Hotel with the Falls themselves and making them more accessible to the elderly and to children. These trolleys were manually operated and lasted until 1957 when they were replaced by mini-buses. Two of the trolleys have been preserved, one being kept at the hotel and one in the Bulwayo Railway Museum.

The headquarters of the whole system had, in the meantime, remained in Umtali, but as the railway had reached the Belgian Congo (Zaire) the great distances involved made this arrangement very inconvenient. Consequently, it was decided to move everything to Bulawayo in October 1910. This was done in one vast operation which took a whole week and brought complete chaos to normal operations. At the same time the opportunity was also taken to establish a Railway Medical Service in Bulawayo. Re-using the old wood and iron buildings from Umtali proved unsatisfactory and so, two years later, new brick-built Head Offices and a new station building were erected and named after Sir Charles Metcalfe, the original Consultant Engineer for the Beira Railways. In the meanwhile, on the Beira line, a new re-crewing depot was built at Gondola in 1911 which enabled the crews from Umtali to have shorter working hours.

For some years after 1918 the Pungwe river failed to flood, causing a severe shortage of water for the locomotives and cranes at Beira. Water had to be ferried in barges from the Busi river, some distance away, and at the same time all trains had to have water

Mocambique Railway locomotive No. 985 ex-Rhodesia Railways 18th Class at Umtali in 1966, taken by author. *(Baxter Collection)*

tanks next to the locomotive from Vila Machado to Beira. The situation changed dramatically in 1923 when there was a very heavy rainy season. At first this caused the Munene river to flood ten miles from Umtali, closing the line for five days. By March these waters had reached the Pungwe which flooded and demolished the bridge and embankments thirty-four miles from Beira. The hundred-foot gap had to be filled with boulder stone and rock, while everything was ferried across by boat until the line re-opened on April 12th. As a result of these heavy rains considerable track strengthening had to be carried out, particularly in the mountainous areas where derailments were occurring far too often. The track deteriorated so badly that in 1925 night running had to be stopped, as it had in the days of the narrow gauge, because it was considered to be too unsafe.

The whole situation was worsened by the fact that the area then suffered three very heavy rainy seasons in succession, culminating in the closing of the line for the whole of February 1925. It was decided to raise nine miles of the track by a couple of feet near the Pungwe delta; but the work was not carried out quickly enough to finish it before the next rainy season. This turned out to be even heavier than the previous two seasons and caused the worst flooding ever recorded. In January 1926 the results of the flooding in the Amatongas were devastating and included the undermining of a high bank which collapsed under a train, overturning the locomotive and killing the driver.

The floods continued down to the Pungwe river which rose eighteen feet and covered the whole countryside. Fourteen miles of the railway were under water to an average depth of five feet and the Pungwe bridge was in great danger of being washed off its foundations. Following a hazardous boat trip along the flooded line, the Chief Engineer closed it for twenty-six miles. After two months and the off-loading of many trains of boulder stone and rock the line was finally re-opened. This experience led to a great deal of re-thinking to prevent the recurrence of such a disastrous situation and the enormous costs involved. Finally it was decided to replace the 800ft Pungwe bridge by a new one of 1000ft span and to deviate the approaches to it with 7500ft of concrete viaduct. In addition to this, fifteen miles of embankment across the flats were raised to three feet above the highest known flood level. The planning was good and no further problems were experienced with the Pungwe river after that.

Mocambique Railway 0-8-2T No. 58 shunting at Beira Docks in 1958, taken by author.
(Baxter Collection)

Concurrently with these water problems the traffic was growing considerably and it was felt that the gradients should be eased to 1 in 70 compensated. Deviations were therefore built in the Gondola area and in the Siluvu hills. It was becoming increasingly difficult in 1924 to handle the freight loads over the 1 in 50 uncompensated gradients and thus it was decided to order twelve Beyer-Garratt locomotives which were delivered in 1925 as Class 13. This, coupled with the improvements to the gradients, enabled the loads to be doubled on the lower sections of the line.

Trouble still continued with wild life, particularly in the Amatongas Forest and on the Pungwe Flats. Stationmasters in particular had to be very watchful for lions when signalling trains in and out of stations. Signalling and telegraph communications were still very uncertain because of the playful habits of elephants and giraffes!

In 1927 a start was made on a programme to stone ballast the main line whilst replacing the old 60lbs rail with 80lbs rails. In that year also, the Beira and Mashonaland, and Rhodesia Railways were both amalgamated to become the Rhodesia Railways Ltd. This amalgamation lasted until 1948 when the Company was nationalised. The Beira part of the railway, including the port of Beira, became a section of the Caminhos de Ferro da Mozambique in April 1949 and operation by them started in October of that year.

During this period, and particularly during the Second World War, traffic continued to grow. Larger Beyer-Garratt locomotives were required and the 16th Class were built specially for the Beira section. After the war was over and nationalisation had taken place, the C.F.M. bought the 17th and 18th Classes from R.R. Later still, as traffic was

Beira Railway in its later days:- Cape-gauge train from Beira entering Michipanda Station in 1958, headed by a Beyer-Garratt locomotive. *(Antony Baxter)*

still increasing, they bought their own 4-8-2 + 2-8-4 Garratts, first from Haine St. Pierre of Belgium in 1952, and then from Henschel of Germany in 1956.

Matters continued uneventfully until Rhodesia unilaterally declared its independence in 1965 when the United Nations imposed sanctions on the country. Traffic dropped considerably, and later the line closed completely when civil war broke out within Rhodesia. It resumed slightly when the new, independent Republic of Zimbabwe came into existence in 1980. This resumption did not last long as another civil war had broken out in Mozambique and the tracks were constantly being sabotaged. The train service was reduced to an average of one per week.

Lomagunda (Ayreshire) Railway train at El Dorado station with a train for Salisbury in 1912.
(National Archives of Zimbabwe)

Such was the importance to Zimbabwe of an outlet to Beira, in place of exclusive reliance on South Africa, that with the agreement of the Mozambique Government, Zimbabwe formed the Beira Corridor Committee whose job it was, using Zimbabwean personnel, to ensure the security of the road and railway. This arrangement has worked successfully in restoring the use of the railway nearly to normal, and has allowed a great deal of the line to be returned to better main line standards.

Thus, after many years of tribulations, political and otherwise, the Beira Railway is fulfilling the purpose set for it by Cecil John Rhodes one hundred years ago.

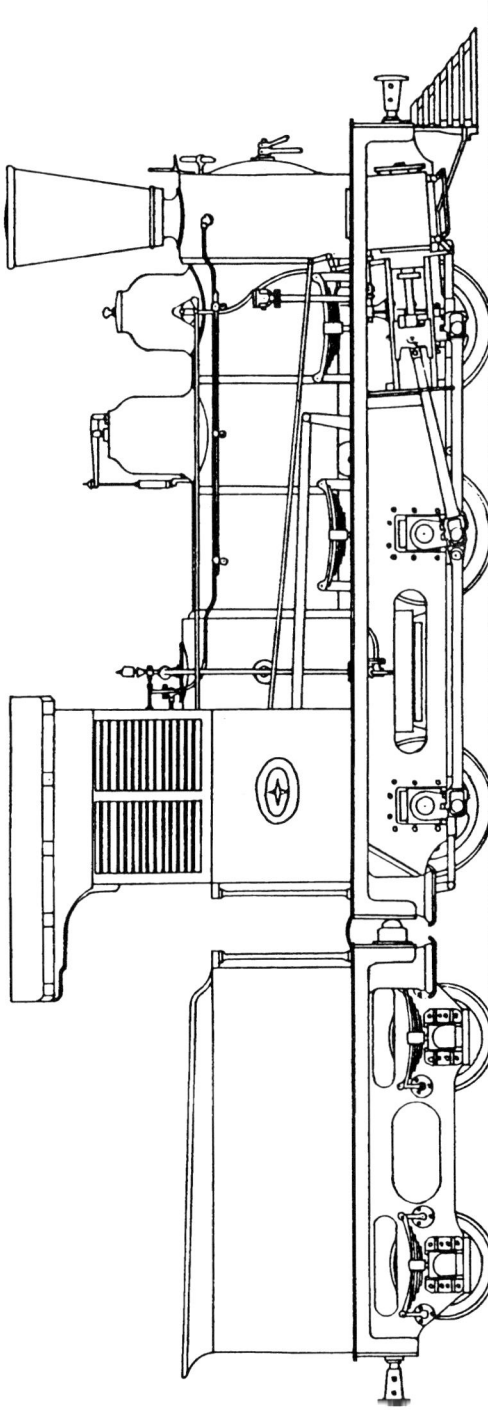

BEIRA RAILWAY COMPANY LTD.

BRUSH ELECTRICAL ENGINEERING COMPANY LTD.
FALCON WORKS LOUGHBOROUGH 0-6-0 1893

0   1ft

BEIRA RAILWAY COMPANY LTD.

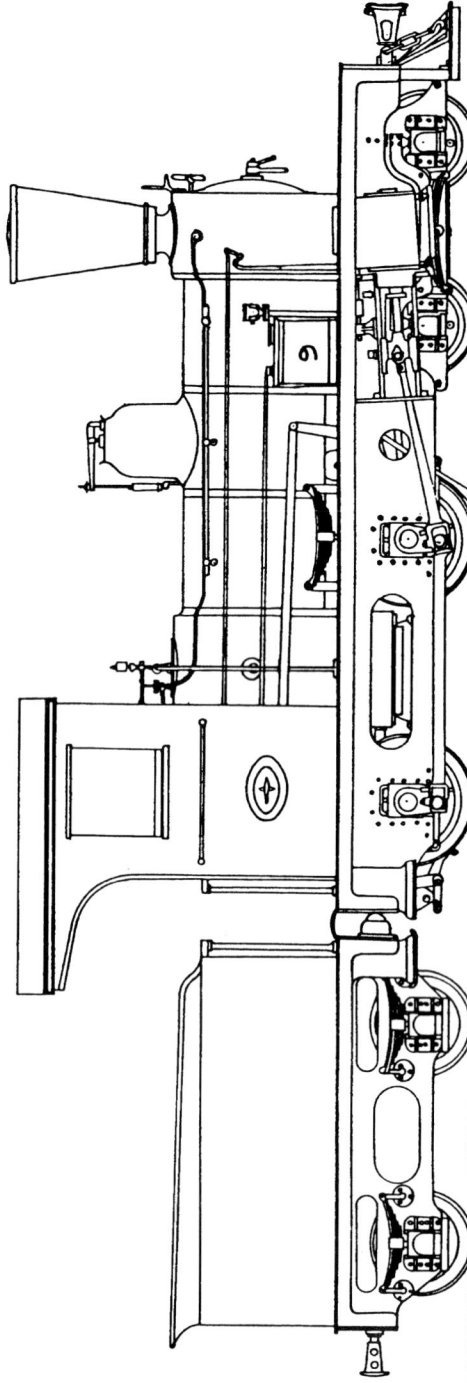

FALCON 4-4-0 CLASS F2 1895

BRUSH ELECTRICAL ENGINEERING COMPANY
LOUGHBOROUGH

0 1ft